COMBAT ZONE
TRUE TALES OF GIs IN IRAQ

WRITER: KARL ZINSMEISTER
PENCILER: DAN JURGENS

INKER: **SANDU FLOREA**
COLORIST: **RAUL TREVINO**
LETTERER: **VIRTUAL CALLIGRAPHY**

ASSOCIATE EDITOR: **WARREN SIMONS**
EDITOR: **AXEL ALONSO**
COLLECTION EDITOR: **JENNIFER GRÜNWALD**
SENIOR EDITOR, SPECIAL PROJECTS: **JEFF YOUNGQUIST**
DIRECTOR OF SALES: **DAVID GABRIEL**
PRODUCTION: **JERRY KALINOWSKI**
BOOK DESIGNER: **JEOF VITA**
CREATIVE DIRECTOR: **TOM MARVELLI**

EDITOR IN CHIEF: **JOE QUESADA**
PUBLISHER: **DAN BUCKLEY**

What you are about to read are real-life accounts of the experiences of American soldiers in the 2003-2004 Iraq War. Names and some details have been changed to protect the privacy of individuals involved, and some incidents have been combined to make for a more condensed read, but the stories are as true to actual events as humanly possible.

What is it like to travel with a corps of fighting men? To come under enemy fire? To cope with the battlefield stresses of sleep deprivation and field rations and brutal heat and dirt for weeks on end?

What kind of technical wizardry takes place when American forces go into battle today?

What are the men behind the fighting machines thinking?

What of the human elements in modern war? How do soldiers separate deadly enemies from nearby civilians? How powerful are the bonds of affection, trust, humor, fear, and dedication that bind real soldiers as they fight for their country?

In the five installments of COMBAT ZONE, you will get scrupulously true-to-life answers to these questions, and a pungent picture of action on a battlefield.

Karl Zinsmeister

Karl Zinsmeister's firsthand observations as an embedded war reporter were originally published in *The American Enterprise, National Review,* the *Los Angeles Times,* the *Christian Science Monitor,* and the *Wall Street Journal.* The tales told in *COMBAT ZONE* are adapted from Zinsmeister's two nonfiction books of Iraq War reporting. Readers interested in further details on war as it is experienced by ordinary soldiers should consult *BOOTS ON THE GROUND: A Month With the 82nd Airborne in the Battle for Iraq* and *DAWN OVER BAGHDAD: How the U.S. Military is Using Bullets and Ballots to Remake Iraq.* Or check out Zinsmeister's forthcoming documentary film for PBS entitled *Warriors.*

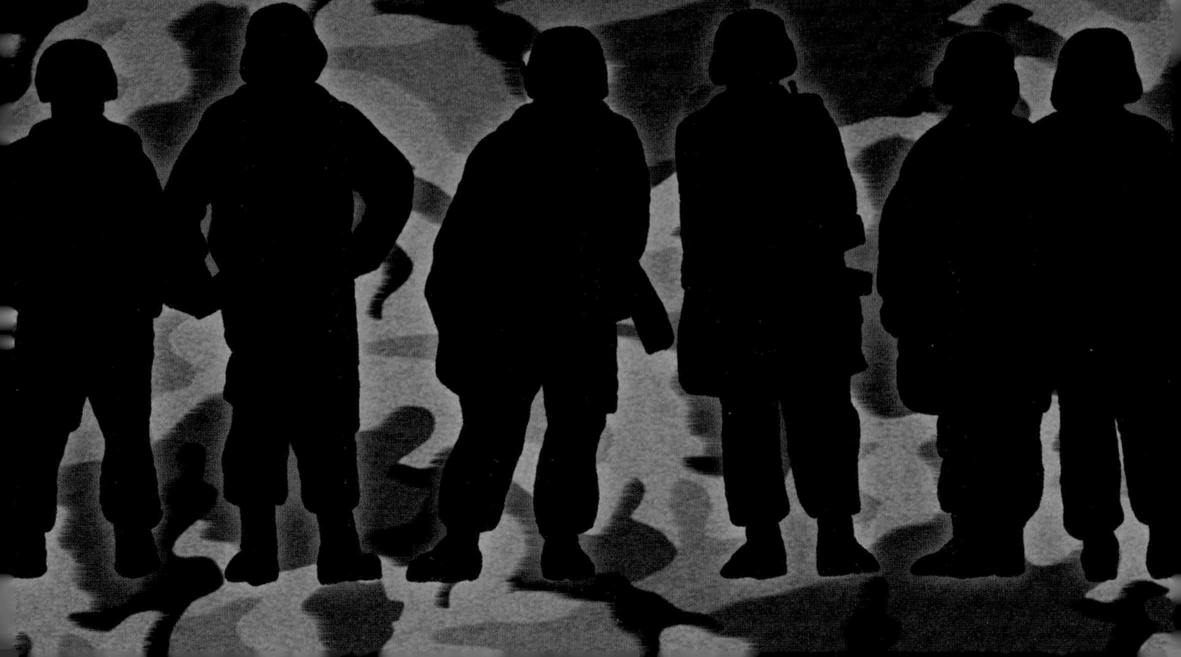

CAST OF CHARACTERS

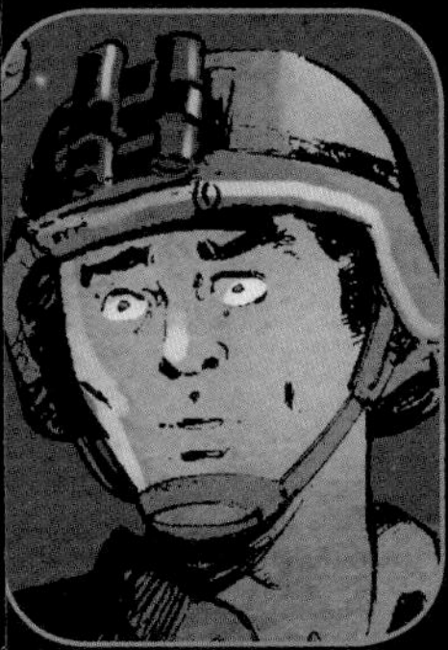

SPECIALIST DUHON

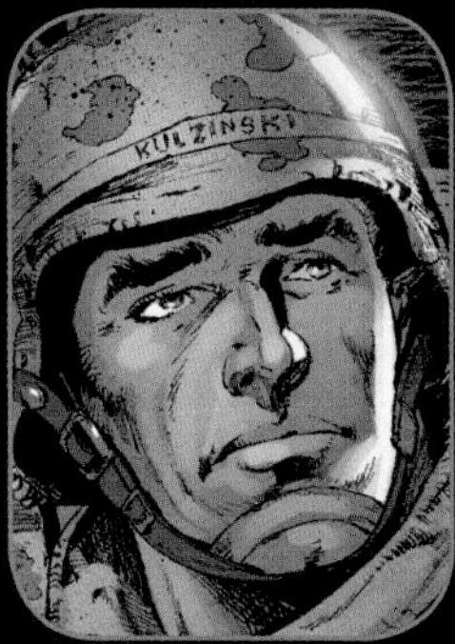

PRIVATE KULZINSKI

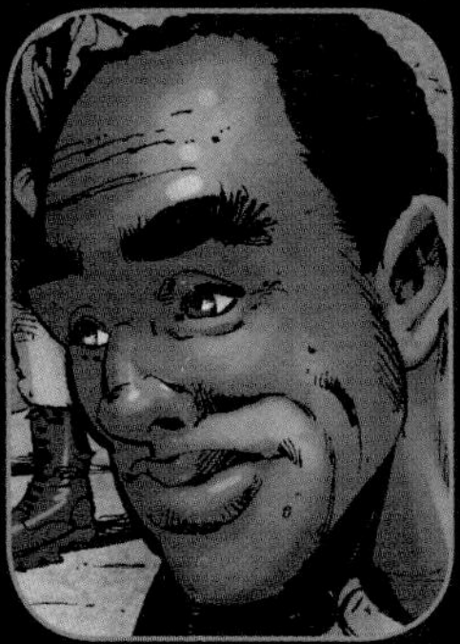

PRIVATE BROWN

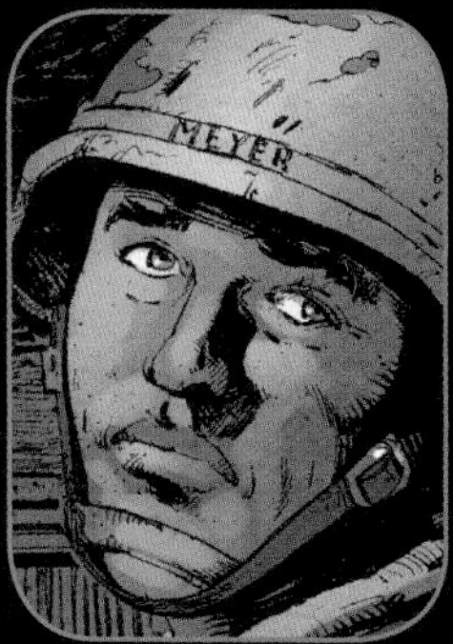

PRIVATE MEYER

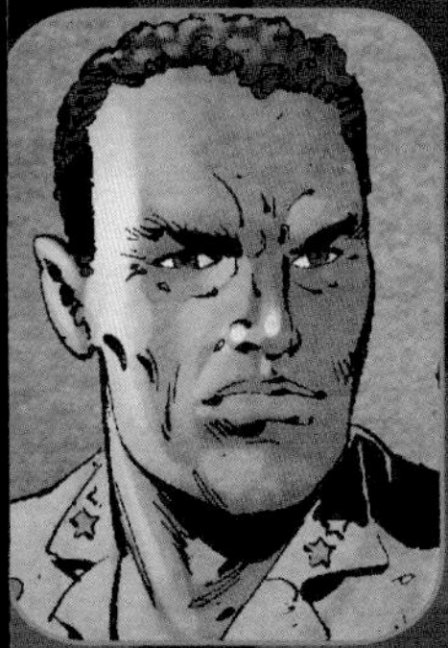

GENERAL SWANK

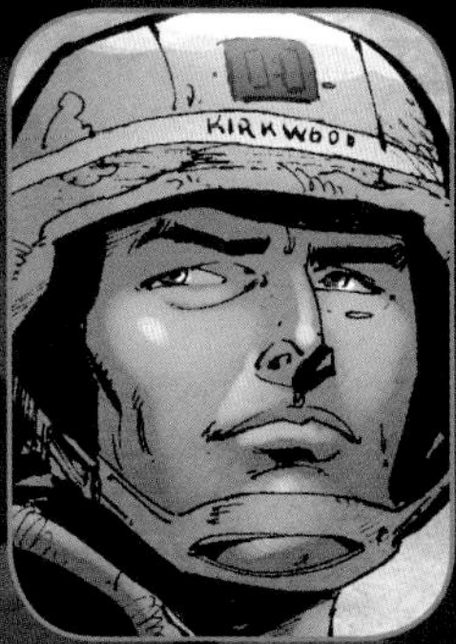

CAPTAIN KIRKWOOD

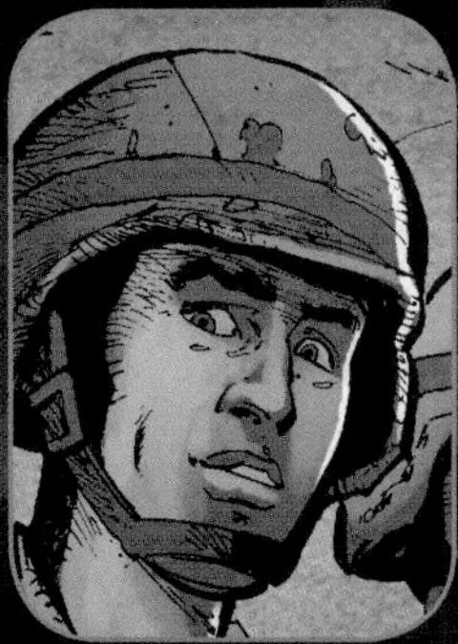

REPORTER

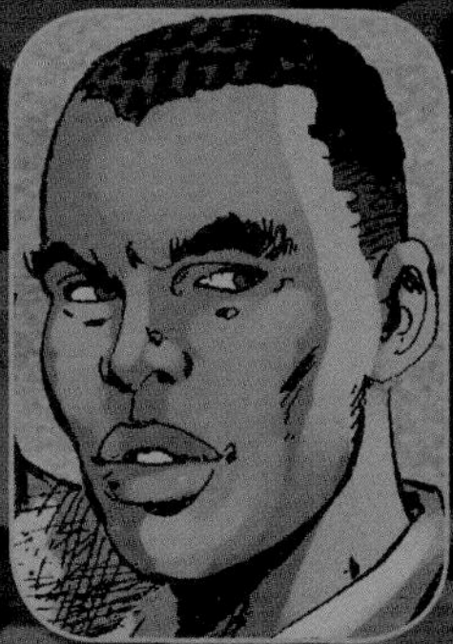

COLONEL FALCON

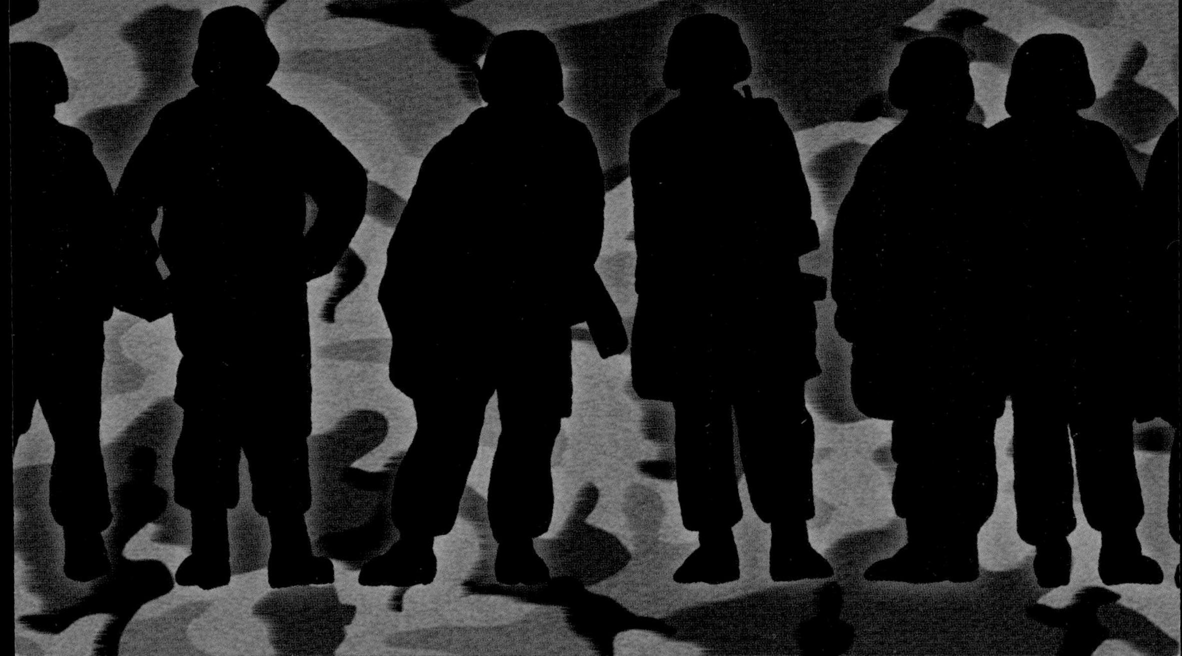

CAST OF CHARACTERS

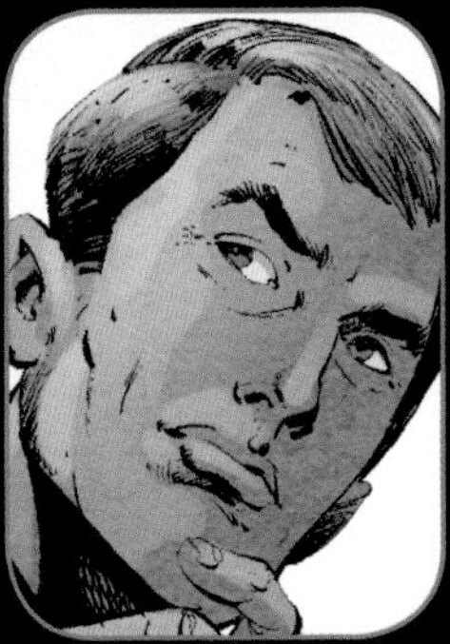

PRIVATE DEAN

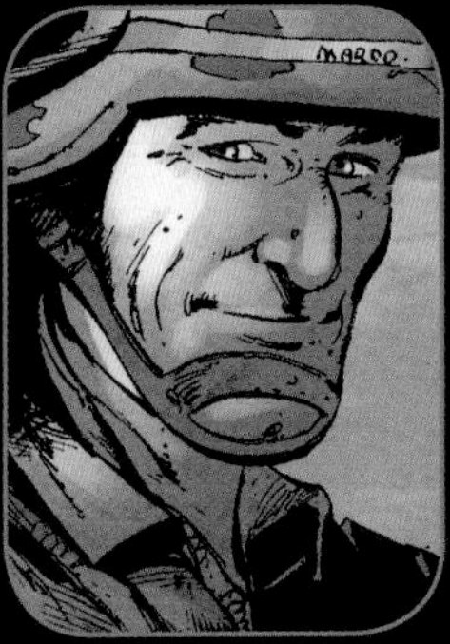
MARCO

PRIVATE MARCO

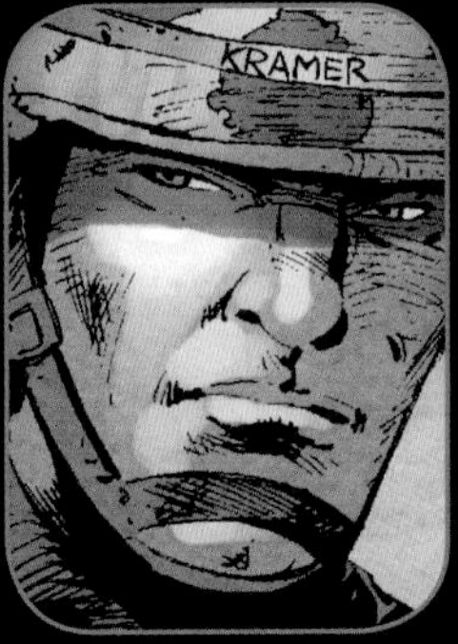
KRAMER

SERGEANT KRAMER

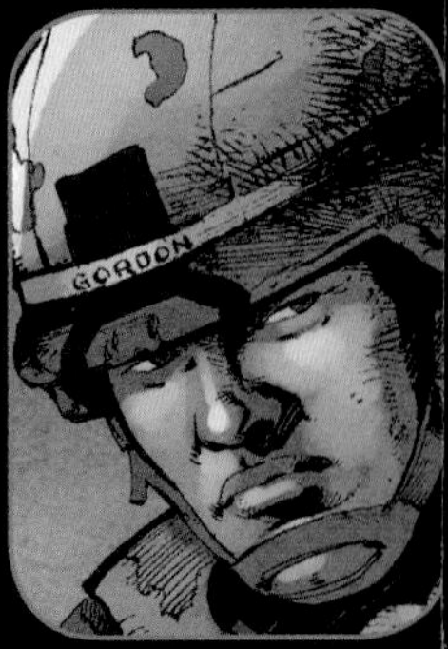
GORDON

LIEUTENANT GORDON

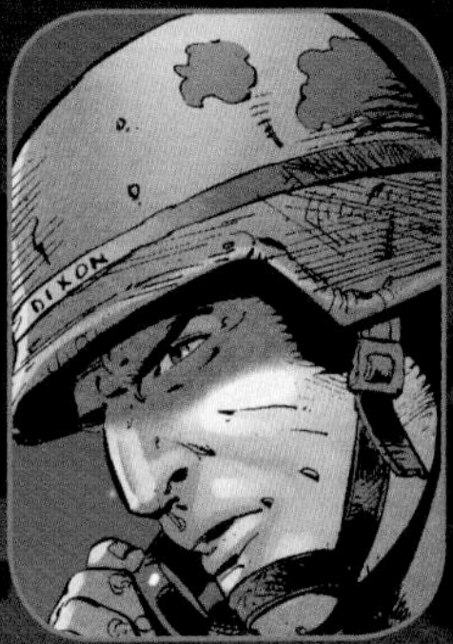
DIXON

SERGEANT DIXON

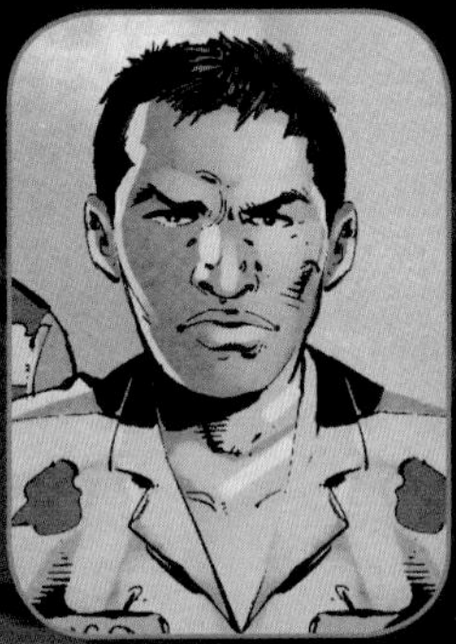

SERGEANT RICO

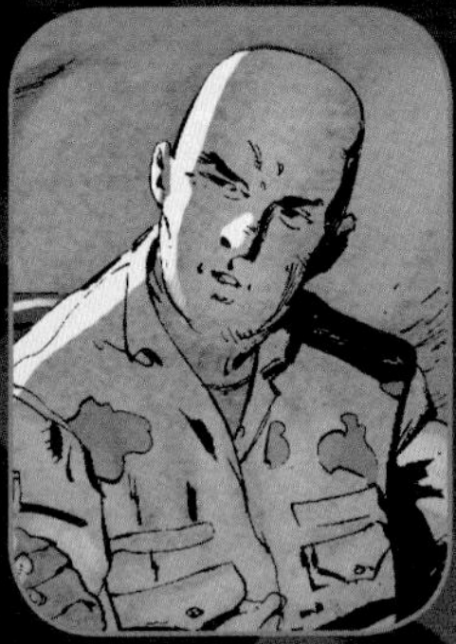

SERGEANT WAYNE

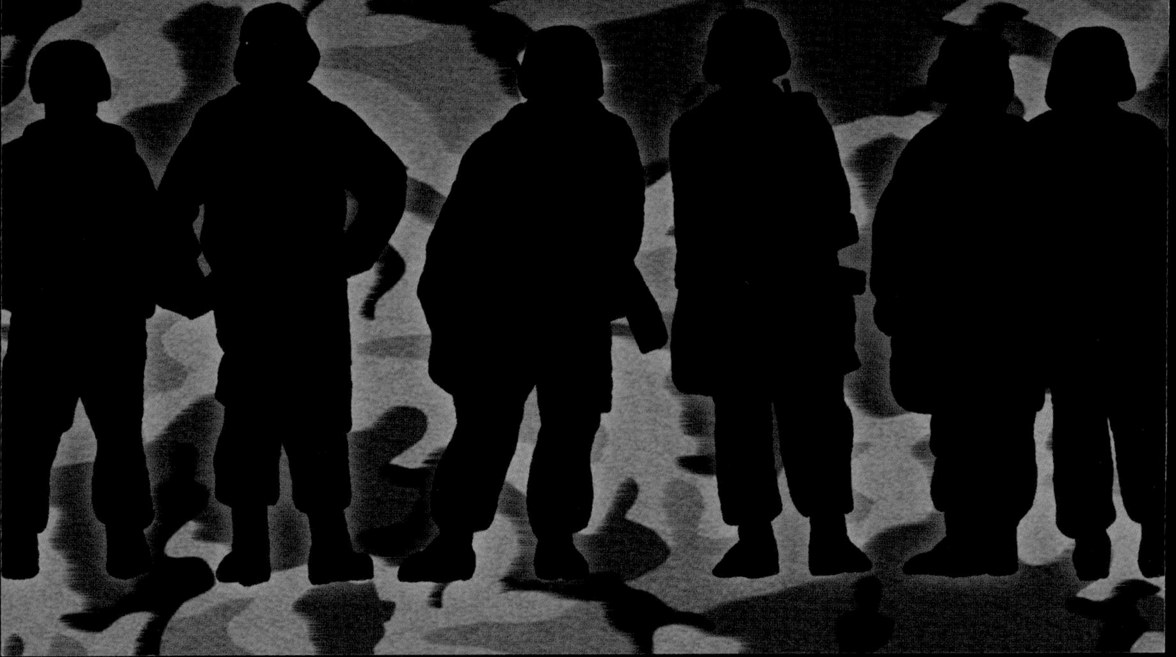

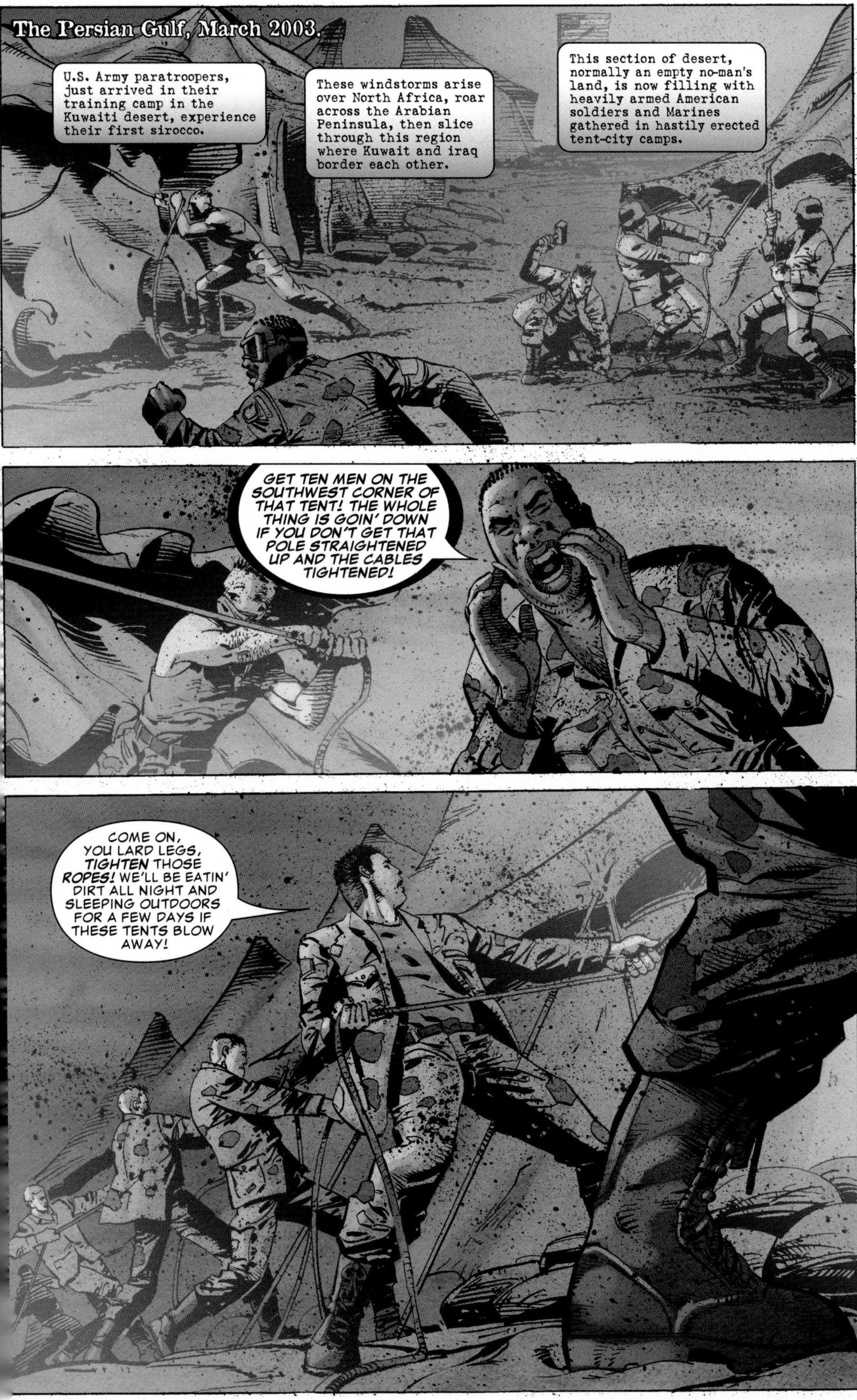
The Persian Gulf, March 2003.
U.S. Army paratroopers, just arrived in their training camp in the Kuwaiti desert, experience their first sirocco.
These windstorms arise over North Africa, roar across the Arabian Peninsula, then slice through this region where Kuwait and iraq border each other.
This section of desert, normally an empty no-man's land, is now filling with heavily armed American soldiers and Marines gathered in hastily erected tent-city camps.
GET TEN MEN ON THE SOUTHWEST CORNER OF THAT TENT! THE WHOLE THING IS GOIN' DOWN IF YOU DON'T GET THAT POLE STRAIGHTENED UP AND THE CABLES TIGHTENED!
COME ON, YOU LARD LEGS, TIGHTEN THOSE ROPES! WE'LL BE EATIN' DIRT ALL NIGHT AND SLEEPING OUTDOORS FOR A FEW DAYS IF THESE TENTS BLOW AWAY!

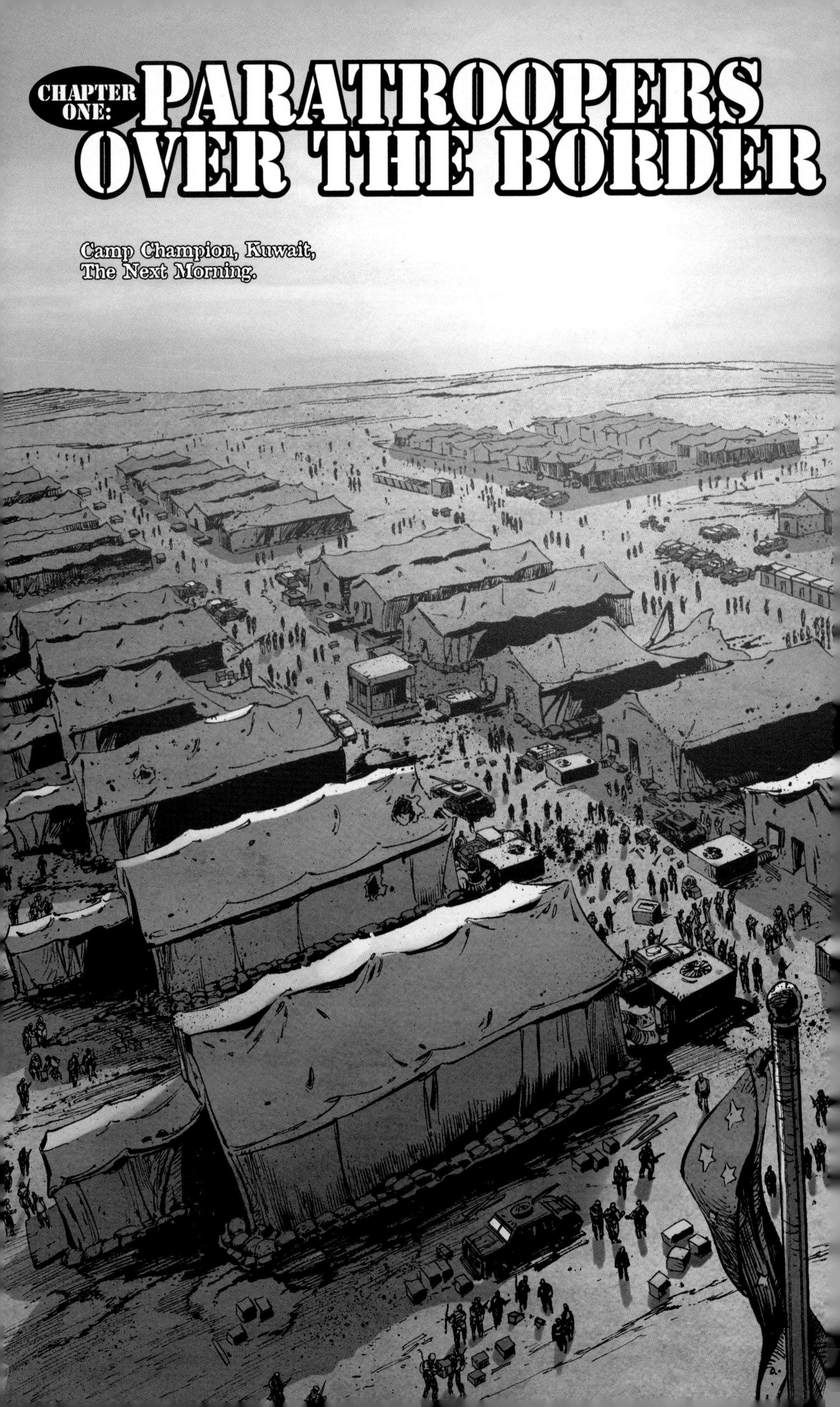
CHAPTER ONE: PARATROOPERS OVER THE BORDER
Camp Champion, Kuwait,
The Next Morning.

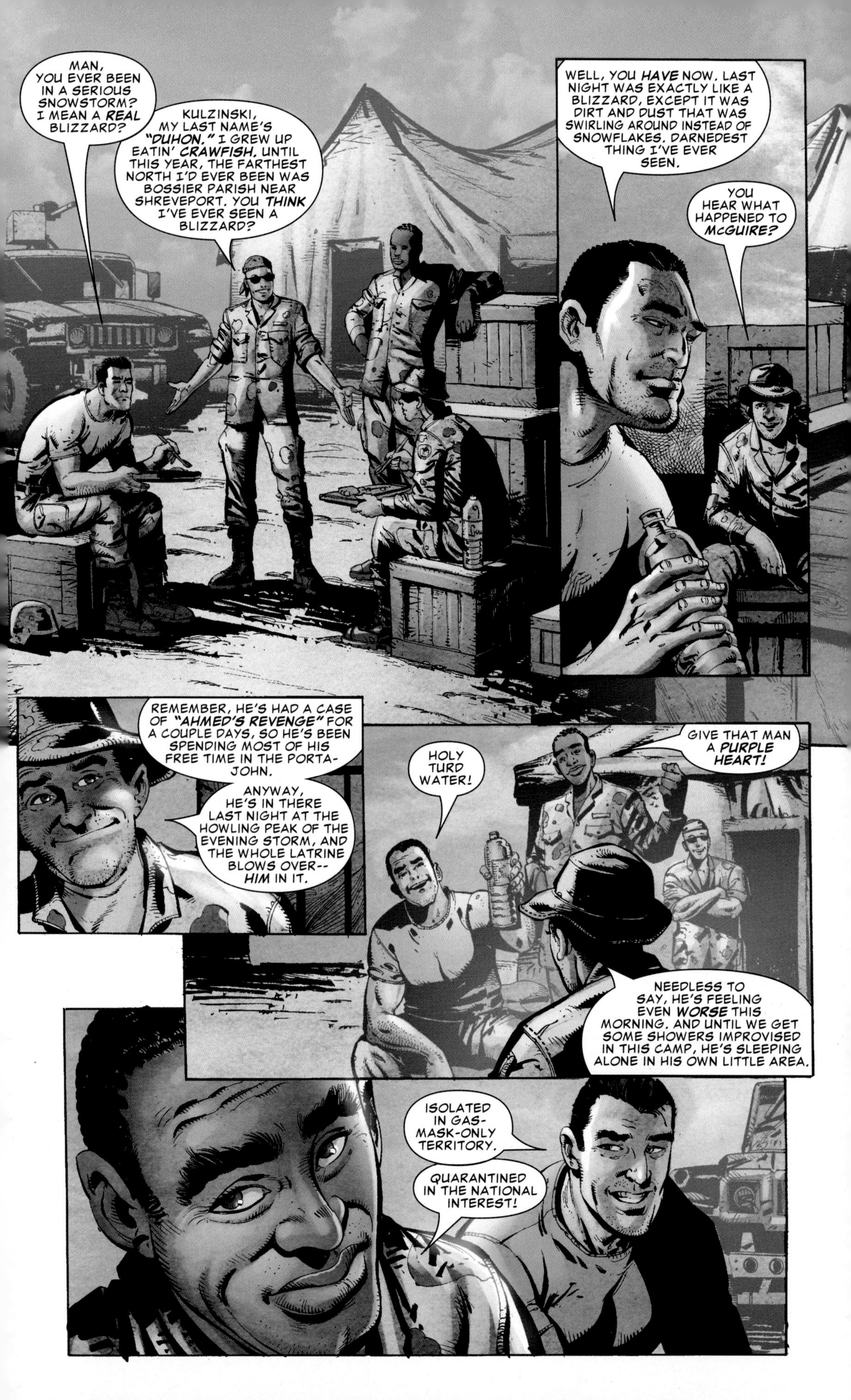
MAN, YOU EVER BEEN IN A SERIOUS SNOWSTORM? I MEAN A REAL BLIZZARD?
KULZINSKI, MY LAST NAME'S "DUHON." I GREW UP EATIN' CRAWFISH. UNTIL THIS YEAR, THE FARTHEST NORTH I'D EVER BEEN WAS BOSSIER PARISH NEAR SHREVEPORT. YOU THINK I'VE EVER SEEN A BLIZZARD?
WELL, YOU HAVE NOW. LAST NIGHT WAS EXACTLY LIKE A BLIZZARD, EXCEPT IT WAS DIRT AND DUST THAT WAS SWIRLING AROUND INSTEAD OF SNOWFLAKES. DARNEDEST THING I'VE EVER SEEN.
YOU HEAR WHAT HAPPENED TO McGUIRE?
REMEMBER, HE'S HAD A CASE OF "AHMED'S REVENGE" FOR A COUPLE DAYS, SO HE'S BEEN SPENDING MOST OF HIS FREE TIME IN THE PORTA-JOHN.
ANYWAY, HE'S IN THERE LAST NIGHT AT THE HOWLING PEAK OF THE EVENING STORM, AND THE WHOLE LATRINE BLOWS OVER-- HIM IN IT.
HOLY TURD WATER!
GIVE THAT MAN A PURPLE HEART!
NEEDLESS TO SAY, HE'S FEELING EVEN WORSE THIS MORNING. AND UNTIL WE GET SOME SHOWERS IMPROVISED IN THIS CAMP, HE'S SLEEPING ALONE IN HIS OWN LITTLE AREA.
ISOLATED IN GAS-MASK-ONLY TERRITORY.
QUARANTINED IN THE NATIONAL INTEREST!

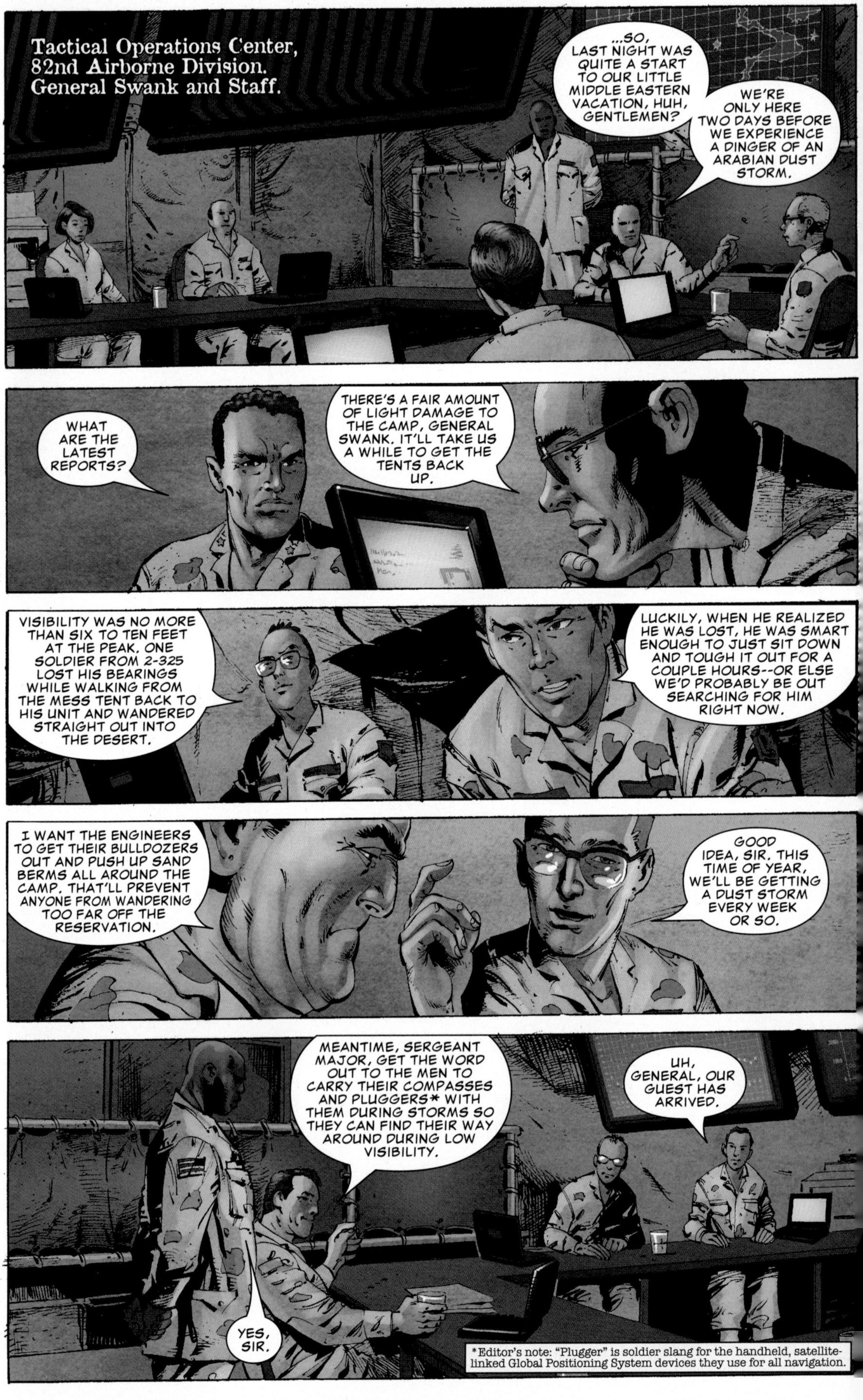
Tactical Operations Center, 82nd Airborne Division. General Swank and Staff.
...SO, LAST NIGHT WAS QUITE A START TO OUR LITTLE MIDDLE EASTERN VACATION, HUH, GENTLEMEN?
WE'RE ONLY HERE TWO DAYS BEFORE WE EXPERIENCE A DINGER OF AN ARABIAN DUST STORM.
WHAT ARE THE LATEST REPORTS?
THERE'S A FAIR AMOUNT OF LIGHT DAMAGE TO THE CAMP, GENERAL SWANK. IT'LL TAKE US A WHILE TO GET THE TENTS BACK UP.
VISIBILITY WAS NO MORE THAN SIX TO TEN FEET AT THE PEAK. ONE SOLDIER FROM 2-325 LOST HIS BEARINGS WHILE WALKING FROM THE MESS TENT BACK TO HIS UNIT AND WANDERED STRAIGHT OUT INTO THE DESERT.
LUCKILY, WHEN HE REALIZED HE WAS LOST, HE WAS SMART ENOUGH TO JUST SIT DOWN AND TOUGH IT OUT FOR A COUPLE HOURS--OR ELSE WE'D PROBABLY BE OUT SEARCHING FOR HIM RIGHT NOW.
I WANT THE ENGINEERS TO GET THEIR BULLDOZERS OUT AND PUSH UP SAND BERMS ALL AROUND THE CAMP. THAT'LL PREVENT ANYONE FROM WANDERING TOO FAR OFF THE RESERVATION.
GOOD IDEA, SIR. THIS TIME OF YEAR, WE'LL BE GETTING A DUST STORM EVERY WEEK OR SO.
MEANTIME, SERGEANT MAJOR, GET THE WORD OUT TO THE MEN TO CARRY THEIR COMPASSES AND PLUGGERS* WITH THEM DURING STORMS SO THEY CAN FIND THEIR WAY AROUND DURING LOW VISIBILITY.
UH, GENERAL, OUR GUEST HAS ARRIVED.
YES, SIR.
*Editor's note: "Plugger" is soldier slang for the handheld, satellite-linked Global Positioning System devices they use for all navigation.

IF YOU DON'T MIND ME SAYING, SIR--THIS IS QUITE AN EXPERIMENT, LETTING THE PRESS RIGHT INTO THE MIDDLE OF A SECRET COMBAT OPERATION--

BUT I THINK IT'S A GOOD THING.

WHEN WE WERE IN AFGHANISTAN, AS SOON AS WE'D FINISH A BATTLE, TALIBAN SYMPATHIZERS WOULD CRAWL OUT OF THE WOODWORK AND START TELLING NEWLY ARRIVING REPORTERS HOW WE'D CARRIED OUT SOME ATROCITY OR OTHER, AND WE'D HAVE NO WAY TO DISPROVE IT.

WITH REPORTERS RIGHT ON THE SCENE, THAT KIND OF DISINFORMATION CAN'T TAKE ROOT.

ROGER, SIR. CAPTAIN KIRKWOOD HERE WILL SHOW THE REPORTER AROUND OVER THE NEXT FEW DAYS.

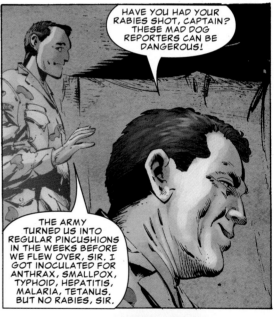

HAVE YOU HAD YOUR RABIES SHOT, CAPTAIN? THESE MAD DOG REPORTERS CAN BE DANGEROUS!

THE ARMY TURNED US INTO REGULAR PINCUSHIONS IN THE WEEKS BEFORE WE FLEW OVER, SIR. I GOT INOCULATED FOR ANTHRAX, SMALLPOX, TYPHOID, HEPATITIS, MALARIA, TETANUS, BUT NO RABIES, SIR.

TETANUS-- THAT'S LOCKJAW, RIGHT? WELL, THAT OUGHTA HELP KEEP YOU SAFE AROUND A REPORTER!

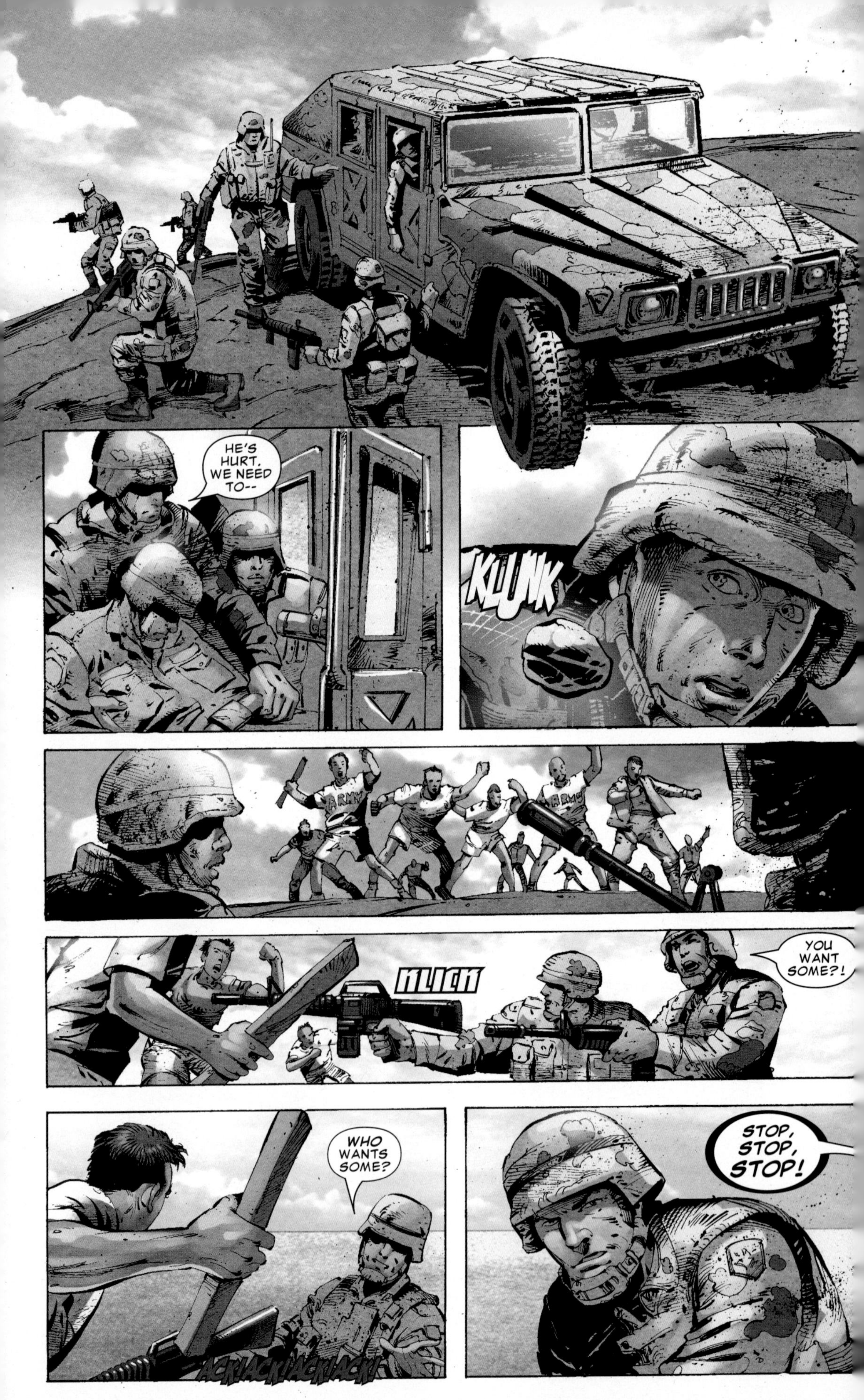

HE'S HURT. WE NEED TO--
KLUNK
KLICK
YOU WANT SOME?!
WHO WANTS SOME?
ACK!ACK!ACK!ACK!
STOP, STOP, STOP!

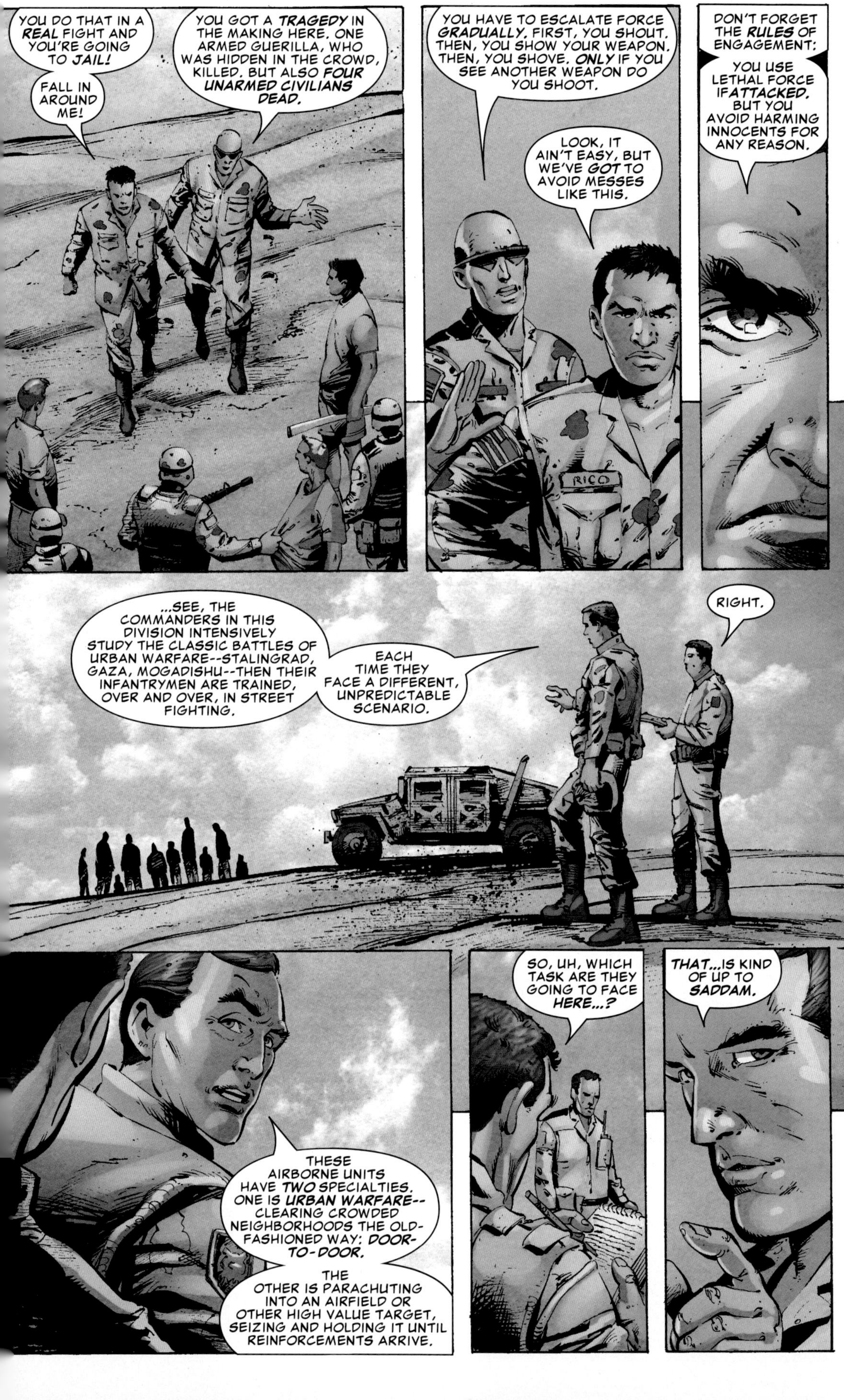
YOU DO THAT IN A REAL FIGHT AND YOU'RE GOING TO JAIL!
FALL IN AROUND ME!
YOU GOT A TRAGEDY IN THE MAKING HERE. ONE ARMED GUERILLA, WHO WAS HIDDEN IN THE CROWD, KILLED. BUT ALSO FOUR UNARMED CIVILIANS DEAD.
YOU HAVE TO ESCALATE FORCE GRADUALLY. FIRST, YOU SHOUT. THEN, YOU SHOW YOUR WEAPON. THEN, YOU SHOVE. ONLY IF YOU SEE ANOTHER WEAPON DO YOU SHOOT.
LOOK, IT AIN'T EASY, BUT WE'VE GOT TO AVOID MESSES LIKE THIS.
RICO
DON'T FORGET THE RULES OF ENGAGEMENT:
YOU USE LETHAL FORCE IFATTACKED. BUT YOU AVOID HARMING INNOCENTS FOR ANY REASON.
...SEE, THE COMMANDERS IN THIS DIVISION INTENSIVELY STUDY THE CLASSIC BATTLES OF URBAN WARFARE--STALINGRAD, GAZA, MOGADISHU--THEN THEIR INFANTRYMEN ARE TRAINED, OVER AND OVER, IN STREET FIGHTING.
EACH TIME THEY FACE A DIFFERENT, UNPREDICTABLE SCENARIO.
RIGHT.
THESE AIRBORNE UNITS HAVE TWO SPECIALTIES. ONE IS URBAN WARFARE--CLEARING CROWDED NEIGHBORHOODS THE OLD-FASHIONED WAY: DOOR-TO-DOOR.
THE OTHER IS PARACHUTING INTO AN AIRFIELD OR OTHER HIGH VALUE TARGET, SEIZING AND HOLDING IT UNTIL REINFORCEMENTS ARRIVE.
SO, UH, WHICH TASK ARE THEY GOING TO FACE HERE...?
THAT...IS KIND OF UP TO SADDAM.

1900 Hours, In The Infantry Tents.

...THAT WAS SOME *STRANGE* FOOD THEY SERVED TONIGHT.

TELL ME ABOUT IT, BROWN. THAT SPAGHETTI SAUCE TASTED LIKE *ITALIAN* FOOD AS INTERPRETED BY A *FILIPINO* COOK WORKING FOR AN *ARAB* FOOD SERVICE COMPANY.

QUITE TASTY, IN MY OPINION, BUT I AGREE THERE WERE DEFINITE *TACO* AND *SHISH KEBAB* OVERTONES IN THAT BOLOGNESE SAUCE.

I'M ALREADY STARTING TO THINK ABOUT THE FOOD FROM HOME I'M GONNA BE CRAVING BEFORE WE GET BACK.

LIKE MY MOM'S HOMEMADE APPLE BUTTER.

RED HOT DOGS.

PIG'S FEET.

OR I'LL TELL YOU WHAT I COULD USE RIGHT NOW: SOME OF MY GRANDDADDY'S *CURE-ALL*...

A SMALL GLASS OF BOILING WATER WITH A PIECE OF PEPPERMINT MELTED IN IT. A SPOONFUL OF WHISKEY. AND A DOLLOP OF HONEY.

LET IT COOL A LITTLE AND THAT'D BE *JUST* THE THING FOR THIS HACKING COUGH WE'VE ALL GOT FROM THE DUST IN THE AIR.

WE USED TO PRETEND WE WERE SICK JUST TO HAVE A LITTLE OF THAT.

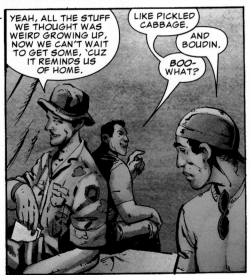

YEAH, ALL THE STUFF WE THOUGHT WAS WEIRD GROWING UP, NOW WE CAN'T WAIT TO GET SOME, 'CUZ IT REMINDS US OF HOME.

LIKE PICKLED CABBAGE.

AND BOUDIN.

BOO-WHAT?

CAJUN RICE-AND-BLOOD SAUSAGE, KULZINSKI-- YOU KNOW-NOTHING YANKEE.

HEY, DOO-HON, I BET YOU NEVER ATE MOUNTAIN *OYSTERS* DOWN IN YOUR SWAMP.

WHAT KIND OF OYSTERS YOU GONNA FIND IN UPSTATE NEWYORK?

FRIED BULL TESTICLES, THAT'S WHAT.

DO YOU REALIZE THAT YOU EASTERN EUROPEAN TYPES ARE COMPLETE BARBARIANS?

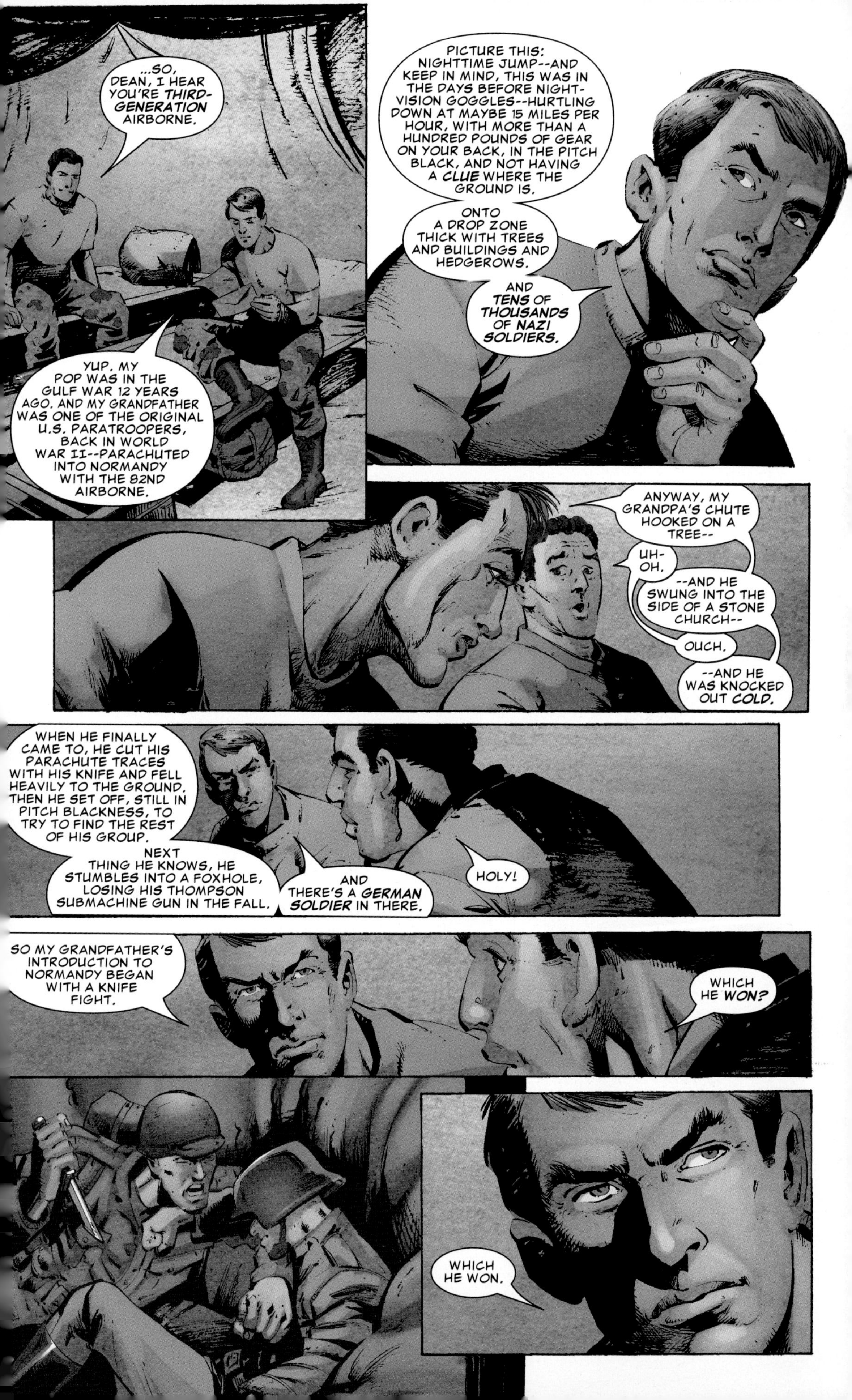
...SO, DEAN, I HEAR YOU'RE THIRD-GENERATION AIRBORNE.
YUP. MY POP WAS IN THE GULF WAR 12 YEARS AGO. AND MY GRANDFATHER WAS ONE OF THE ORIGINAL U.S. PARATROOPERS, BACK IN WORLD WAR II--PARACHUTED INTO NORMANDY WITH THE 82ND AIRBORNE.
PICTURE THIS: NIGHTTIME JUMP--AND KEEP IN MIND, THIS WAS IN THE DAYS BEFORE NIGHT-VISION GOGGLES--HURTLING DOWN AT MAYBE 15 MILES PER HOUR, WITH MORE THAN A HUNDRED POUNDS OF GEAR ON YOUR BACK, IN THE PITCH BLACK, AND NOT HAVING A CLUE WHERE THE GROUND IS.
ONTO A DROP ZONE THICK WITH TREES AND BUILDINGS AND HEDGEROWS.
AND TENS OF THOUSANDS OF NAZI SOLDIERS.
ANYWAY, MY GRANDPA'S CHUTE HOOKED ON A TREE--
UH-OH.
--AND HE SWUNG INTO THE SIDE OF A STONE CHURCH--
OUCH.
--AND HE WAS KNOCKED OUT COLD.
WHEN HE FINALLY CAME TO, HE CUT HIS PARACHUTE TRACES WITH HIS KNIFE AND FELL HEAVILY TO THE GROUND. THEN HE SET OFF, STILL IN PITCH BLACKNESS, TO TRY TO FIND THE REST OF HIS GROUP.
NEXT THING HE KNOWS, HE STUMBLES INTO A FOXHOLE, LOSING HIS THOMPSON SUBMACHINE GUN IN THE FALL.
AND THERE'S A GERMAN SOLDIER IN THERE.
HOLY!
SO MY GRANDFATHER'S INTRODUCTION TO NORMANDY BEGAN WITH A KNIFE FIGHT.
WHICH HE WON?
WHICH HE WON.

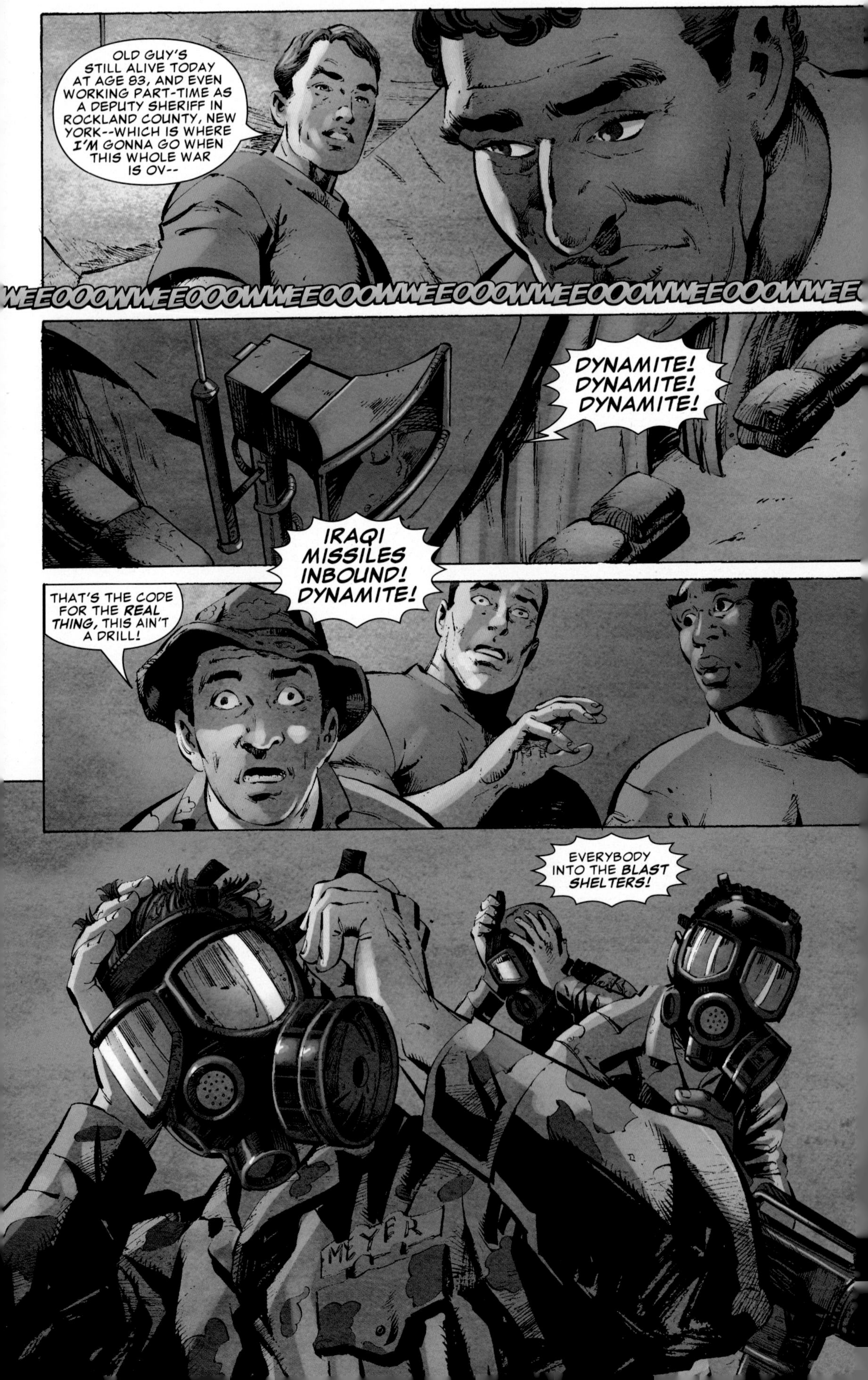
OLD GUY'S STILL ALIVE TODAY AT AGE 83, AND EVEN WORKING PART-TIME AS A DEPUTY SHERIFF IN ROCKLAND COUNTY, NEW YORK--WHICH IS WHERE I'M GONNA GO WHEN THIS WHOLE WAR IS OV--
WEEOOOWWEEOOOWWEEOOOWWEEOOOWWEEOOOWWEEOOOWWEE
DYNAMITE! DYNAMITE! DYNAMITE!
IRAQI MISSILES INBOUND! DYNAMITE!
THAT'S THE CODE FOR THE REAL THING, THIS AIN'T A DRILL!
EVERYBODY INTO THE BLAST SHELTERS!
MEYER

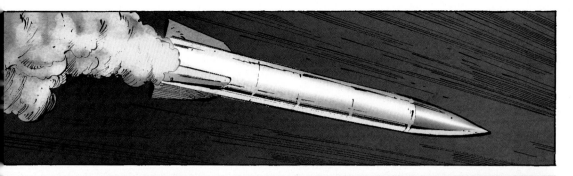

Inside The Patriot Missile Command Post.

SIR! DIRECT HIT. THE PATRIOT INTERCEPTED THE IRAQI MISSILE.

QR 36 SHOWS THAT LAST LAUNCH COMING FROM APPROXIMATELY 135 MILES AWAY.

WELL. SO MUCH FOR THE THEORY THAT SADDAM GOT RID OF ALL HIS INTERMEDIATE-RANGE BALLISTIC MISSILES.

OUR SOLDIERS ARE PACKED INTO THOSE CAMPS 500 MEN TO THE ACRE, WITH NOTHING BUT *CANVAS* OVERHEAD TO PROTECT THEM.

IF THE IRAQIS MANAGE TO LAND ONE OF THOSE ROCKETS IN THEIR MIDST BEFORE WE CAN SHOOT IT DOWN, IT'S GOING TO BE A *KILLING FIELD.*

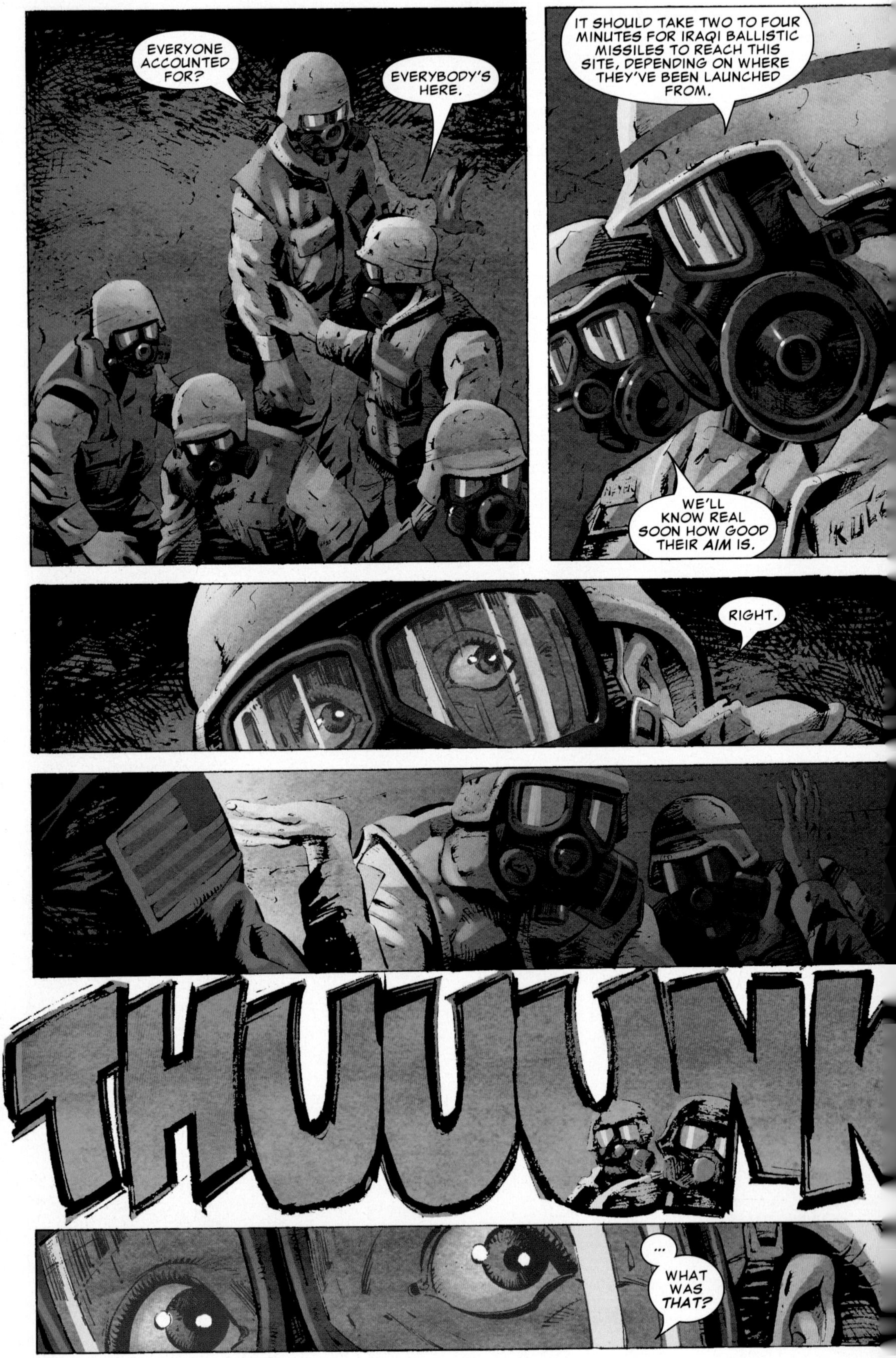
EVERYONE ACCOUNTED FOR?
EVERYBODY'S HERE.
IT SHOULD TAKE TWO TO FOUR MINUTES FOR IRAQI BALLISTIC MISSILES TO REACH THIS SITE, DEPENDING ON WHERE THEY'VE BEEN LAUNCHED FROM.
WE'LL KNOW REAL SOON HOW GOOD THEIR *AIM* IS.
RIGHT.
THUUUNK
...
WHAT WAS *THAT?*

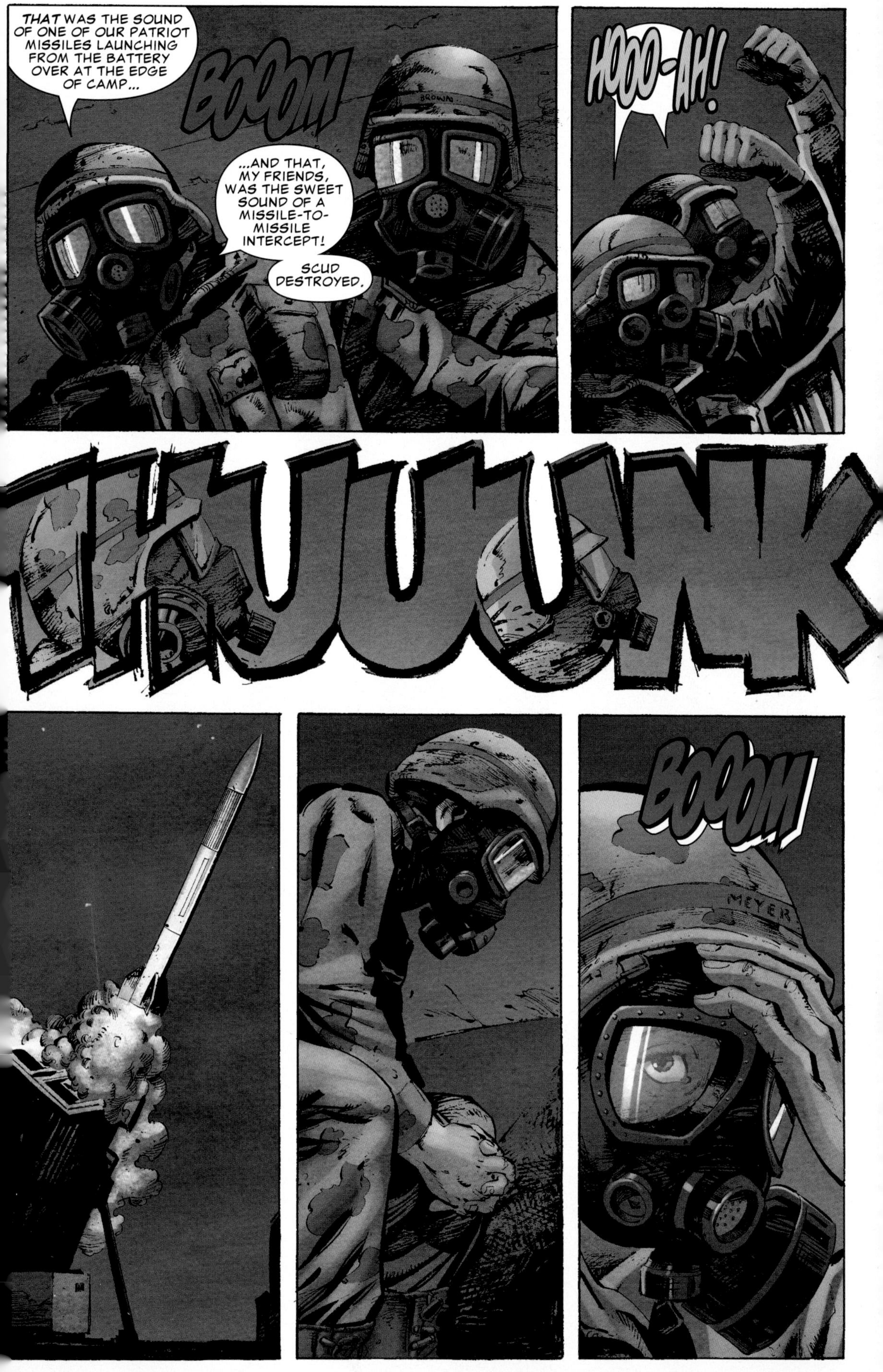
THAT WAS THE SOUND OF ONE OF OUR PATRIOT MISSILES LAUNCHING FROM THE BATTERY OVER AT THE EDGE OF CAMP...
BOOOM
...AND THAT, MY FRIENDS, WAS THE SWEET SOUND OF A MISSILE-TO-MISSILE INTERCEPT!
SCUD DESTROYED.
BROWN
HOOO-AH!
THUUUNK
BOOOM
MEYER

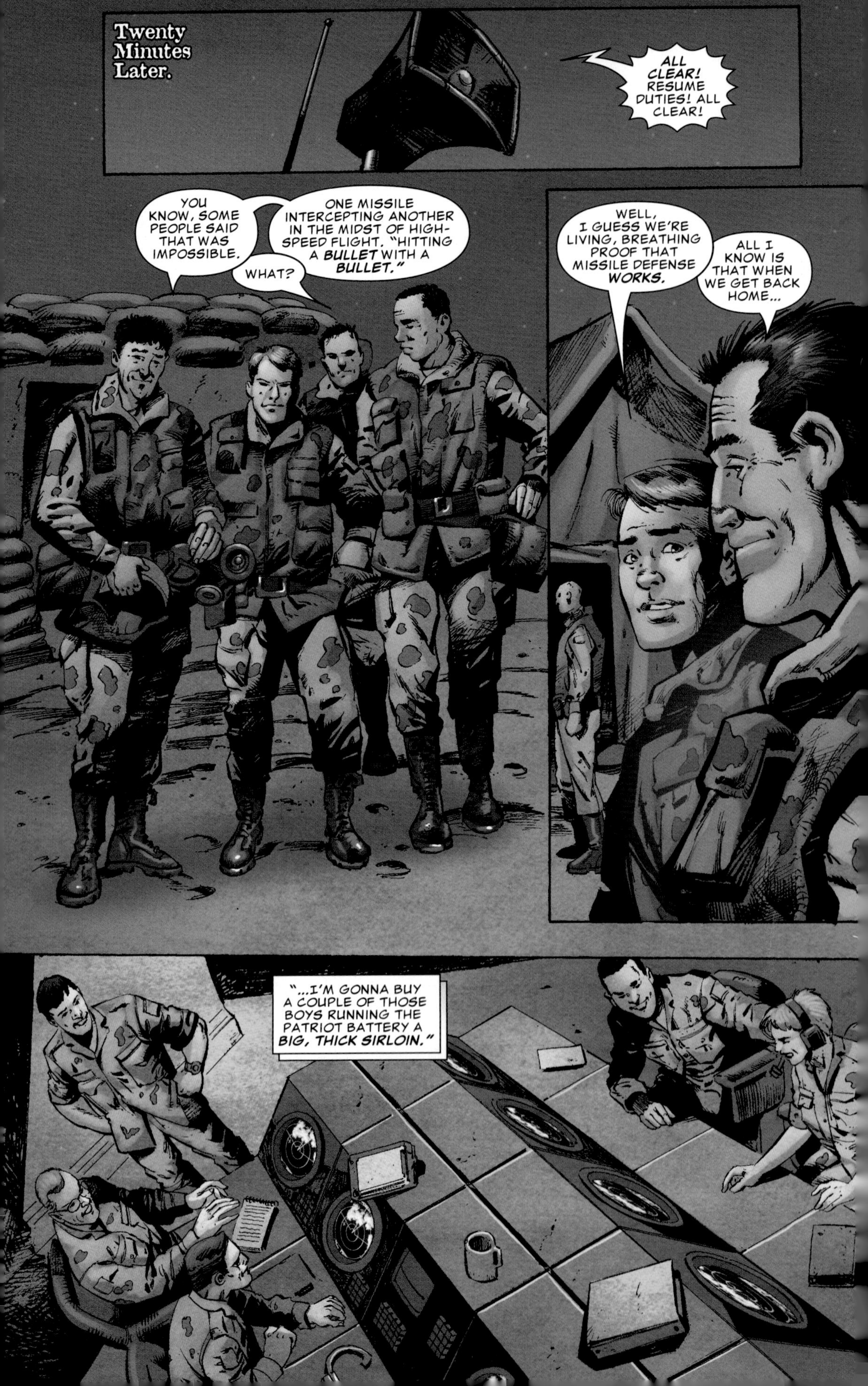
Twenty Minutes Later.
ALL CLEAR! RESUME DUTIES! ALL CLEAR!
YOU KNOW, SOME PEOPLE SAID THAT WAS IMPOSSIBLE.
WHAT?
ONE MISSILE INTERCEPTING ANOTHER IN THE MIDST OF HIGH-SPEED FLIGHT. "HITTING A BULLET WITH A BULLET."
WELL, I GUESS WE'RE LIVING, BREATHING PROOF THAT MISSILE DEFENSE WORKS.
ALL I KNOW IS THAT WHEN WE GET BACK HOME...
"...I'M GONNA BUY A COUPLE OF THOSE BOYS RUNNING THE PATRIOT BATTERY A BIG, THICK SIRLOIN."

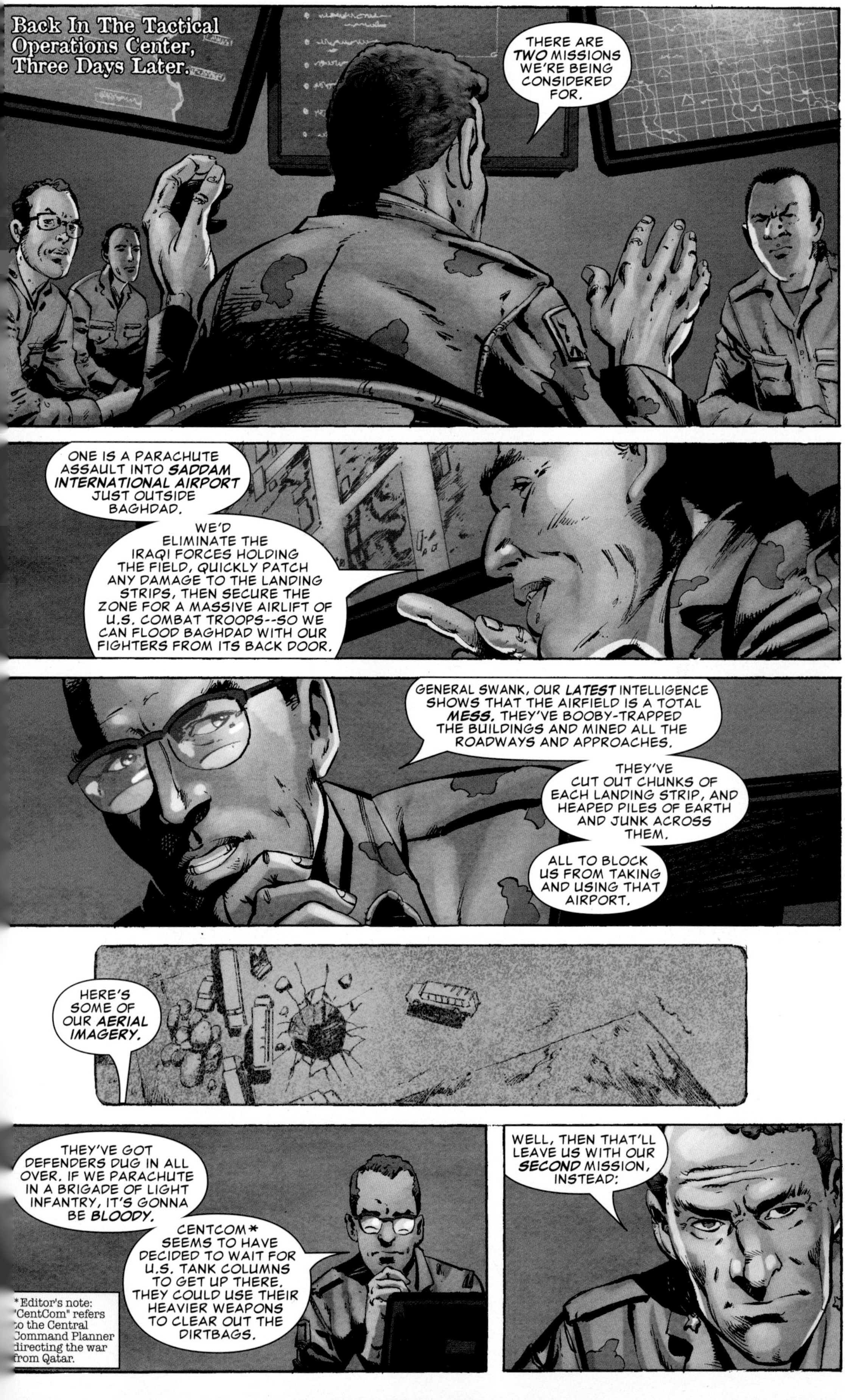
Back In The Tactical Operations Center, Three Days Later.
THERE ARE TWO MISSIONS WE'RE BEING CONSIDERED FOR.
ONE IS A PARACHUTE ASSAULT INTO SADDAM INTERNATIONAL AIRPORT JUST OUTSIDE BAGHDAD.
WE'D ELIMINATE THE IRAQI FORCES HOLDING THE FIELD, QUICKLY PATCH ANY DAMAGE TO THE LANDING STRIPS, THEN SECURE THE ZONE FOR A MASSIVE AIRLIFT OF U.S. COMBAT TROOPS--SO WE CAN FLOOD BAGHDAD WITH OUR FIGHTERS FROM ITS BACK DOOR.
GENERAL SWANK, OUR LATEST INTELLIGENCE SHOWS THAT THE AIRFIELD IS A TOTAL MESS. THEY'VE BOOBY-TRAPPED THE BUILDINGS AND MINED ALL THE ROADWAYS AND APPROACHES.
THEY'VE CUT OUT CHUNKS OF EACH LANDING STRIP, AND HEAPED PILES OF EARTH AND JUNK ACROSS THEM.
ALL TO BLOCK US FROM TAKING AND USING THAT AIRPORT.
HERE'S SOME OF OUR AERIAL IMAGERY.
THEY'VE GOT DEFENDERS DUG IN ALL OVER. IF WE PARACHUTE IN A BRIGADE OF LIGHT INFANTRY, IT'S GONNA BE BLOODY.
CENTCOM* SEEMS TO HAVE DECIDED TO WAIT FOR U.S. TANK COLUMNS TO GET UP THERE. THEY COULD USE THEIR HEAVIER WEAPONS TO CLEAR OUT THE DIRTBAGS.
*Editor's note: "CentCom" refers to the Central Command Planner directing the war from Qatar.
WELL, THEN THAT'LL LEAVE US WITH OUR SECOND MISSION, INSTEAD:

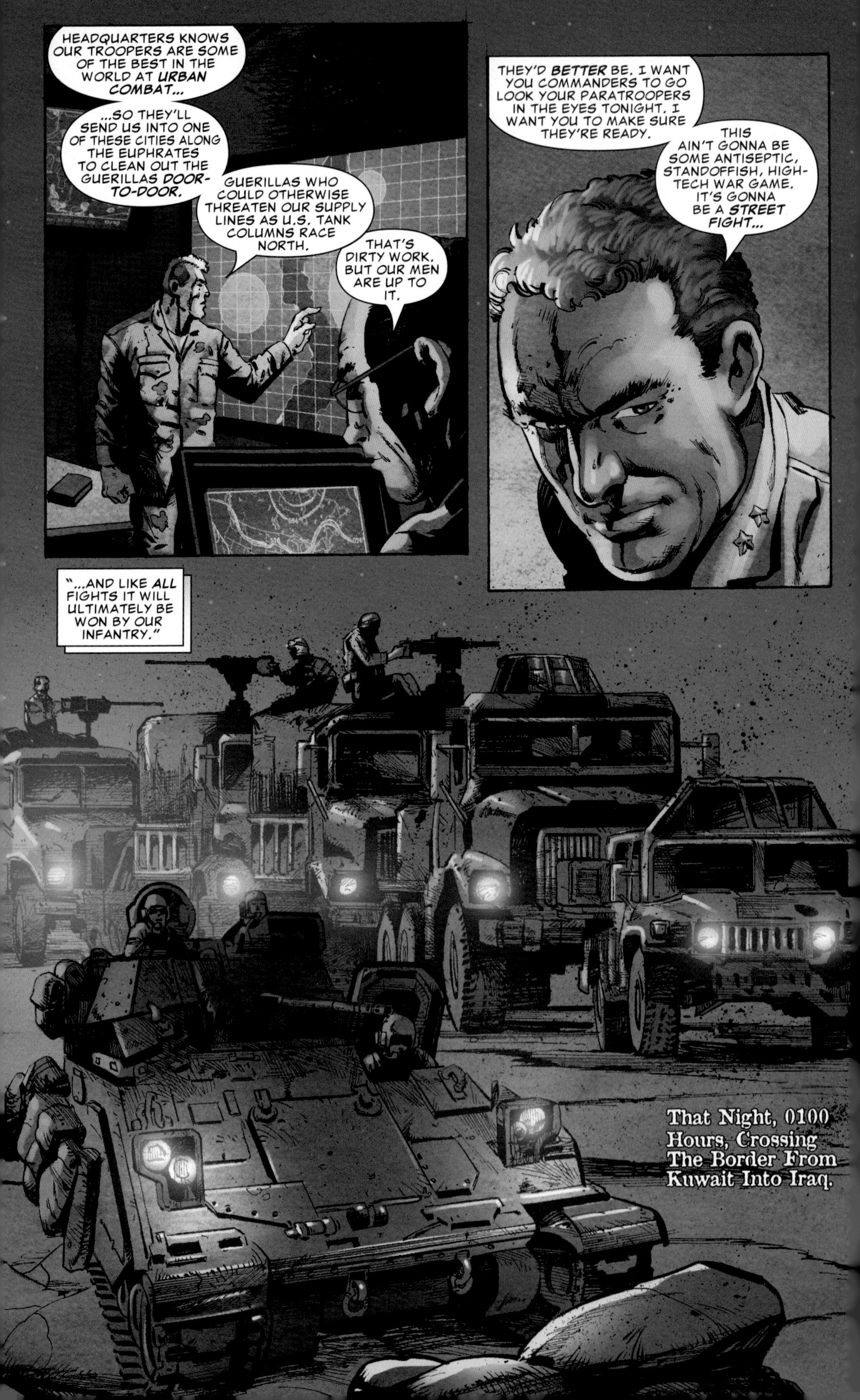
HEADQUARTERS KNOWS OUR TROOPERS ARE SOME OF THE BEST IN THE WORLD AT URBAN COMBAT...
...SO THEY'LL SEND US INTO ONE OF THESE CITIES ALONG THE EUPHRATES TO CLEAN OUT THE GUERILLAS DOOR-TO-DOOR.
GUERILLAS WHO COULD OTHERWISE THREATEN OUR SUPPLY LINES AS U.S. TANK COLUMNS RACE NORTH.
THAT'S DIRTY WORK. BUT OUR MEN ARE UP TO IT.
THEY'D BETTER BE. I WANT YOU COMMANDERS TO GO LOOK YOUR PARATROOPERS IN THE EYES TONIGHT. I WANT YOU TO MAKE SURE THEY'RE READY.
THIS AIN'T GONNA BE SOME ANTISEPTIC, STANDOFFISH, HIGH-TECH WAR GAME. IT'S GONNA BE A STREET FIGHT...
"...AND LIKE ALL FIGHTS IT WILL ULTIMATELY BE WON BY OUR INFANTRY."
That Night, 0100 Hours, Crossing The Border From Kuwait Into Iraq.

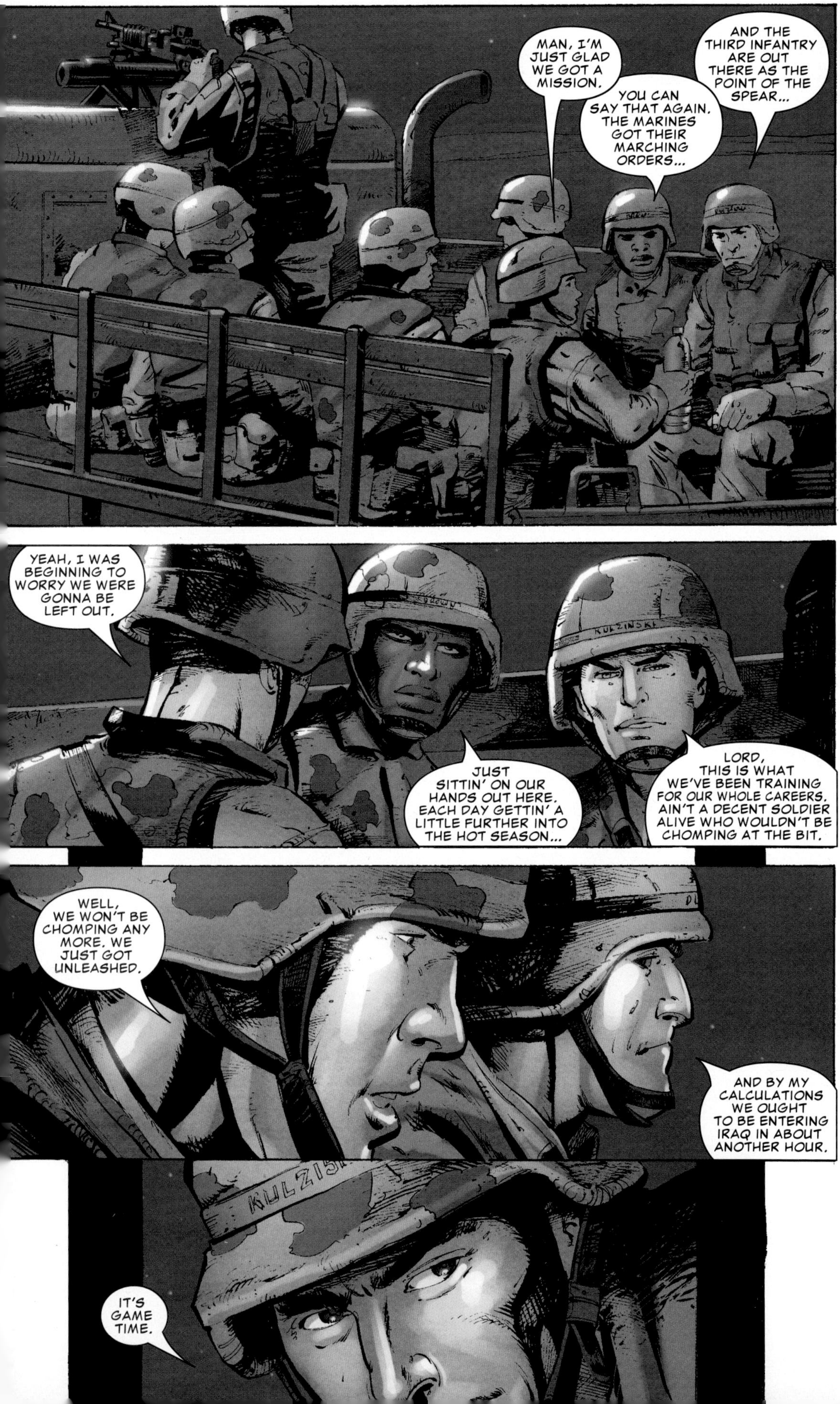
MAN, I'M JUST GLAD WE GOT A MISSION.
YOU CAN SAY THAT AGAIN. THE MARINES GOT THEIR MARCHING ORDERS...
AND THE THIRD INFANTRY ARE OUT THERE AS THE POINT OF THE SPEAR...
YEAH, I WAS BEGINNING TO WORRY WE WERE GONNA BE LEFT OUT.
JUST SITTIN' ON OUR HANDS OUT HERE. EACH DAY GETTIN' A LITTLE FURTHER INTO THE HOT SEASON...
LORD, THIS IS WHAT WE'VE BEEN TRAINING FOR OUR WHOLE CAREERS. AIN'T A DECENT SOLDIER ALIVE WHO WOULDN'T BE CHOMPING AT THE BIT.
WELL, WE WON'T BE CHOMPING ANY MORE. WE JUST GOT UNLEASHED.
AND BY MY CALCULATIONS WE OUGHT TO BE ENTERING IRAQ IN ABOUT ANOTHER HOUR.
IT'S GAME TIME.

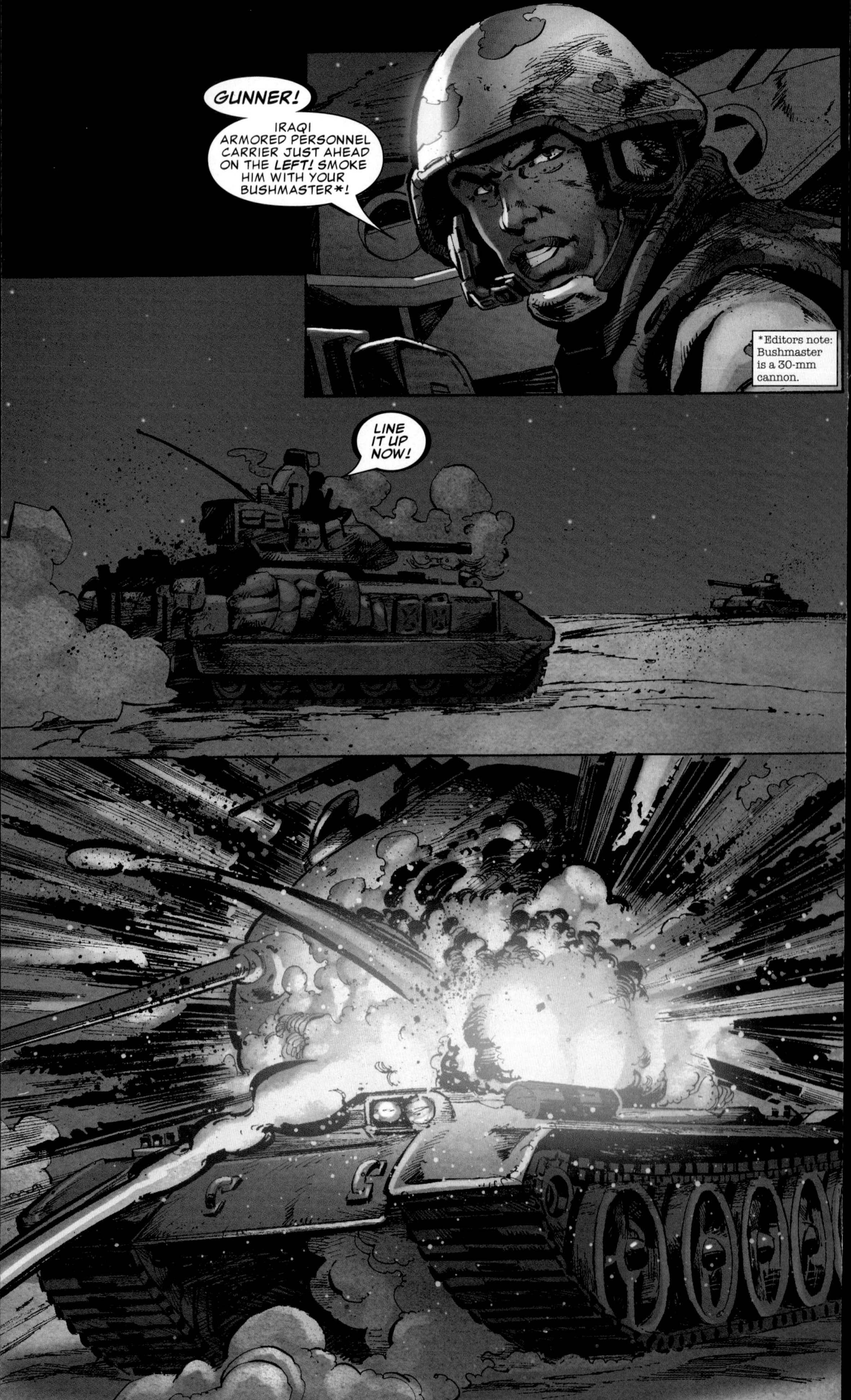
GUNNER!
IRAQI ARMORED PERSONNEL CARRIER JUST AHEAD ON THE LEFT! SMOKE HIM WITH YOUR BUSHMASTER*!
*Editors note: Bushmaster is a 30-mm cannon.
LINE IT UP NOW!

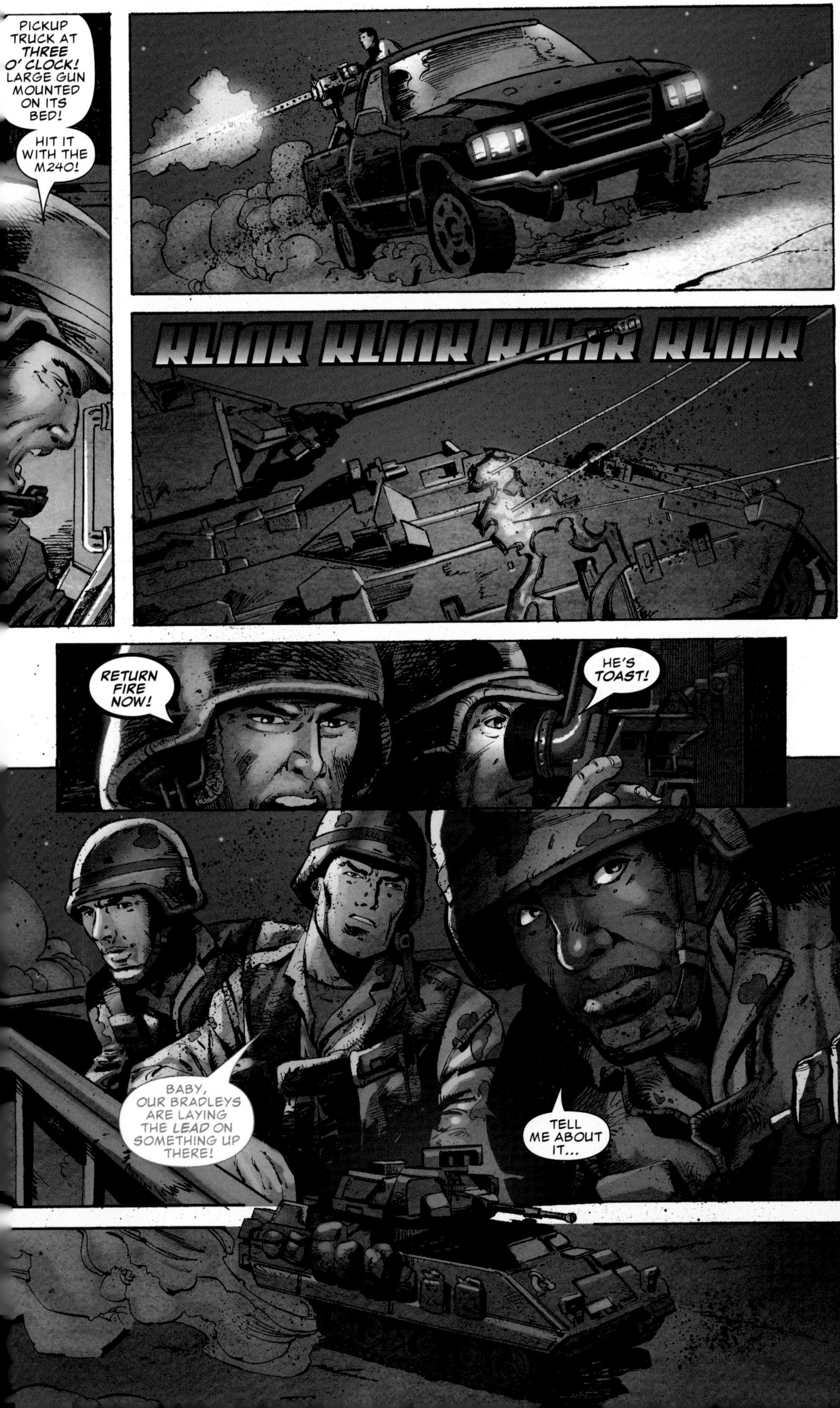

PICKUP TRUCK AT THREE O' CLOCK! LARGE GUN MOUNTED ON ITS BED!
HIT IT WITH THE M240!
KLINK KLINK KLINK KLINK
RETURN FIRE NOW!
HE'S TOAST!
BABY, OUR BRADLEYS ARE LAYING THE LEAD ON SOMETHING UP THERE!
TELL ME ABOUT IT...

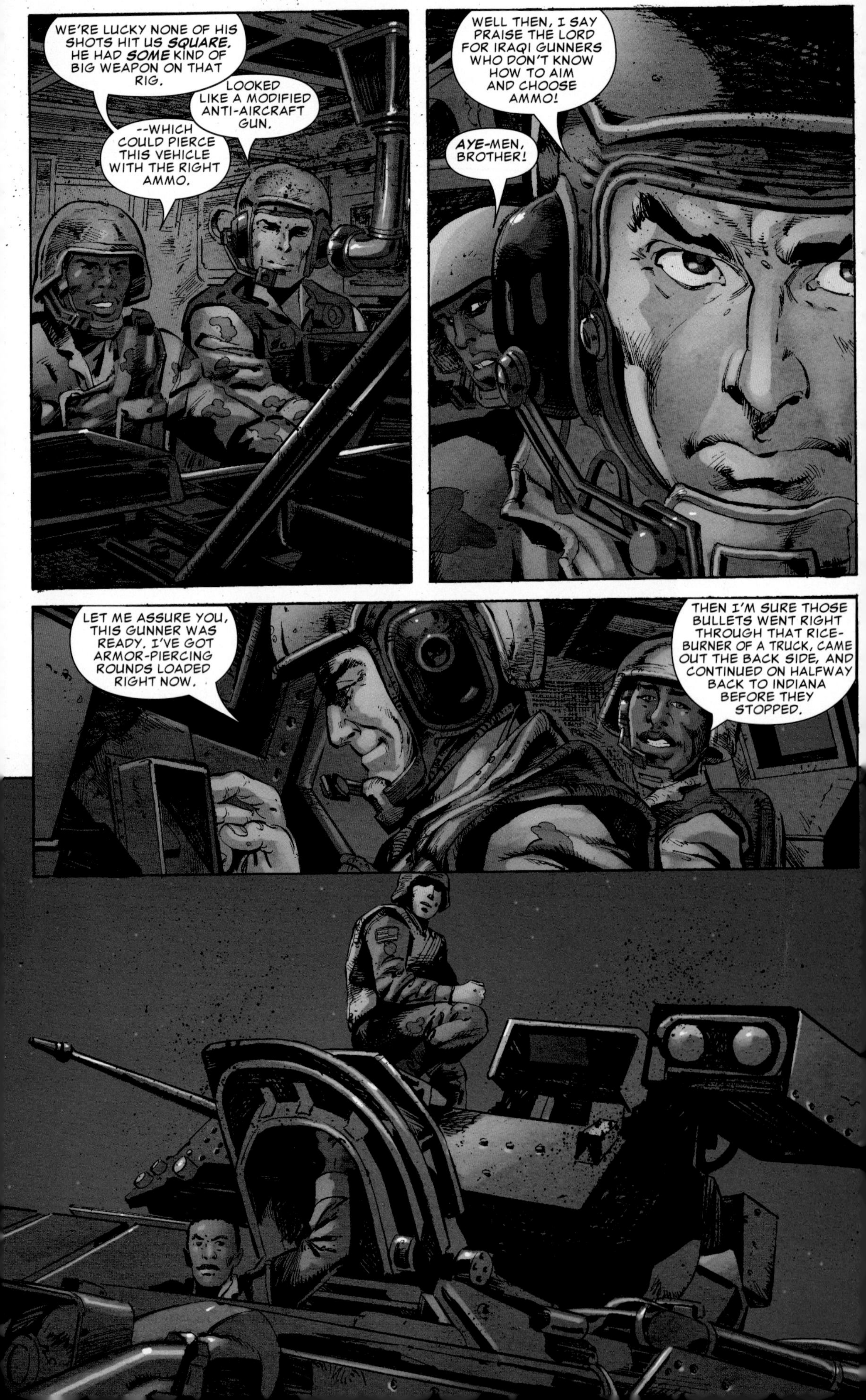
WE'RE LUCKY NONE OF HIS SHOTS HIT US SQUARE. HE HAD SOME KIND OF BIG WEAPON ON THAT RIG.
LOOKED LIKE A MODIFIED ANTI-AIRCRAFT GUN.
--WHICH COULD PIERCE THIS VEHICLE WITH THE RIGHT AMMO.
WELL THEN, I SAY PRAISE THE LORD FOR IRAQI GUNNERS WHO DON'T KNOW HOW TO AIM AND CHOOSE AMMO!
AYE-MEN, BROTHER!
LET ME ASSURE YOU, THIS GUNNER WAS READY. I'VE GOT ARMOR-PIERCING ROUNDS LOADED RIGHT NOW.
THEN I'M SURE THOSE BULLETS WENT RIGHT THROUGH THAT RICE-BURNER OF A TRUCK, CAME OUT THE BACK SIDE, AND CONTINUED ON HALFWAY BACK TO INDIANA BEFORE THEY STOPPED.

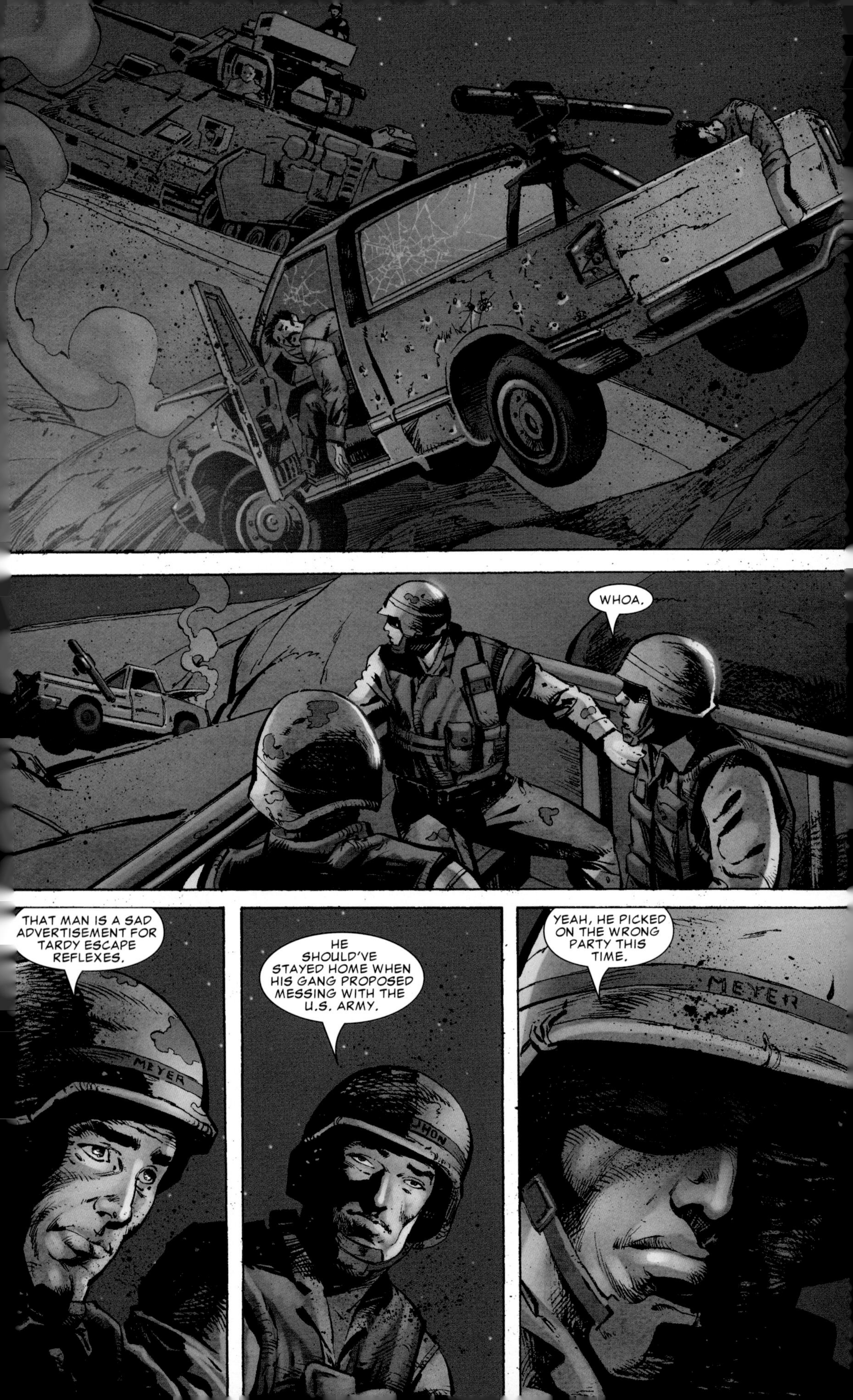
WHOA.
THAT MAN IS A SAD ADVERTISEMENT FOR TARDY ESCAPE REFLEXES.
HE SHOULD'VE STAYED HOME WHEN HIS GANG PROPOSED MESSING WITH THE U.S. ARMY.
YEAH, HE PICKED ON THE WRONG PARTY THIS TIME.

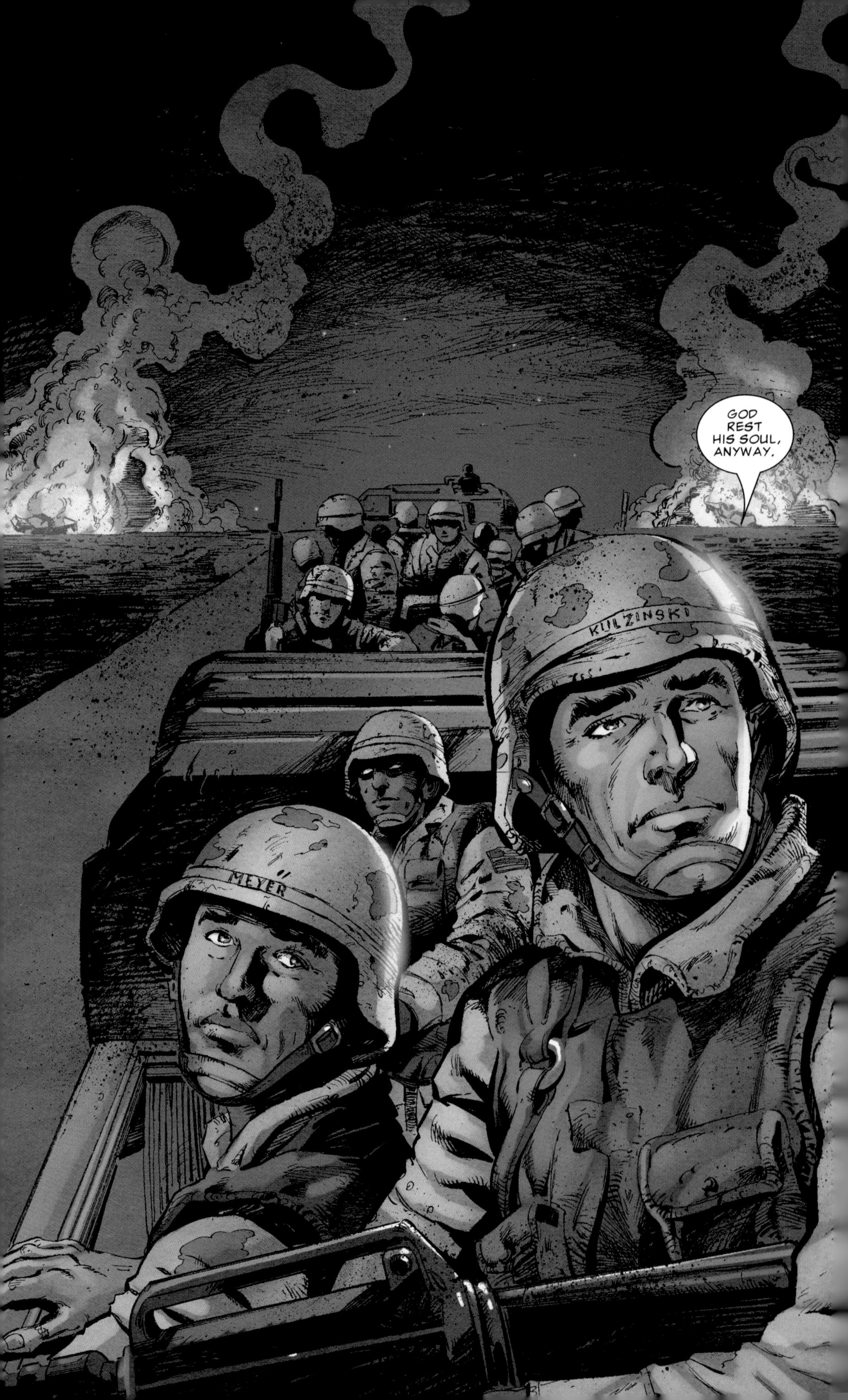
GOD REST HIS SOUL, ANYWAY.
KULZINSKI
MEYER

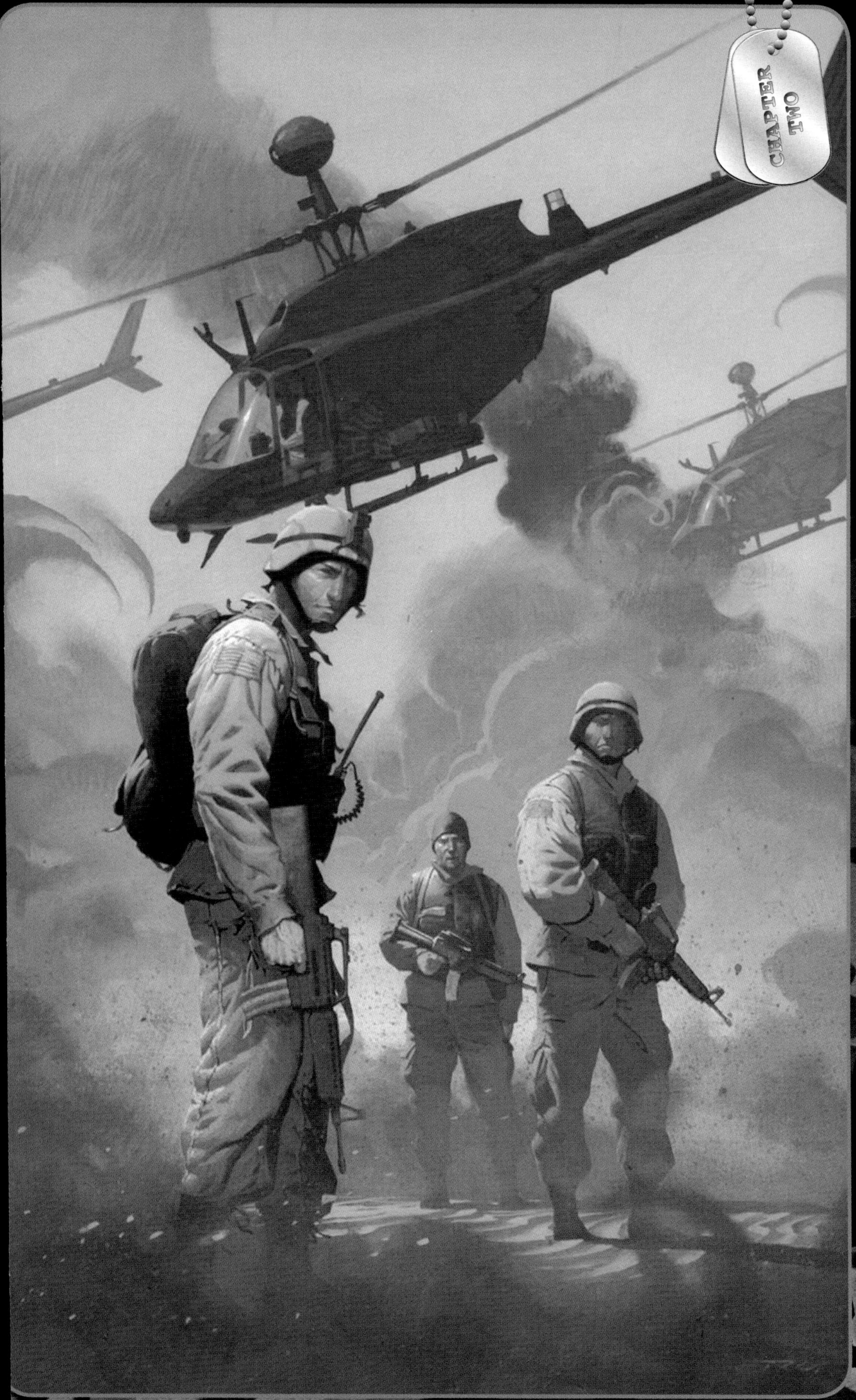
CHAPTER
TWO

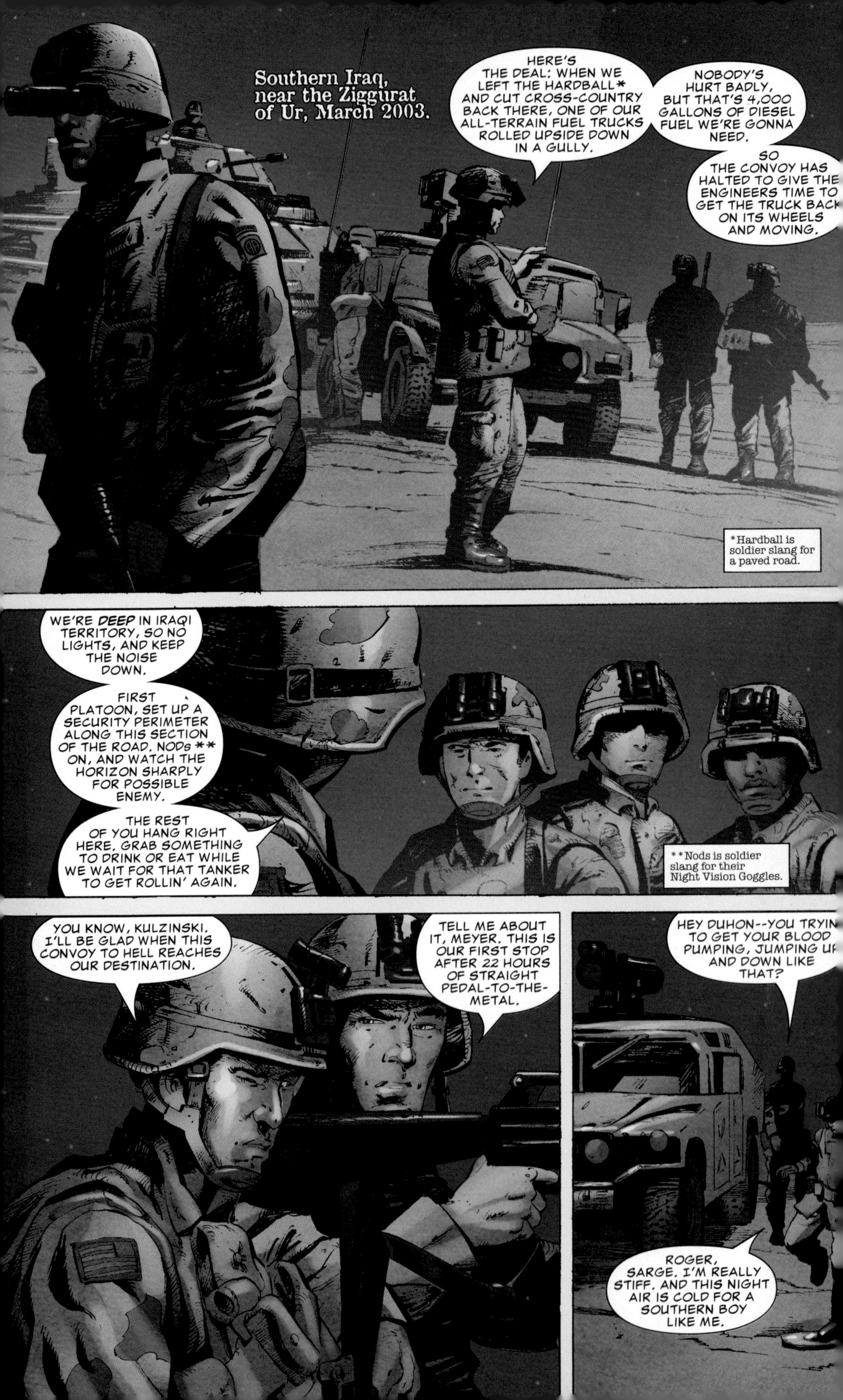
Southern Iraq, near the Ziggurat of Ur, March 2003.
HERE'S THE DEAL: WHEN WE LEFT THE HARDBALL* AND CUT CROSS-COUNTRY BACK THERE, ONE OF OUR ALL-TERRAIN FUEL TRUCKS ROLLED UPSIDE DOWN IN A GULLY.
NOBODY'S HURT BADLY, BUT THAT'S 4,000 GALLONS OF DIESEL FUEL WE'RE GONNA NEED.
SO THE CONVOY HAS HALTED TO GIVE THE ENGINEERS TIME TO GET THE TRUCK BACK ON ITS WHEELS AND MOVING.
*Hardball is soldier slang for a paved road.
WE'RE DEEP IN IRAQI TERRITORY, SO NO LIGHTS, AND KEEP THE NOISE DOWN.
FIRST PLATOON, SET UP A SECURITY PERIMETER ALONG THIS SECTION OF THE ROAD. NODs ** ON, AND WATCH THE HORIZON SHARPLY FOR POSSIBLE ENEMY.
THE REST OF YOU HANG RIGHT HERE. GRAB SOMETHING TO DRINK OR EAT WHILE WE WAIT FOR THAT TANKER TO GET ROLLIN' AGAIN.
**Nods is soldier slang for their Night Vision Goggles.
YOU KNOW, KULZINSKI, I'LL BE GLAD WHEN THIS CONVOY TO HELL REACHES OUR DESTINATION.
TELL ME ABOUT IT, MEYER. THIS IS OUR FIRST STOP AFTER 22 HOURS OF STRAIGHT PEDAL-TO-THE-METAL.
HEY DUHON--YOU TRYIN TO GET YOUR BLOOD PUMPING, JUMPING UP AND DOWN LIKE THAT?
ROGER, SARGE. I'M REALLY STIFF, AND THIS NIGHT AIR IS COLD FOR A SOUTHERN BOY LIKE ME.

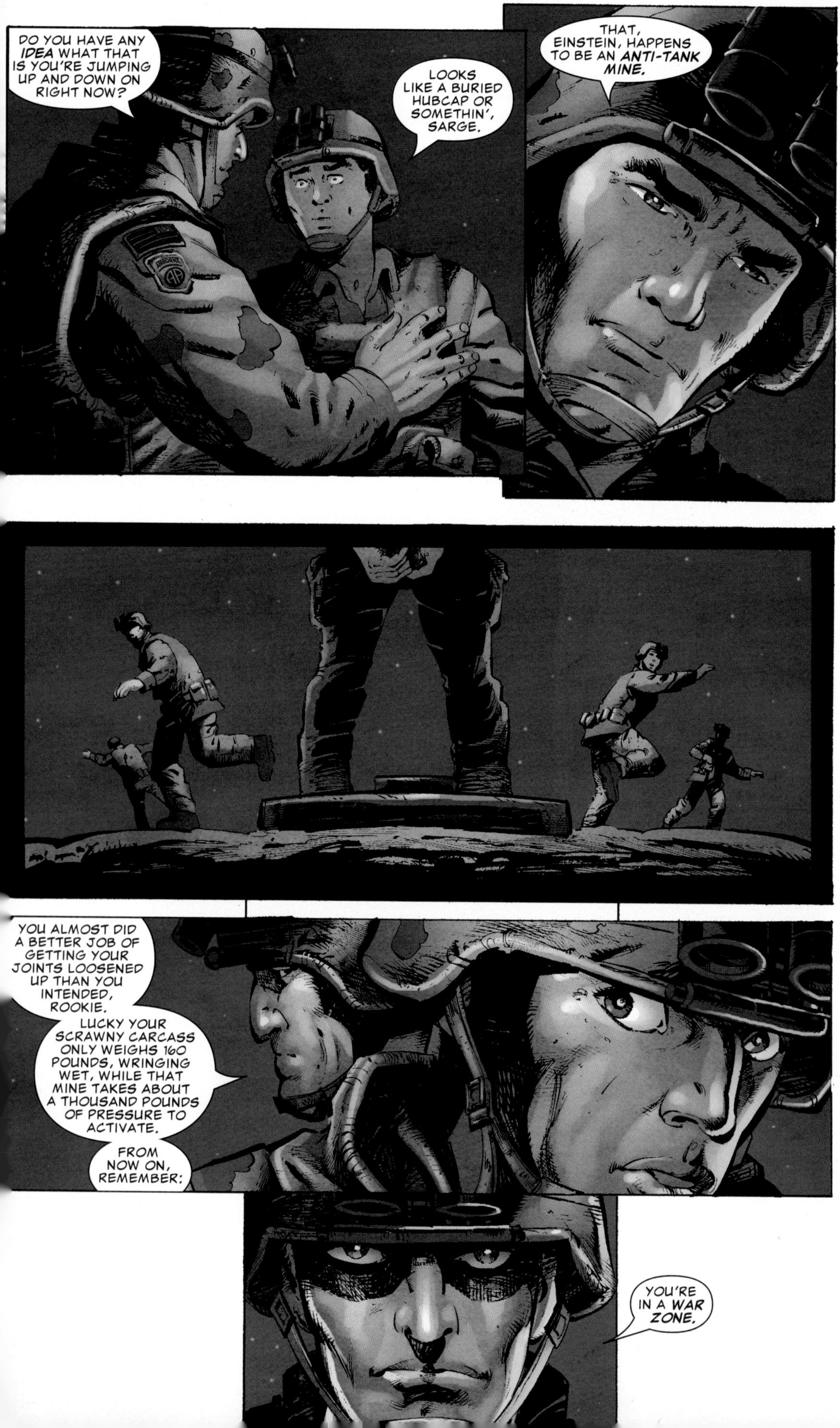
DO YOU HAVE ANY IDEA WHAT THAT IS YOU'RE JUMPING UP AND DOWN ON RIGHT NOW?
LOOKS LIKE A BURIED HUBCAP OR SOMETHIN', SARGE.
THAT, EINSTEIN, HAPPENS TO BE AN ANTI-TANK MINE.
YOU ALMOST DID A BETTER JOB OF GETTING YOUR JOINTS LOOSENED UP THAN YOU INTENDED, ROOKIE.
LUCKY YOUR SCRAWNY CARCASS ONLY WEIGHS 160 POUNDS, WRINGING WET, WHILE THAT MINE TAKES ABOUT A THOUSAND POUNDS OF PRESSURE TO ACTIVATE.
FROM NOW ON, REMEMBER:
YOU'RE IN A WAR ZONE.

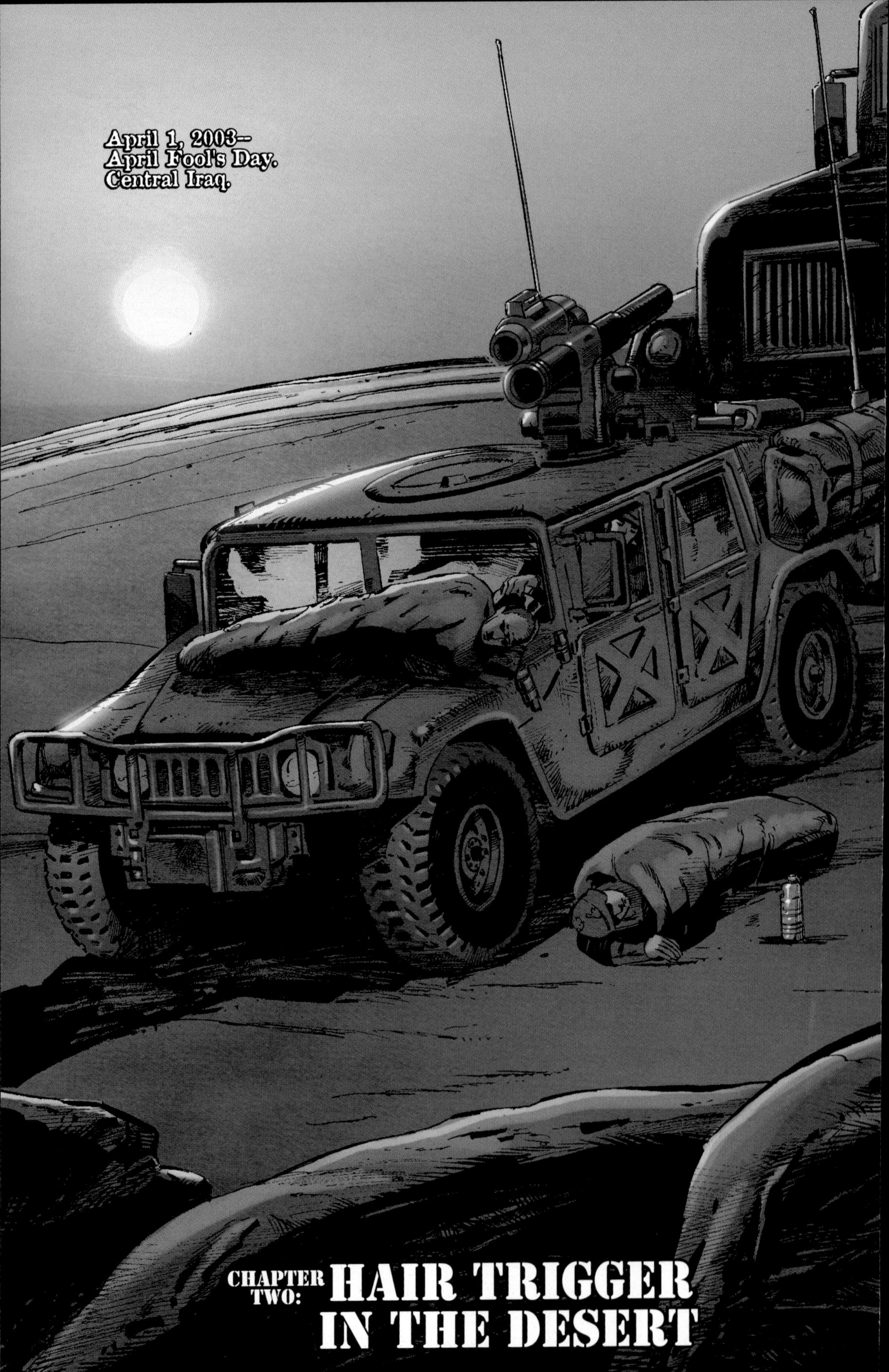
April 1, 2003--
April Fool's Day.
Central Iraq.
CHAPTER TWO: HAIR TRIGGER IN THE DESERT

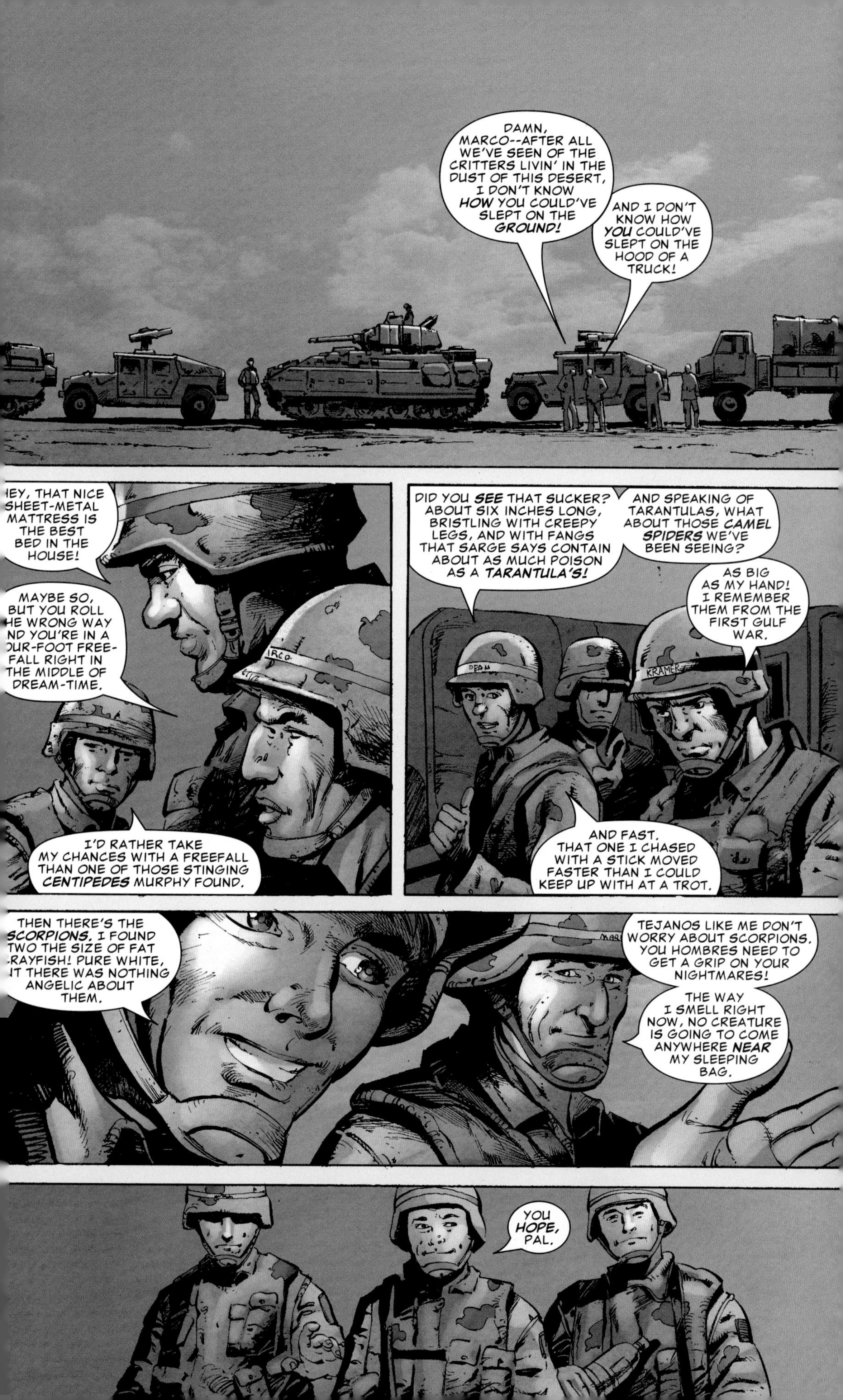
DAMN, MARCO--AFTER ALL WE'VE SEEN OF THE CRITTERS LIVIN' IN THE DUST OF THIS DESERT, I DON'T KNOW HOW YOU COULD'VE SLEPT ON THE GROUND!
AND I DON'T KNOW HOW YOU COULD'VE SLEPT ON THE HOOD OF A TRUCK!
EY, THAT NICE SHEET-METAL MATTRESS IS THE BEST BED IN THE HOUSE!
MAYBE SO, BUT YOU ROLL HE WRONG WAY ND YOU'RE IN A OUR-FOOT FREE-FALL RIGHT IN THE MIDDLE OF DREAM-TIME.
I'D RATHER TAKE MY CHANCES WITH A FREEFALL THAN ONE OF THOSE STINGING CENTIPEDES MURPHY FOUND.
DID YOU SEE THAT SUCKER? ABOUT SIX INCHES LONG, BRISTLING WITH CREEPY LEGS, AND WITH FANGS THAT SARGE SAYS CONTAIN ABOUT AS MUCH POISON AS A TARANTULA'S!
AND SPEAKING OF TARANTULAS, WHAT ABOUT THOSE CAMEL SPIDERS WE'VE BEEN SEEING?
AS BIG AS MY HAND! I REMEMBER THEM FROM THE FIRST GULF WAR.
KRAMER
AND FAST. THAT ONE I CHASED WITH A STICK MOVED FASTER THAN I COULD KEEP UP WITH AT A TROT.
THEN THERE'S THE SCORPIONS. I FOUND TWO THE SIZE OF FAT RAYFISH! PURE WHITE, T THERE WAS NOTHING ANGELIC ABOUT THEM.
TEJANOS LIKE ME DON'T WORRY ABOUT SCORPIONS. YOU HOMBRES NEED TO GET A GRIP ON YOUR NIGHTMARES!
THE WAY I SMELL RIGHT NOW, NO CREATURE IS GOING TO COME ANYWHERE NEAR MY SLEEPING BAG.
YOU HOPE, PAL.

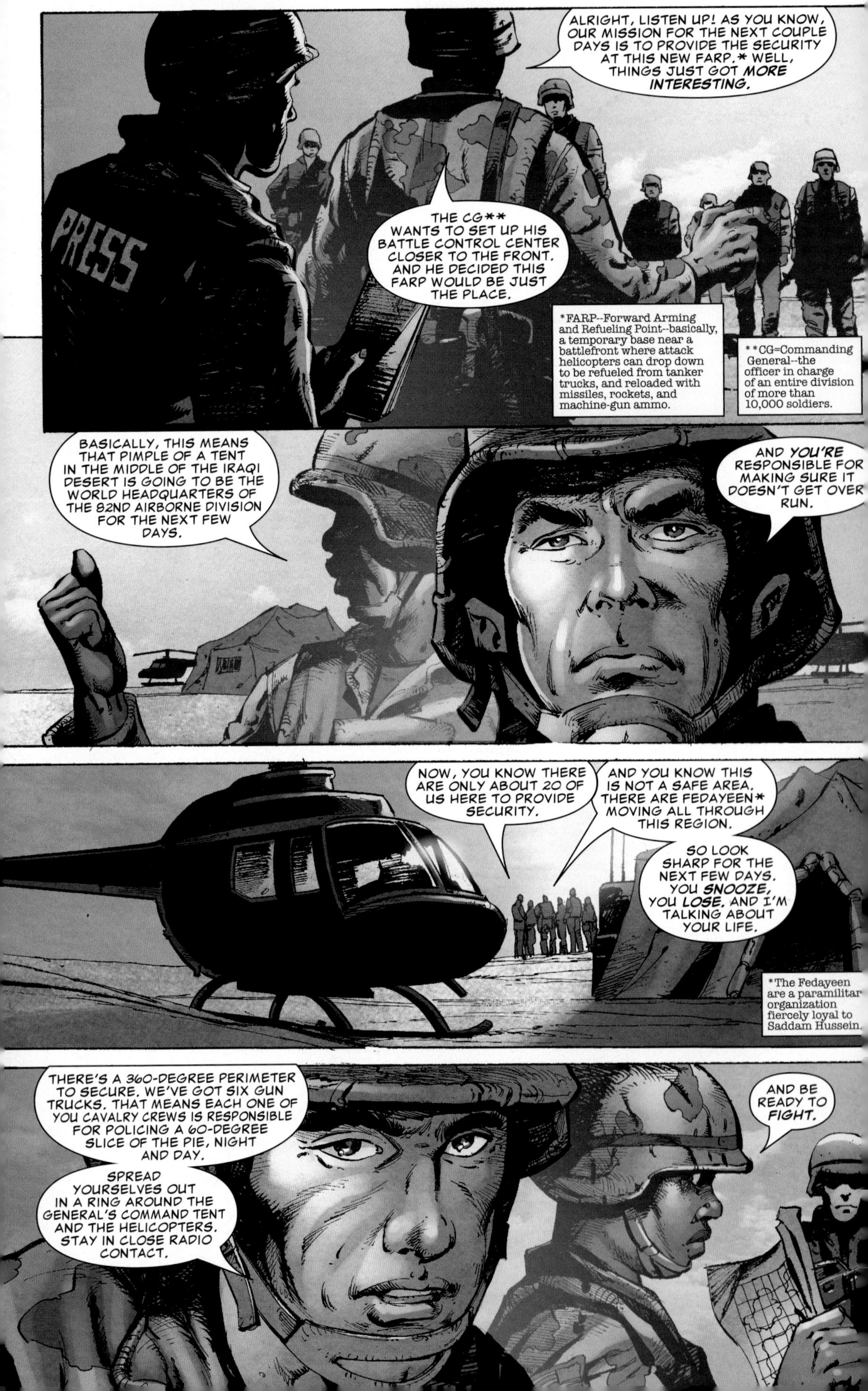
ALRIGHT, LISTEN UP! AS YOU KNOW, OUR MISSION FOR THE NEXT COUPLE DAYS IS TO PROVIDE THE SECURITY AT THIS NEW FARP.* WELL, THINGS JUST GOT MORE INTERESTING.
THE CG** WANTS TO SET UP HIS BATTLE CONTROL CENTER CLOSER TO THE FRONT. AND HE DECIDED THIS FARP WOULD BE JUST THE PLACE.
PRESS
*FARP--Forward Arming and Refueling Point--basically, a temporary base near a battlefront where attack helicopters can drop down to be refueled from tanker trucks, and reloaded with missiles, rockets, and machine-gun ammo.
**CG=Commanding General--the officer in charge of an entire division of more than 10,000 soldiers.
BASICALLY, THIS MEANS THAT PIMPLE OF A TENT IN THE MIDDLE OF THE IRAQI DESERT IS GOING TO BE THE WORLD HEADQUARTERS OF THE 82ND AIRBORNE DIVISION FOR THE NEXT FEW DAYS.
AND YOU'RE RESPONSIBLE FOR MAKING SURE IT DOESN'T GET OVER RUN.
NOW, YOU KNOW THERE ARE ONLY ABOUT 20 OF US HERE TO PROVIDE SECURITY.
AND YOU KNOW THIS IS NOT A SAFE AREA. THERE ARE FEDAYEEN* MOVING ALL THROUGH THIS REGION.
SO LOOK SHARP FOR THE NEXT FEW DAYS. YOU SNOOZE, YOU LOSE. AND I'M TALKING ABOUT YOUR LIFE.
*The Fedayeen are a paramilitar organization fiercely loyal to Saddam Hussein.
THERE'S A 360-DEGREE PERIMETER TO SECURE. WE'VE GOT SIX GUN TRUCKS. THAT MEANS EACH ONE OF YOU CAVALRY CREWS IS RESPONSIBLE FOR POLICING A 60-DEGREE SLICE OF THE PIE, NIGHT AND DAY.
SPREAD YOURSELVES OUT IN A RING AROUND THE GENERAL'S COMMAND TENT AND THE HELICOPTERS. STAY IN CLOSE RADIO CONTACT.
AND BE READY TO FIGHT.

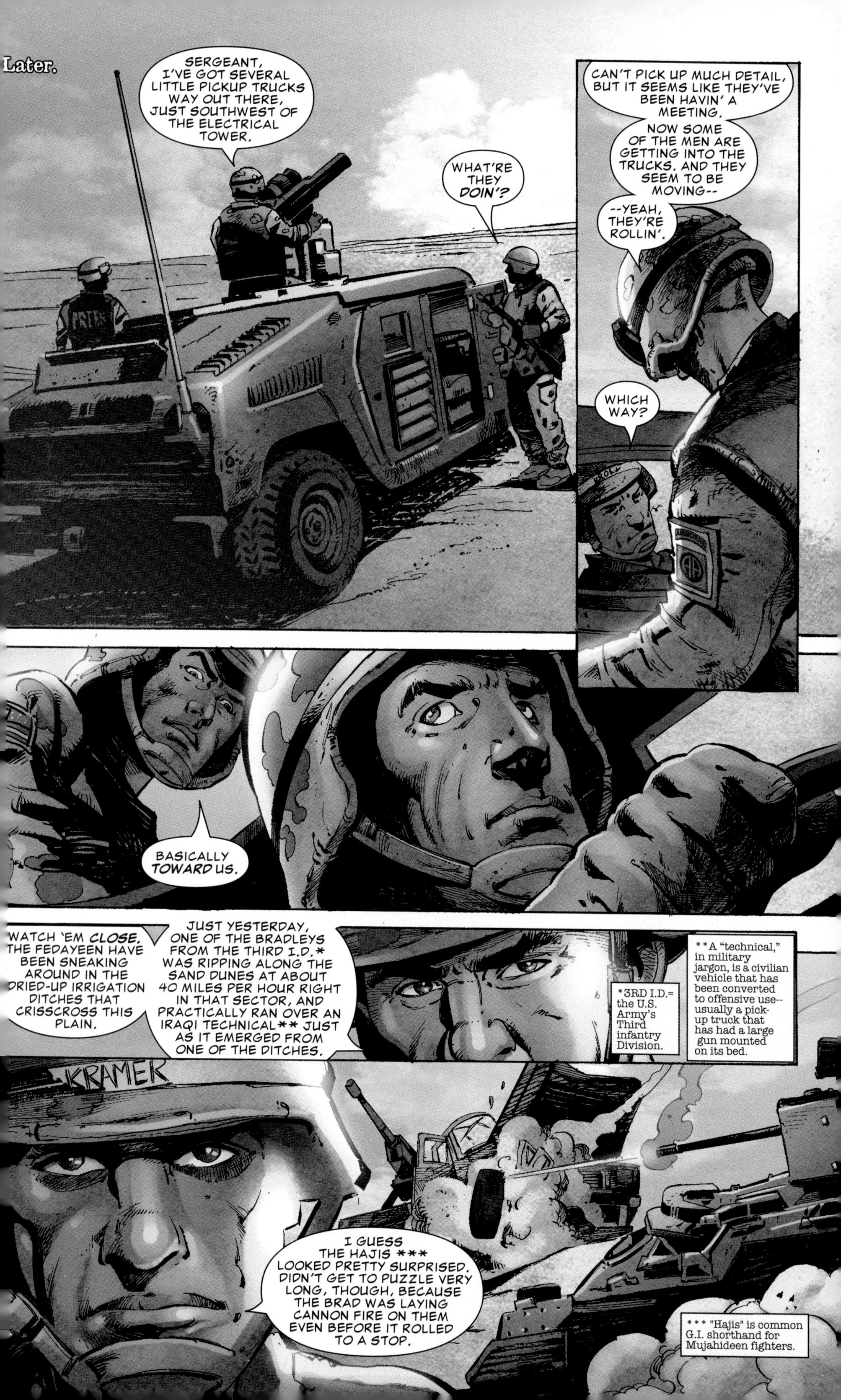
Later.
SERGEANT, I'VE GOT SEVERAL LITTLE PICKUP TRUCKS WAY OUT THERE, JUST SOUTHWEST OF THE ELECTRICAL TOWER.
WHAT'RE THEY DOIN'?
CAN'T PICK UP MUCH DETAIL, BUT IT SEEMS LIKE THEY'VE BEEN HAVIN' A MEETING.
NOW SOME OF THE MEN ARE GETTING INTO THE TRUCKS, AND THEY SEEM TO BE MOVING--
--YEAH, THEY'RE ROLLIN'.
WHICH WAY?
BASICALLY TOWARD US.
WATCH 'EM CLOSE. THE FEDAYEEN HAVE BEEN SNEAKING AROUND IN THE DRIED-UP IRRIGATION DITCHES THAT CRISSCROSS THIS PLAIN.
JUST YESTERDAY, ONE OF THE BRADLEYS FROM THE THIRD I.D.* WAS RIPPING ALONG THE SAND DUNES AT ABOUT 40 MILES PER HOUR RIGHT IN THAT SECTOR, AND PRACTICALLY RAN OVER AN IRAQI TECHNICAL** JUST AS IT EMERGED FROM ONE OF THE DITCHES.
*3RD I.D.= the U.S. Army's Third infantry Division.
**A "technical," in military jargon, is a civilian vehicle that has been converted to offensive use--usually a pick-up truck that has had a large gun mounted on its bed.
KRAMER
I GUESS THE HAJIS *** LOOKED PRETTY SURPRISED. DIDN'T GET TO PUZZLE VERY LONG, THOUGH, BECAUSE THE BRAD WAS LAYING CANNON FIRE ON THEM EVEN BEFORE IT ROLLED TO A STOP.
*** "Hajis" is common G.I. shorthand for Mujahideen fighters.

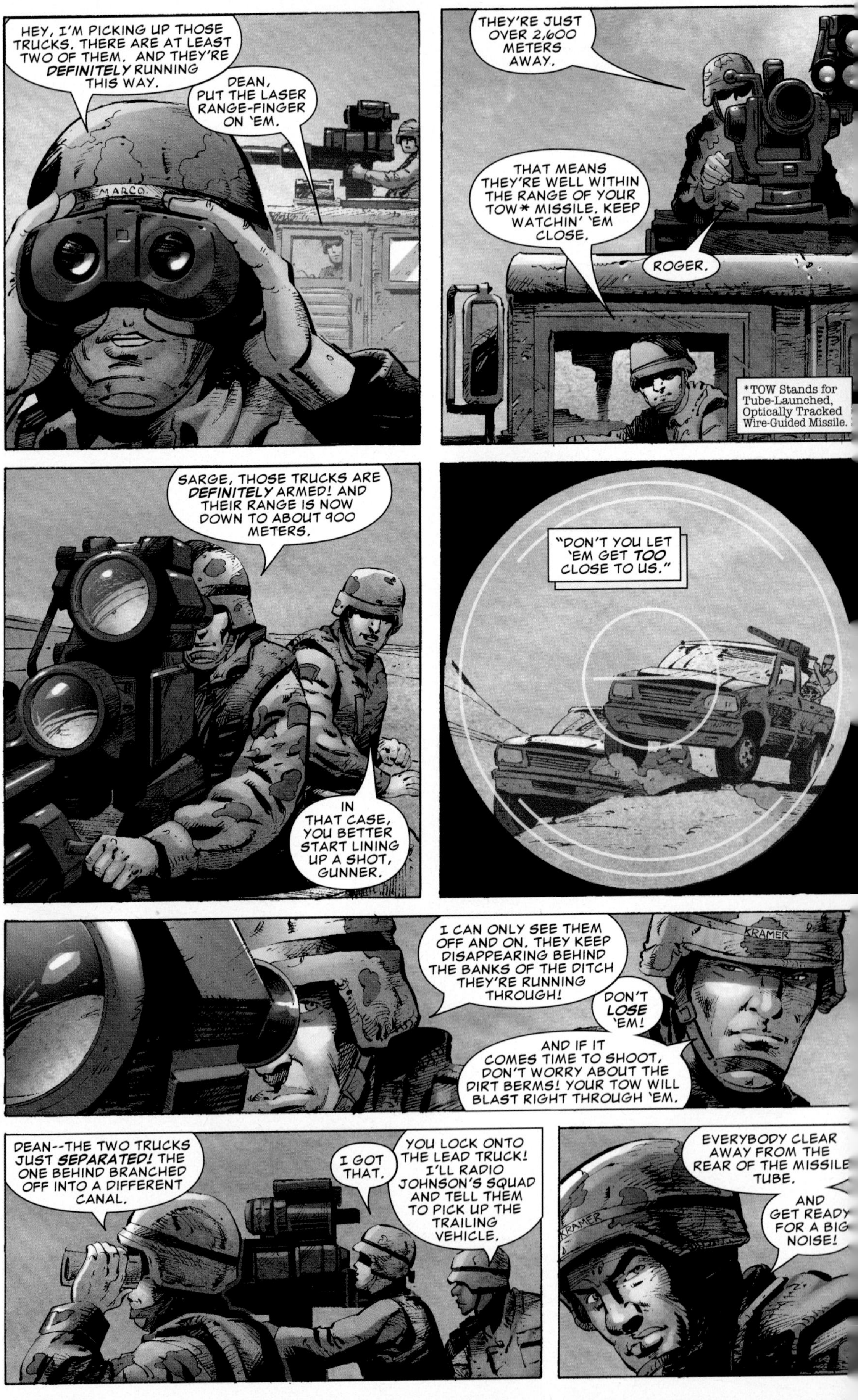
HEY, I'M PICKING UP THOSE TRUCKS. THERE ARE AT LEAST TWO OF THEM. AND THEY'RE DEFINITELY RUNNING THIS WAY.
DEAN, PUT THE LASER RANGE-FINGER ON 'EM.
MARCO
THEY'RE JUST OVER 2,600 METERS AWAY.
THAT MEANS THEY'RE WELL WITHIN THE RANGE OF YOUR TOW* MISSILE. KEEP WATCHIN' 'EM CLOSE.
ROGER.
*TOW Stands for Tube-Launched, Optically Tracked Wire-Guided Missile.
SARGE, THOSE TRUCKS ARE DEFINITELY ARMED! AND THEIR RANGE IS NOW DOWN TO ABOUT 900 METERS.
IN THAT CASE, YOU BETTER START LINING UP A SHOT, GUNNER.
"DON'T YOU LET 'EM GET TOO CLOSE TO US."
I CAN ONLY SEE THEM OFF AND ON. THEY KEEP DISAPPEARING BEHIND THE BANKS OF THE DITCH THEY'RE RUNNING THROUGH!
KRAMER
DON'T LOSE 'EM!
AND IF IT COMES TIME TO SHOOT, DON'T WORRY ABOUT THE DIRT BERMS! YOUR TOW WILL BLAST RIGHT THROUGH 'EM.
DEAN--THE TWO TRUCKS JUST SEPARATED! THE ONE BEHIND BRANCHED OFF INTO A DIFFERENT CANAL.
I GOT THAT.
YOU LOCK ONTO THE LEAD TRUCK! I'LL RADIO JOHNSON'S SQUAD AND TELL THEM TO PICK UP THE TRAILING VEHICLE.
EVERYBODY CLEAR AWAY FROM THE REAR OF THE MISSILE TUBE.
AND GET READY FOR A BIG NOISE!
KRAMER

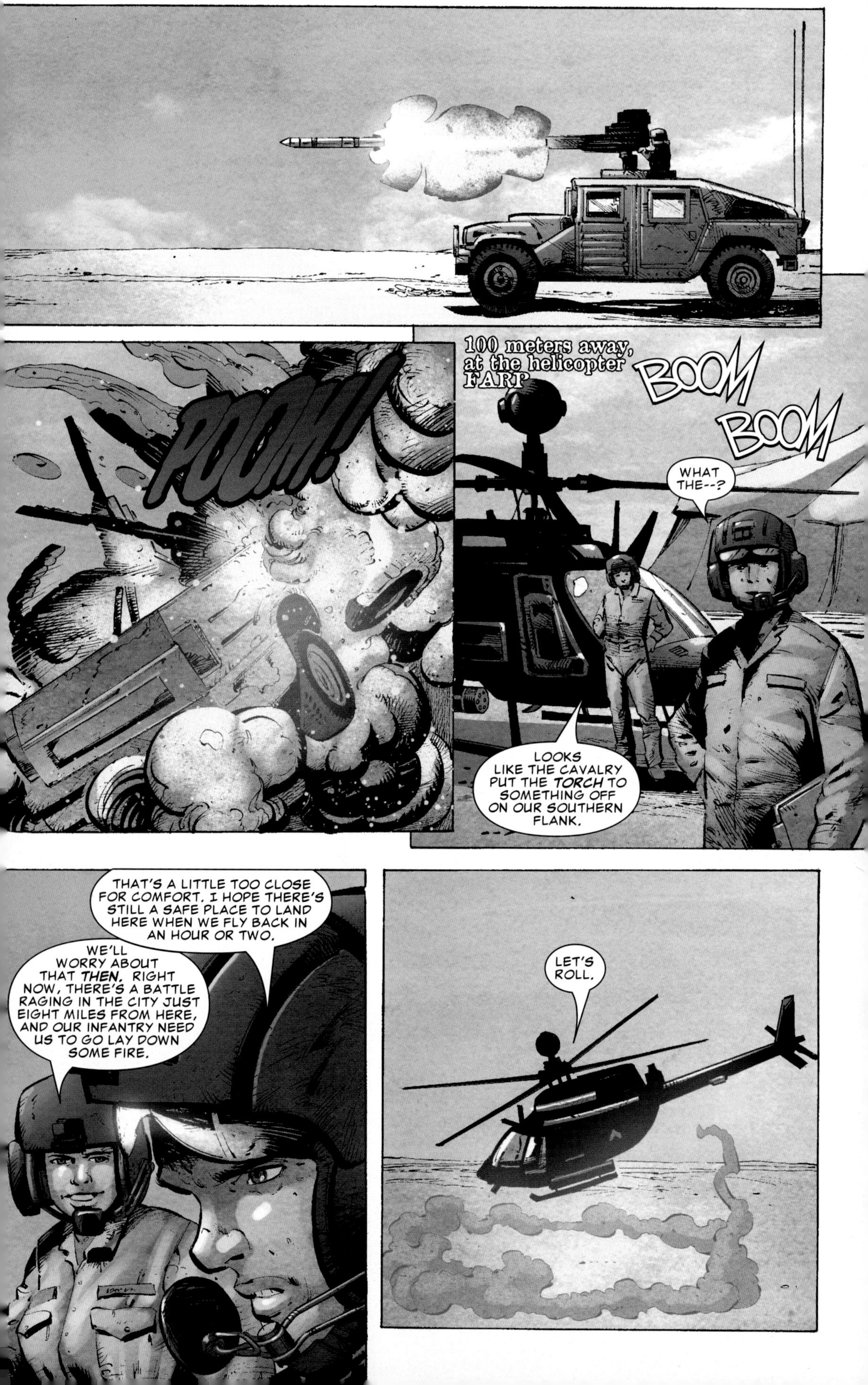

POOM!
100 meters away, at the helicopter FARP
BOOM
BOOM
WHAT THE--?
LOOKS LIKE THE CAVALRY PUT THE *TORCH* TO SOMETHING OFF ON OUR SOUTHERN FLANK.
THAT'S A LITTLE TOO CLOSE FOR COMFORT. I HOPE THERE'S STILL A SAFE PLACE TO LAND HERE WHEN WE FLY BACK IN AN HOUR OR TWO.
WE'LL WORRY ABOUT THAT *THEN.* RIGHT NOW, THERE'S A BATTLE RAGING IN THE CITY JUST EIGHT MILES FROM HERE, AND OUR INFANTRY NEED US TO GO LAY DOWN SOME FIRE.
LET'S ROLL.

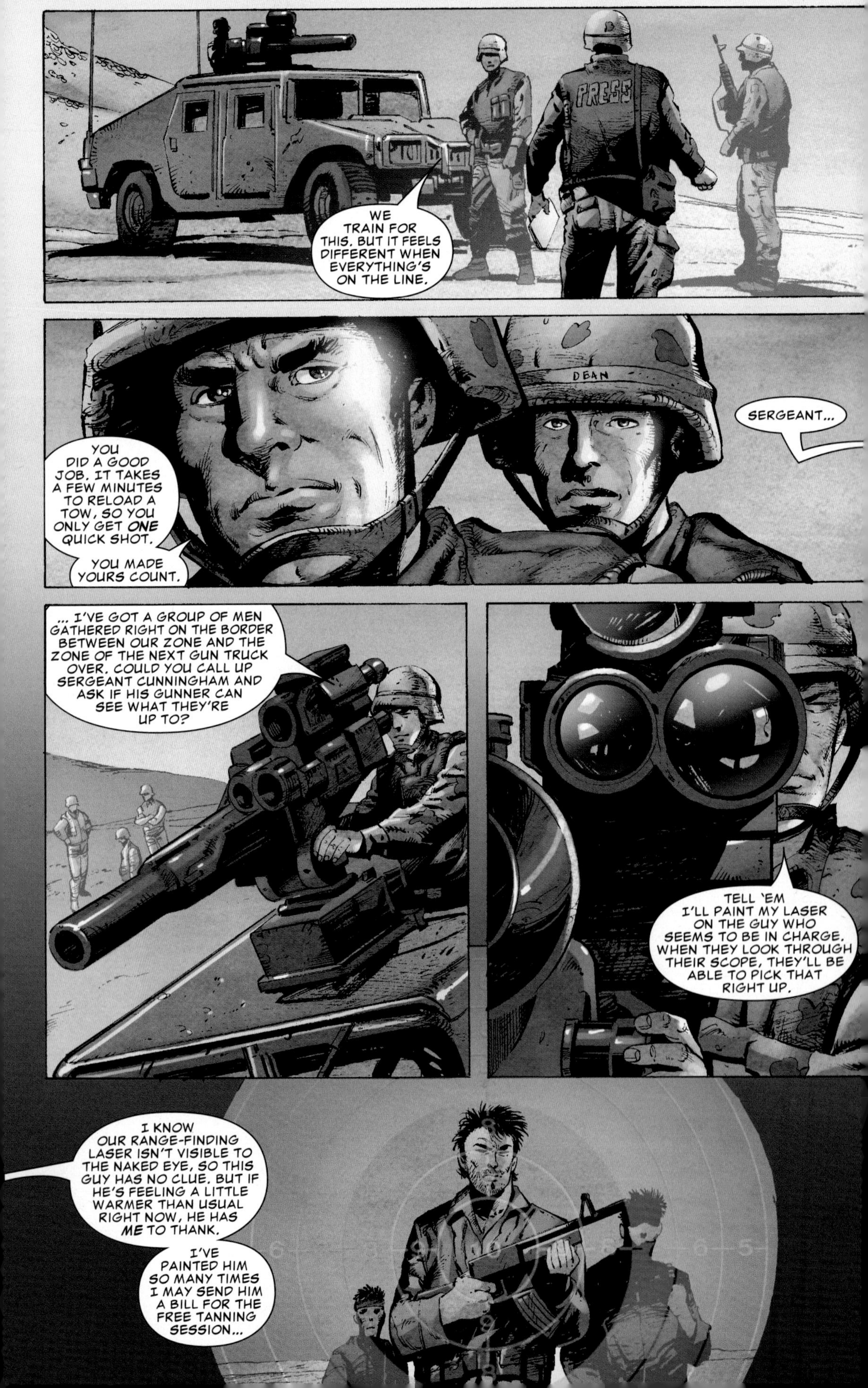
WE TRAIN FOR THIS. BUT IT FEELS DIFFERENT WHEN EVERYTHING'S ON THE LINE.
PRESS
DEAN
YOU DID A GOOD JOB. IT TAKES A FEW MINUTES TO RELOAD A TOW, SO YOU ONLY GET *ONE* QUICK SHOT.
YOU MADE YOURS COUNT.
SERGEANT...
... I'VE GOT A GROUP OF MEN GATHERED RIGHT ON THE BORDER BETWEEN OUR ZONE AND THE ZONE OF THE NEXT GUN TRUCK OVER. COULD YOU CALL UP SERGEANT CUNNINGHAM AND ASK IF HIS GUNNER CAN SEE WHAT THEY'RE UP TO?
TELL 'EM I'LL PAINT MY LASER ON THE GUY WHO SEEMS TO BE IN CHARGE. WHEN THEY LOOK THROUGH THEIR SCOPE, THEY'LL BE ABLE TO PICK THAT RIGHT UP.
I KNOW OUR RANGE-FINDING LASER ISN'T VISIBLE TO THE NAKED EYE, SO THIS GUY HAS NO CLUE. BUT IF HE'S FEELING A LITTLE WARMER THAN USUAL RIGHT NOW, HE HAS *ME* TO THANK.
I'VE PAINTED HIM SO MANY TIMES I MAY SEND HIM A BILL FOR THE FREE TANNING SESSION...

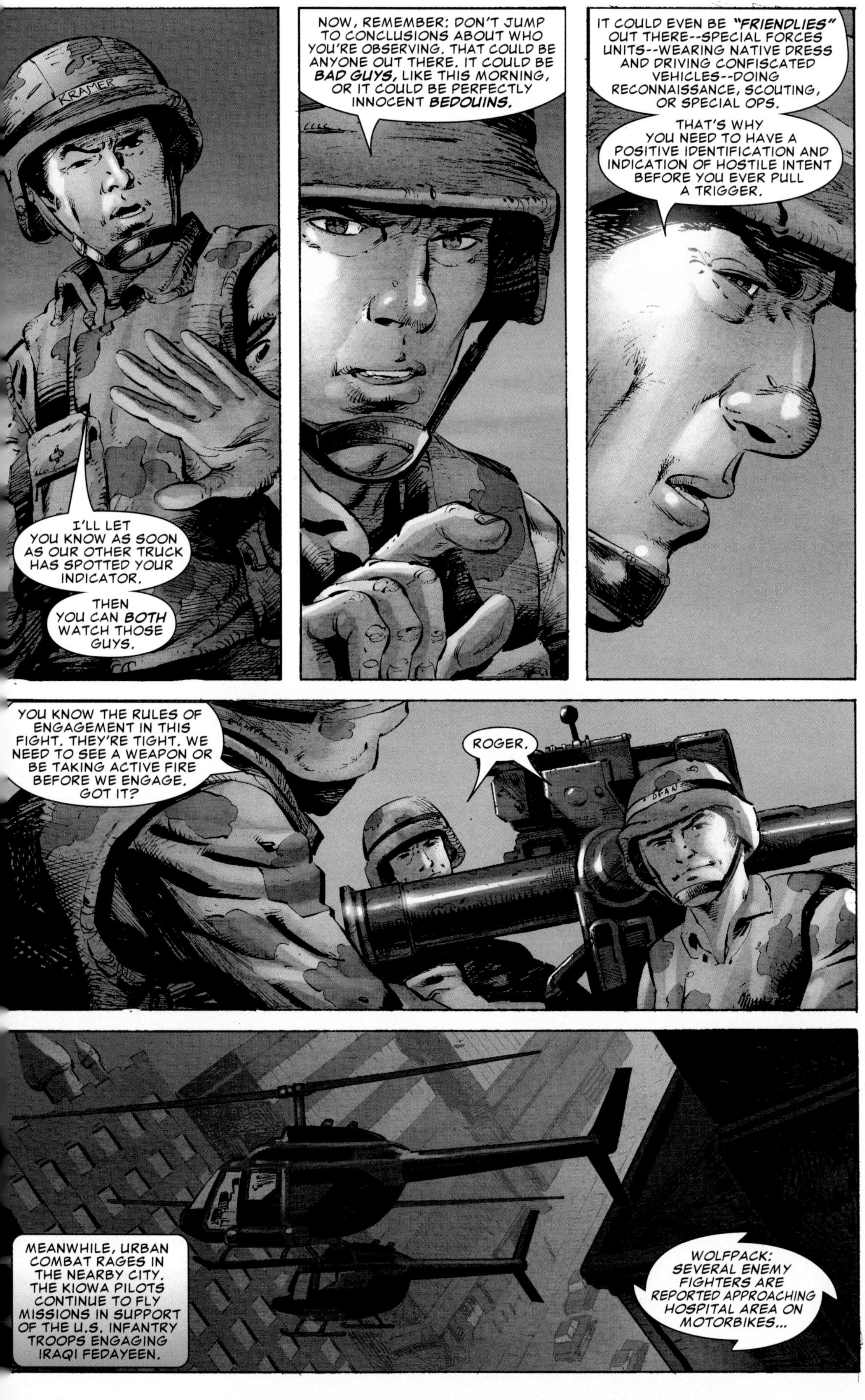
KRAMER
I'LL LET YOU KNOW AS SOON AS OUR OTHER TRUCK HAS SPOTTED YOUR INDICATOR.
THEN YOU CAN BOTH WATCH THOSE GUYS.
NOW, REMEMBER: DON'T JUMP TO CONCLUSIONS ABOUT WHO YOU'RE OBSERVING. THAT COULD BE ANYONE OUT THERE. IT COULD BE BAD GUYS, LIKE THIS MORNING, OR IT COULD BE PERFECTLY INNOCENT BEDOUINS.
IT COULD EVEN BE "FRIENDLIES" OUT THERE--SPECIAL FORCES UNITS--WEARING NATIVE DRESS AND DRIVING CONFISCATED VEHICLES--DOING RECONNAISSANCE, SCOUTING, OR SPECIAL OPS.
THAT'S WHY YOU NEED TO HAVE A POSITIVE IDENTIFICATION AND INDICATION OF HOSTILE INTENT BEFORE YOU EVER PULL A TRIGGER.
YOU KNOW THE RULES OF ENGAGEMENT IN THIS FIGHT. THEY'RE TIGHT. WE NEED TO SEE A WEAPON OR BE TAKING ACTIVE FIRE BEFORE WE ENGAGE. GOT IT?
ROGER.
DEAN
MEANWHILE, URBAN COMBAT RAGES IN THE NEARBY CITY. THE KIOWA PILOTS CONTINUE TO FLY MISSIONS IN SUPPORT OF THE U.S. INFANTRY TROOPS ENGAGING IRAQI FEDAYEEN.
WOLFPACK: SEVERAL ENEMY FIGHTERS ARE REPORTED APPROACHING HOSPITAL AREA ON MOTORBIKES...

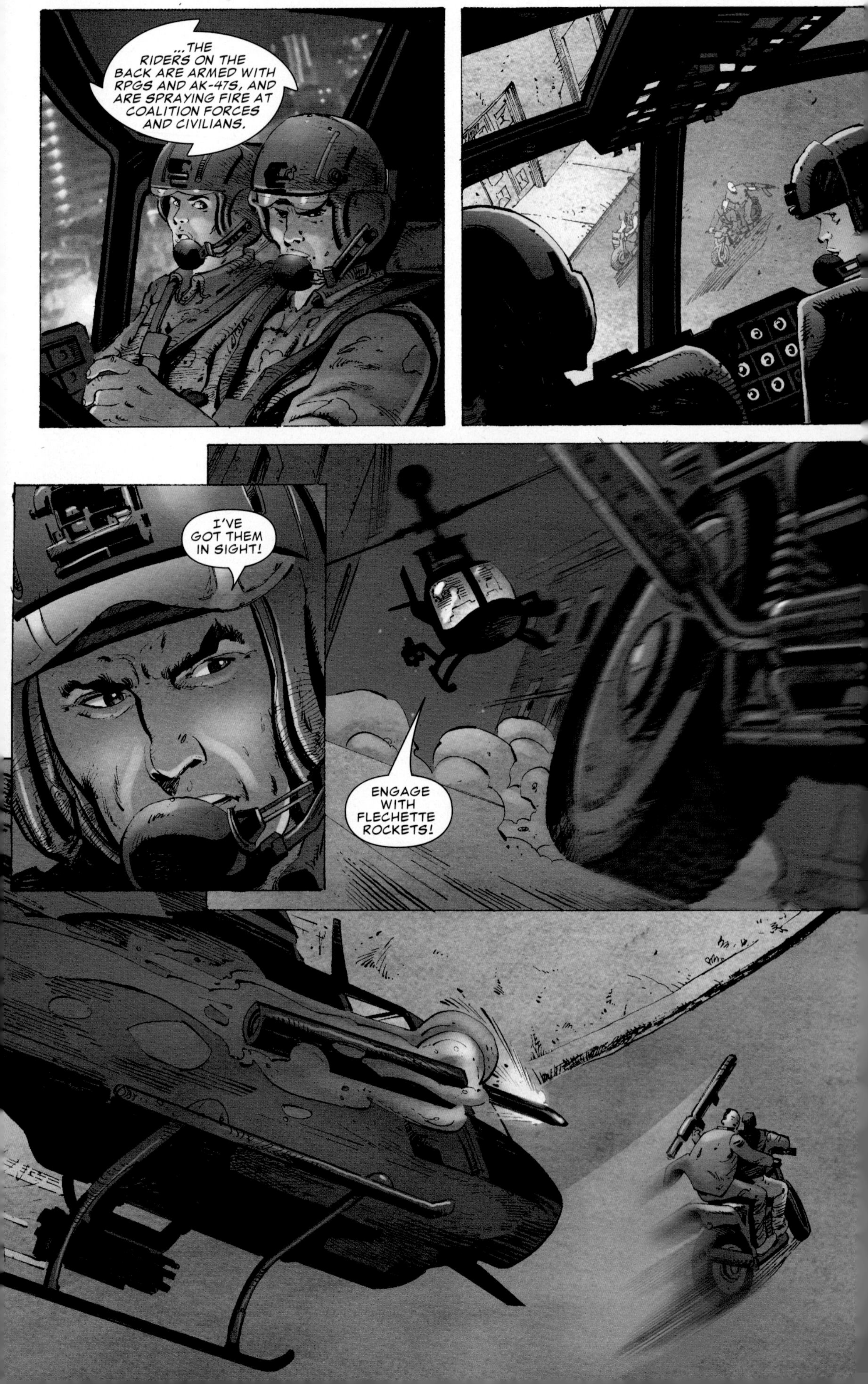
...THE RIDERS ON THE BACK ARE ARMED WITH RPGS AND AK-47S, AND ARE SPRAYING FIRE AT COALITION FORCES AND CIVILIANS.
I'VE GOT THEM IN SIGHT!
ENGAGE WITH FLECHETTE ROCKETS!

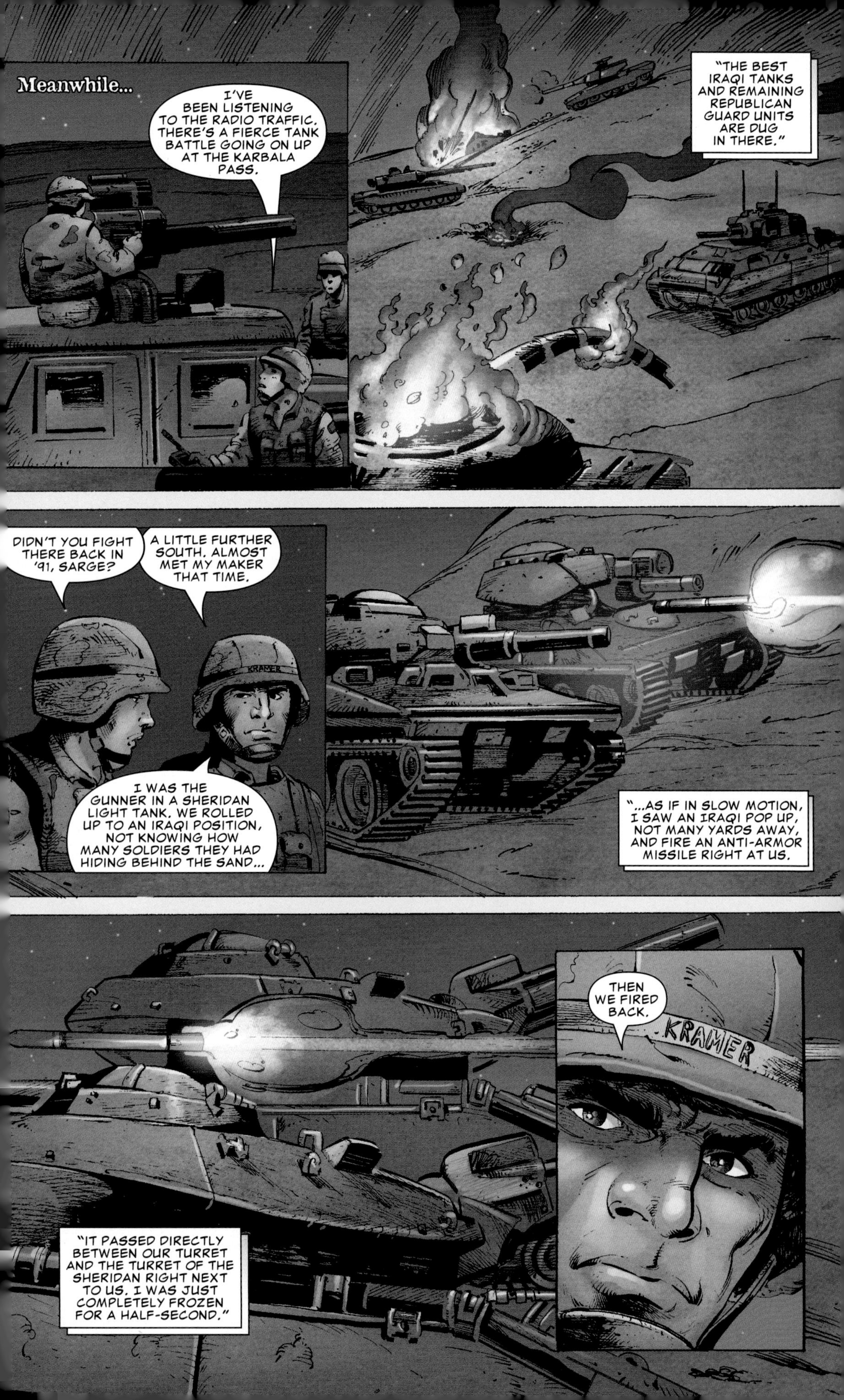
Meanwhile...
I'VE BEEN LISTENING TO THE RADIO TRAFFIC. THERE'S A FIERCE TANK BATTLE GOING ON UP AT THE KARBALA PASS.
"THE BEST IRAQI TANKS AND REMAINING REPUBLICAN GUARD UNITS ARE DUG IN THERE."
DIDN'T YOU FIGHT THERE BACK IN '91, SARGE?
A LITTLE FURTHER SOUTH. ALMOST MET MY MAKER THAT TIME.
KRAMER
I WAS THE GUNNER IN A SHERIDAN LIGHT TANK. WE ROLLED UP TO AN IRAQI POSITION, NOT KNOWING HOW MANY SOLDIERS THEY HAD HIDING BEHIND THE SAND...
"...AS IF IN SLOW MOTION, I SAW AN IRAQI POP UP, NOT MANY YARDS AWAY, AND FIRE AN ANTI-ARMOR MISSILE RIGHT AT US.
"IT PASSED DIRECTLY BETWEEN OUR TURRET AND THE TURRET OF THE SHERIDAN RIGHT NEXT TO US. I WAS JUST COMPLETELY FROZEN FOR A HALF-SECOND."
THEN WE FIRED BACK.
KRAMER

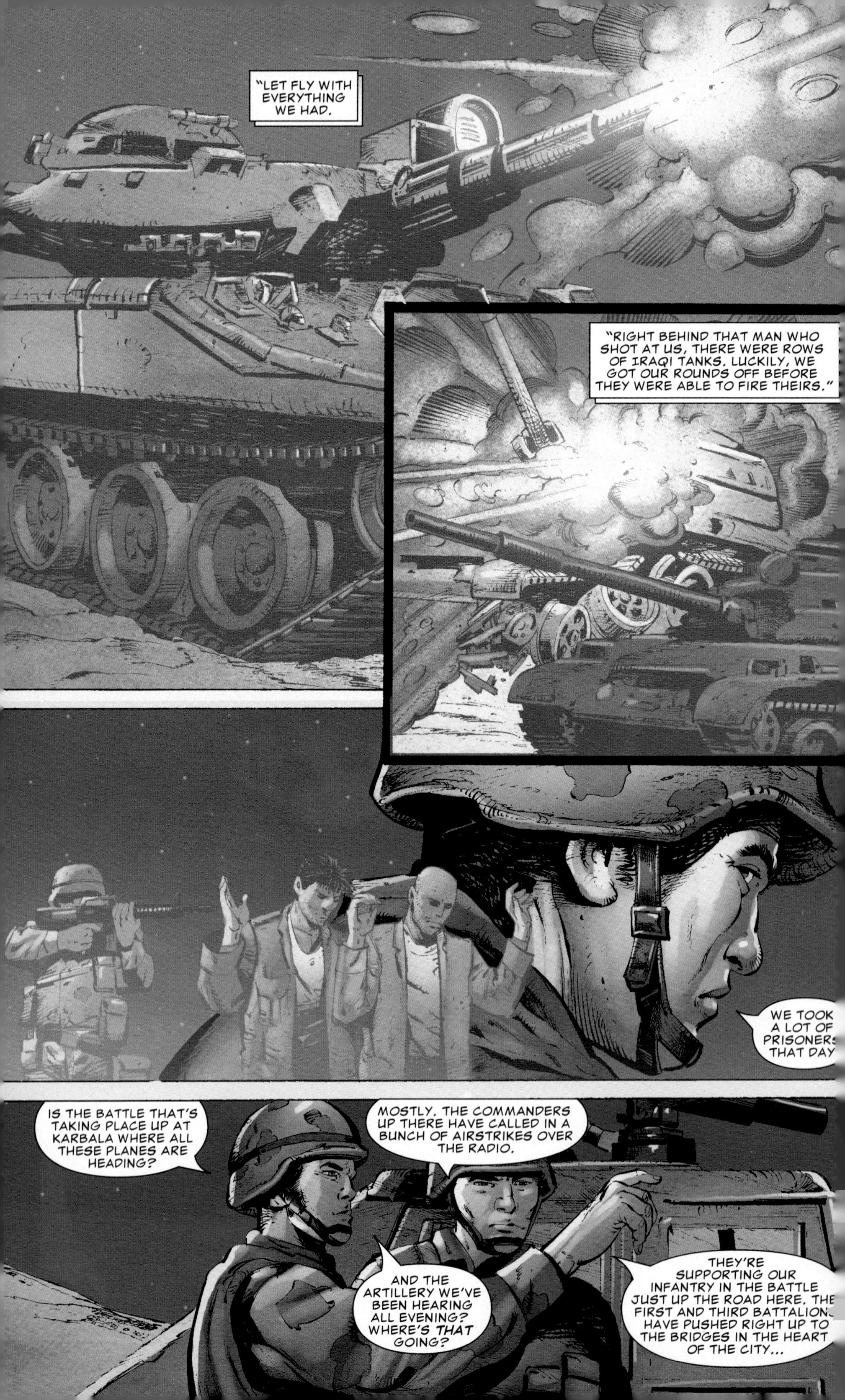
"LET FLY WITH EVERYTHING WE HAD.
"RIGHT BEHIND THAT MAN WHO SHOT AT US, THERE WERE ROWS OF IRAQI TANKS. LUCKILY, WE GOT OUR ROUNDS OFF BEFORE THEY WERE ABLE TO FIRE THEIRS."
WE TOOK A LOT OF PRISONERS THAT DAY
IS THE BATTLE THAT'S TAKING PLACE UP AT KARBALA WHERE ALL THESE PLANES ARE HEADING?
MOSTLY. THE COMMANDERS UP THERE HAVE CALLED IN A BUNCH OF AIRSTRIKES OVER THE RADIO.
AND THE ARTILLERY WE'VE BEEN HEARING ALL EVENING? WHERE'S THAT GOING?
THEY'RE SUPPORTING OUR INFANTRY IN THE BATTLE JUST UP THE ROAD HERE. THE FIRST AND THIRD BATTALIONS HAVE PUSHED RIGHT UP TO THE BRIDGES IN THE HEART OF THE CITY...

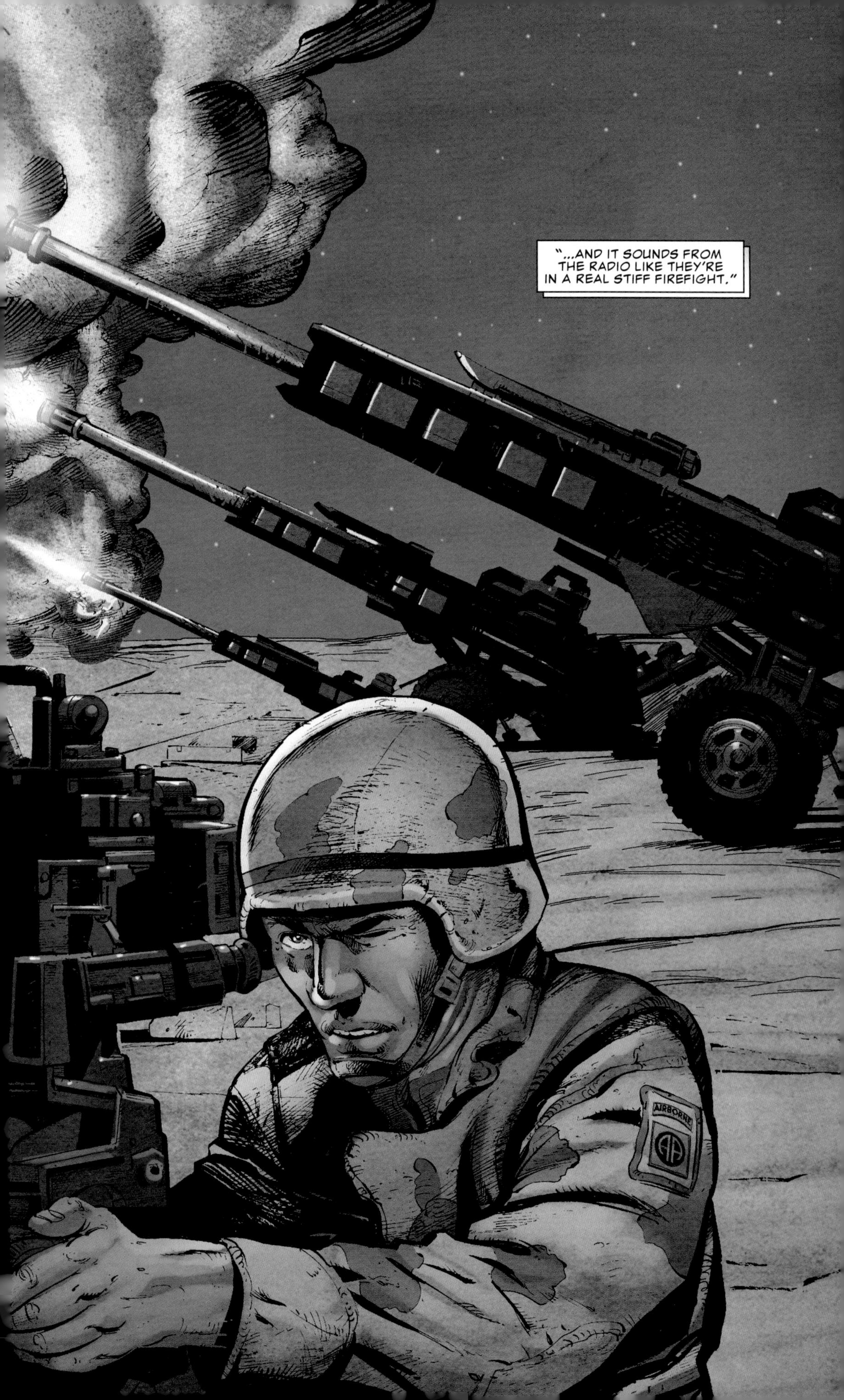
"...AND IT SOUNDS FROM THE RADIO LIKE THEY'RE IN A REAL STIFF FIREFIGHT."
AIRBORNE

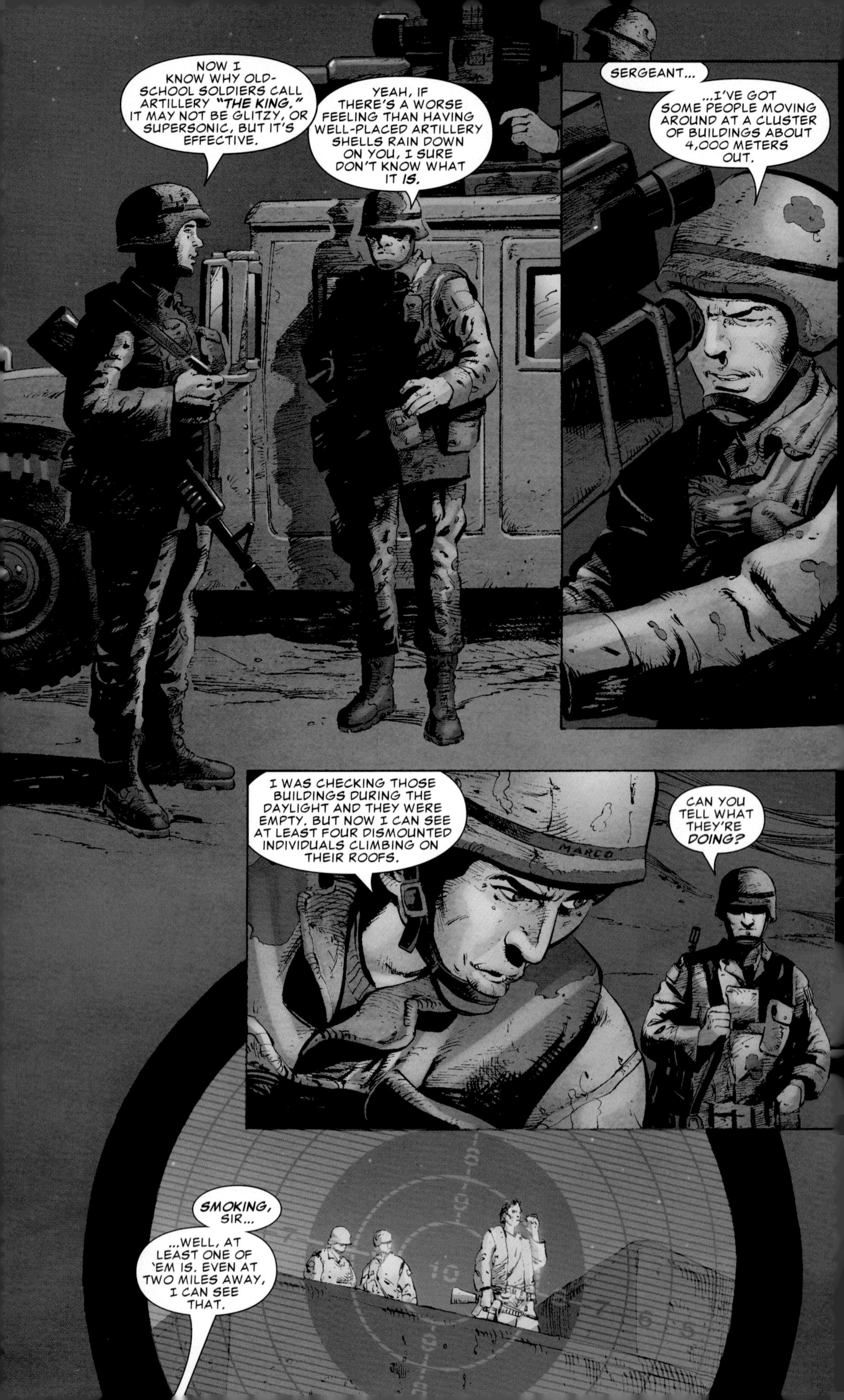
NOW I KNOW WHY OLD-SCHOOL SOLDIERS CALL ARTILLERY "THE KING." IT MAY NOT BE GLITZY, OR SUPERSONIC, BUT IT'S EFFECTIVE.
YEAH, IF THERE'S A WORSE FEELING THAN HAVING WELL-PLACED ARTILLERY SHELLS RAIN DOWN ON YOU, I SURE DON'T KNOW WHAT IT IS.
SERGEANT...
...I'VE GOT SOME PEOPLE MOVING AROUND AT A CLUSTER OF BUILDINGS ABOUT 4,000 METERS OUT.
I WAS CHECKING THOSE BUILDINGS DURING THE DAYLIGHT AND THEY WERE EMPTY. BUT NOW I CAN SEE AT LEAST FOUR DISMOUNTED INDIVIDUALS CLIMBING ON THEIR ROOFS.
CAN YOU TELL WHAT THEY'RE DOING?
SMOKING, SIR...
...WELL, AT LEAST ONE OF 'EM IS. EVEN AT TWO MILES AWAY, I CAN SEE THAT.

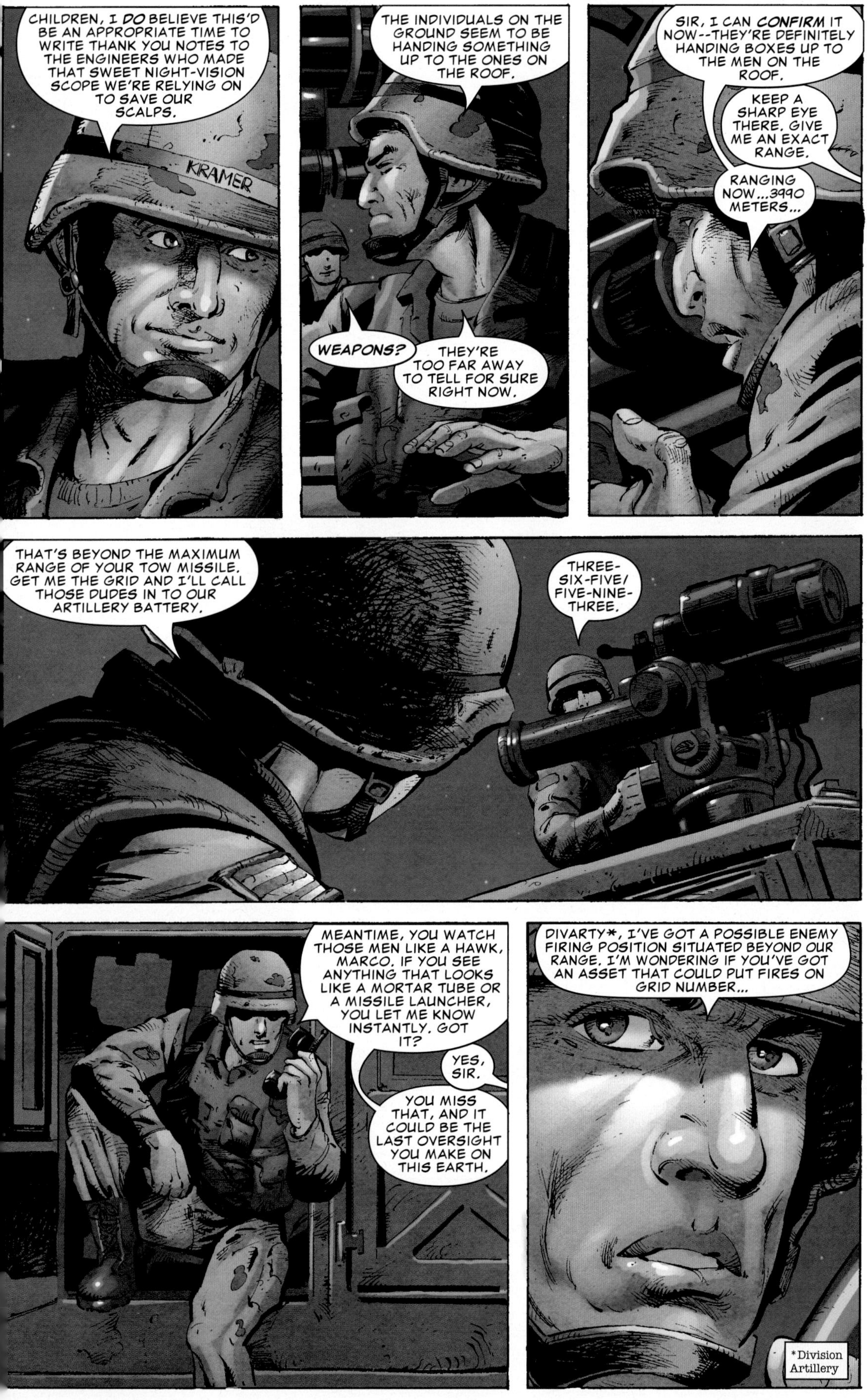

CHILDREN, I DO BELIEVE THIS'D BE AN APPROPRIATE TIME TO WRITE THANK YOU NOTES TO THE ENGINEERS WHO MADE THAT SWEET NIGHT-VISION SCOPE WE'RE RELYING ON TO SAVE OUR SCALPS.
KRAMER
THE INDIVIDUALS ON THE GROUND SEEM TO BE HANDING SOMETHING UP TO THE ONES ON THE ROOF.
WEAPONS?
THEY'RE TOO FAR AWAY TO TELL FOR SURE RIGHT NOW.
SIR, I CAN CONFIRM IT NOW--THEY'RE DEFINITELY HANDING BOXES UP TO THE MEN ON THE ROOF.
KEEP A SHARP EYE THERE. GIVE ME AN EXACT RANGE.
RANGING NOW...3990 METERS...
THAT'S BEYOND THE MAXIMUM RANGE OF YOUR TOW MISSILE. GET ME THE GRID AND I'LL CALL THOSE DUDES IN TO OUR ARTILLERY BATTERY.
THREE-SIX-FIVE/ FIVE-NINE-THREE.
MEANTIME, YOU WATCH THOSE MEN LIKE A HAWK, MARCO. IF YOU SEE ANYTHING THAT LOOKS LIKE A MORTAR TUBE OR A MISSILE LAUNCHER, YOU LET ME KNOW INSTANTLY. GOT IT?
YES, SIR.
YOU MISS THAT, AND IT COULD BE THE LAST OVERSIGHT YOU MAKE ON THIS EARTH.
DIVARTY*, I'VE GOT A POSSIBLE ENEMY FIRING POSITION SITUATED BEYOND OUR RANGE. I'M WONDERING IF YOU'VE GOT AN ASSET THAT COULD PUT FIRES ON GRID NUMBER...
*Division Artillery

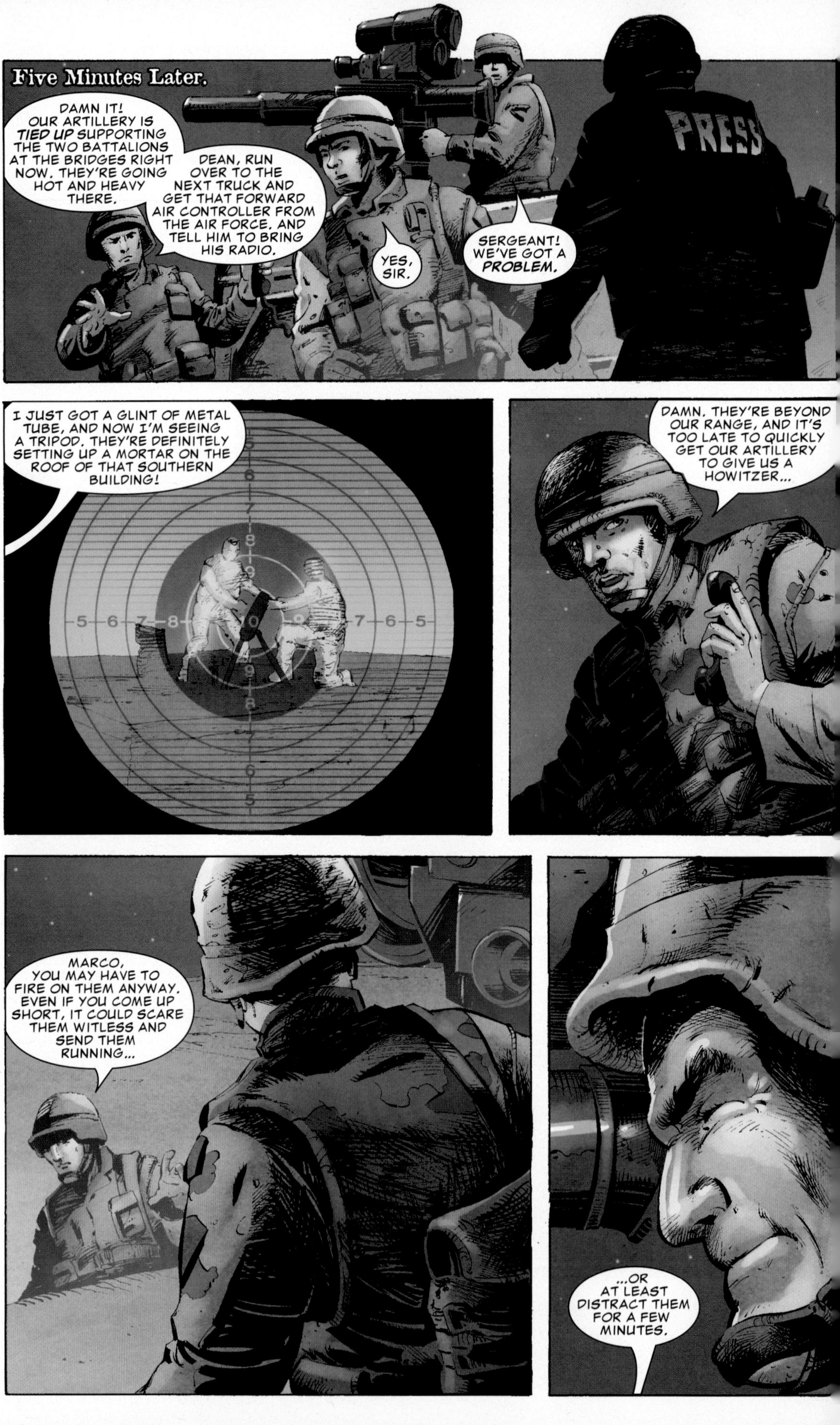
Five Minutes Later.
DAMN IT! OUR ARTILLERY IS TIED UP SUPPORTING THE TWO BATTALIONS AT THE BRIDGES RIGHT NOW. THEY'RE GOING HOT AND HEAVY THERE.
DEAN, RUN OVER TO THE NEXT TRUCK AND GET THAT FORWARD AIR CONTROLLER FROM THE AIR FORCE. AND TELL HIM TO BRING HIS RADIO.
YES, SIR.
SERGEANT! WE'VE GOT A PROBLEM.
PRESS
I JUST GOT A GLINT OF METAL TUBE, AND NOW I'M SEEING A TRIPOD. THEY'RE DEFINITELY SETTING UP A MORTAR ON THE ROOF OF THAT SOUTHERN BUILDING!
DAMN. THEY'RE BEYOND OUR RANGE, AND IT'S TOO LATE TO QUICKLY GET OUR ARTILLERY TO GIVE US A HOWITZER...
MARCO, YOU MAY HAVE TO FIRE ON THEM ANYWAY. EVEN IF YOU COME UP SHORT, IT COULD SCARE THEM WITLESS AND SEND THEM RUNNING...
...OR AT LEAST DISTRACT THEM FOR A FEW MINUTES.

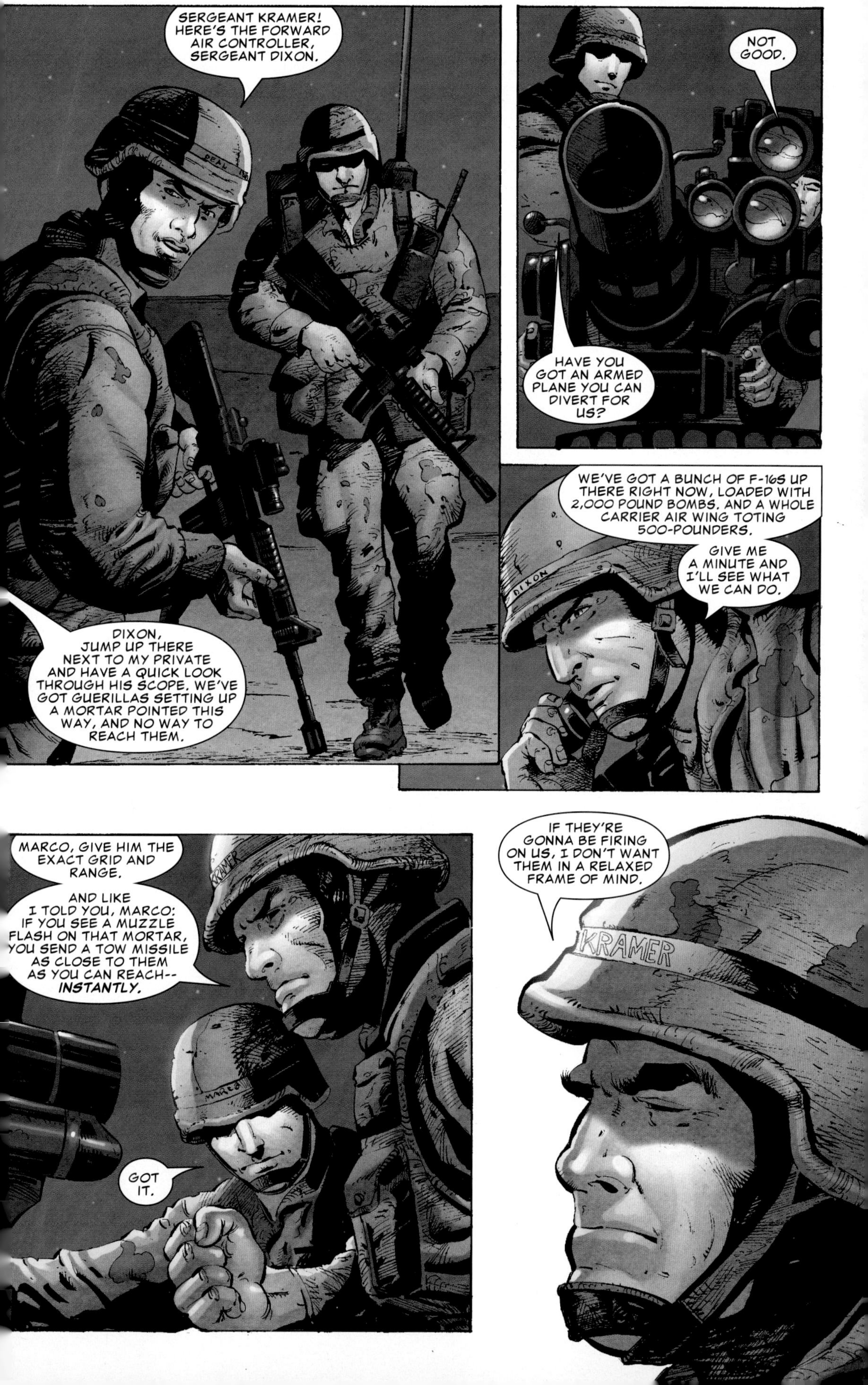
SERGEANT KRAMER! HERE'S THE FORWARD AIR CONTROLLER, SERGEANT DIXON.
DIXON, JUMP UP THERE NEXT TO MY PRIVATE AND HAVE A QUICK LOOK THROUGH HIS SCOPE. WE'VE GOT GUERILLAS SETTING UP A MORTAR POINTED THIS WAY, AND NO WAY TO REACH THEM.
NOT GOOD.
HAVE YOU GOT AN ARMED PLANE YOU CAN DIVERT FOR US?
WE'VE GOT A BUNCH OF F-16S UP THERE RIGHT NOW, LOADED WITH 2,000 POUND BOMBS. AND A WHOLE CARRIER AIR WING TOTING 500-POUNDERS.
GIVE ME A MINUTE AND I'LL SEE WHAT WE CAN DO.
DIXON
MARCO, GIVE HIM THE EXACT GRID AND RANGE.
AND LIKE I TOLD YOU, MARCO: IF YOU SEE A MUZZLE FLASH ON THAT MORTAR, YOU SEND A TOW MISSILE AS CLOSE TO THEM AS YOU CAN REACH-- **INSTANTLY.**
GOT IT.
IF THEY'RE GONNA BE FIRING ON US, I DON'T WANT THEM IN A RELAXED FRAME OF MIND.
KRAMER

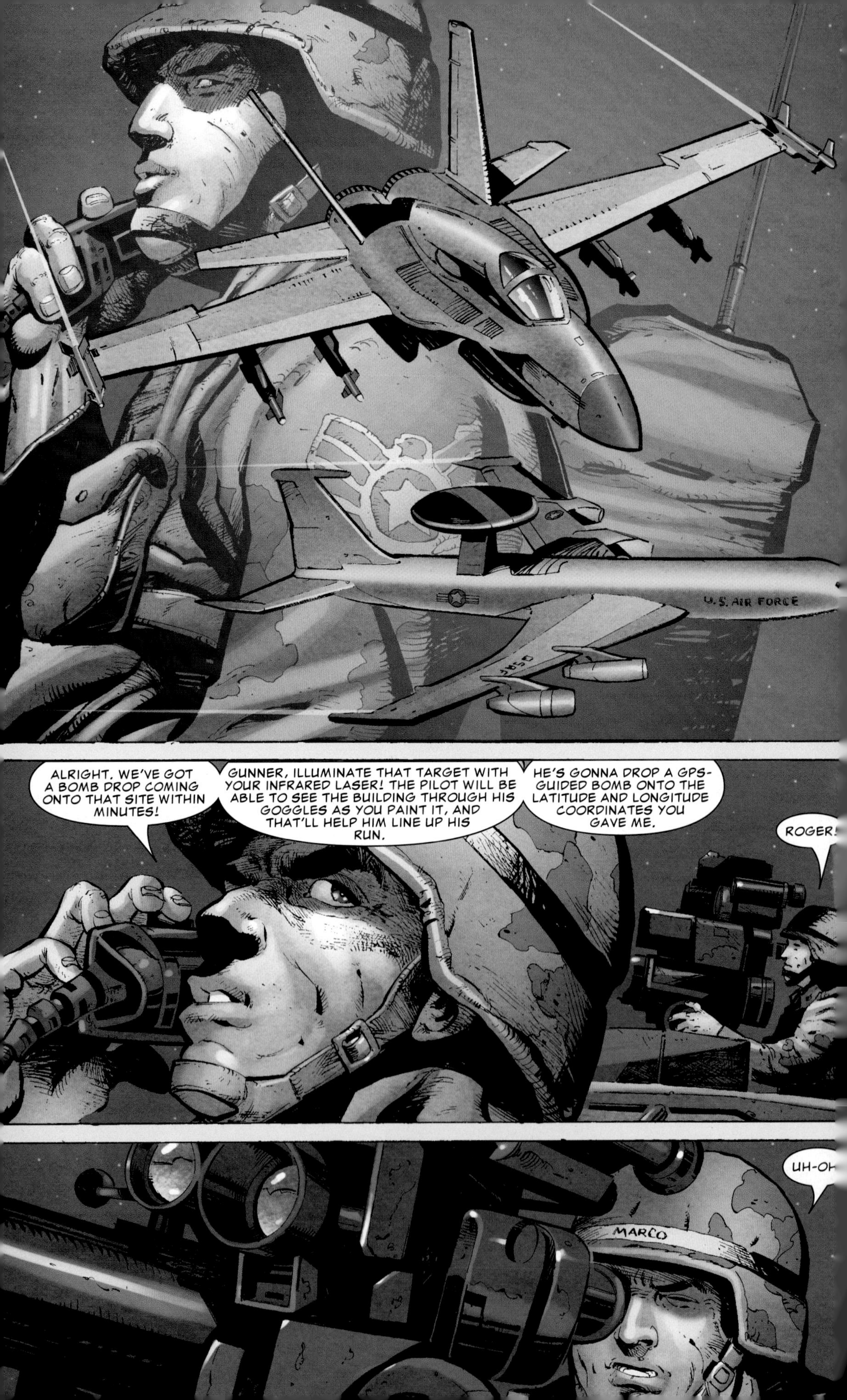
U.S. AIR FORCE
ALRIGHT. WE'VE GOT A BOMB DROP COMING ONTO THAT SITE WITHIN MINUTES!
GUNNER, ILLUMINATE THAT TARGET WITH YOUR INFRARED LASER! THE PILOT WILL BE ABLE TO SEE THE BUILDING THROUGH HIS GOGGLES AS YOU PAINT IT, AND THAT'LL HELP HIM LINE UP HIS RUN.
HE'S GONNA DROP A GPS-GUIDED BOMB ONTO THE LATITUDE AND LONGITUDE COORDINATES YOU GAVE ME.
ROGER!
UH-OH
MARCO

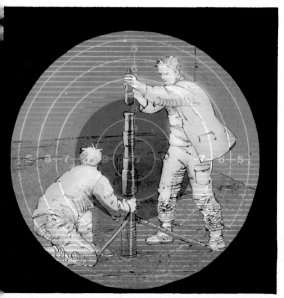

INCOMING! HIT THE DIRT!

JUST ONE...

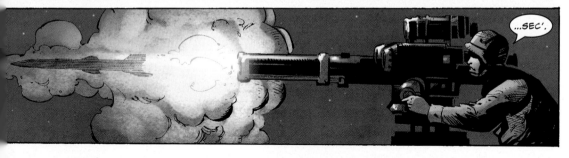

...SEC'.

COME ON, BABY.

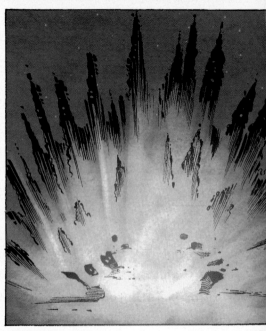

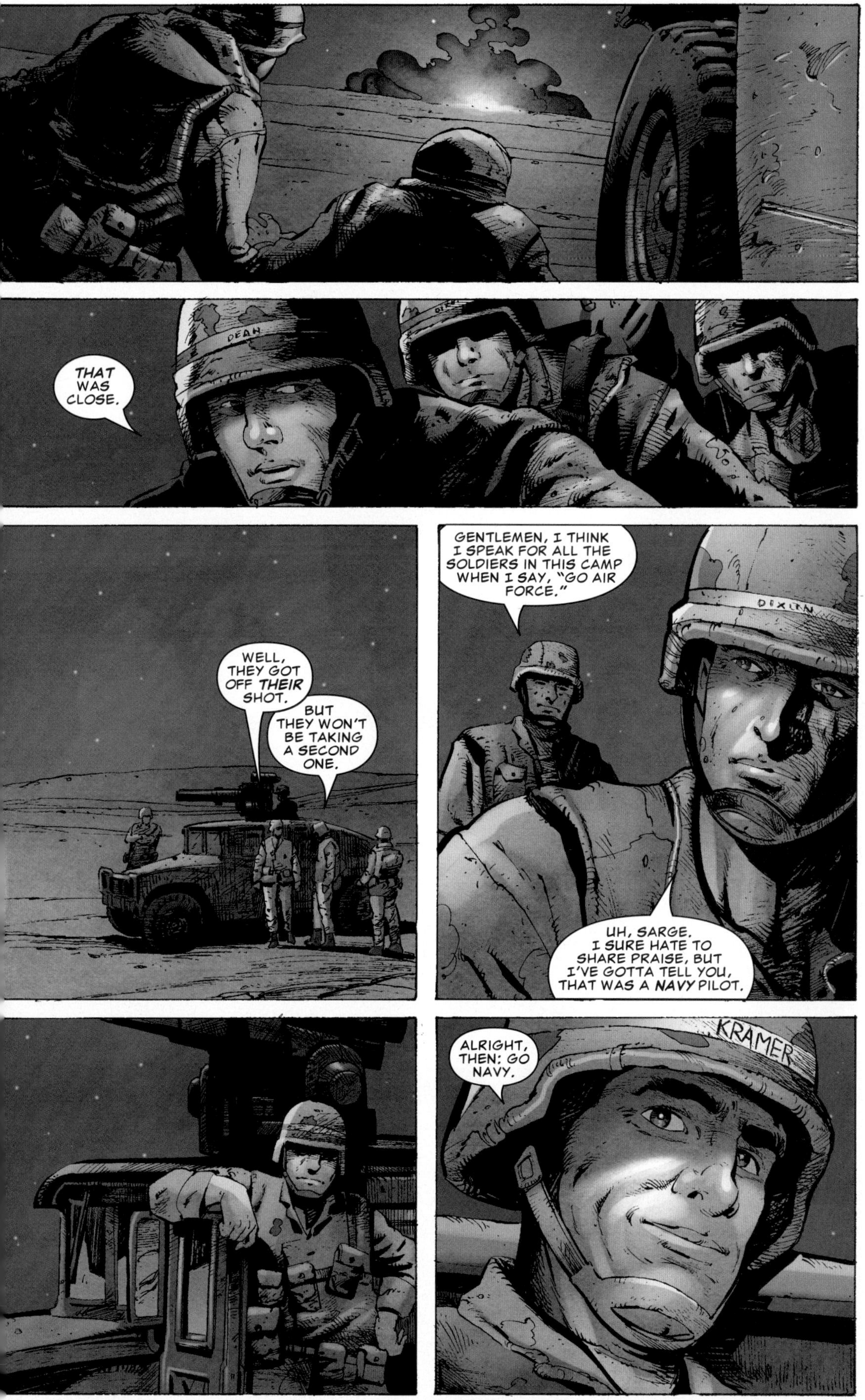
THAT WAS CLOSE.
WELL, THEY GOT OFF THEIR SHOT.
BUT THEY WON'T BE TAKING A SECOND ONE.
GENTLEMEN, I THINK I SPEAK FOR ALL THE SOLDIERS IN THIS CAMP WHEN I SAY, "GO AIR FORCE."
UH, SARGE. I SURE HATE TO SHARE PRAISE, BUT I'VE GOTTA TELL YOU, THAT WAS A NAVY PILOT.
KRAMER
ALRIGHT, THEN: GO NAVY.

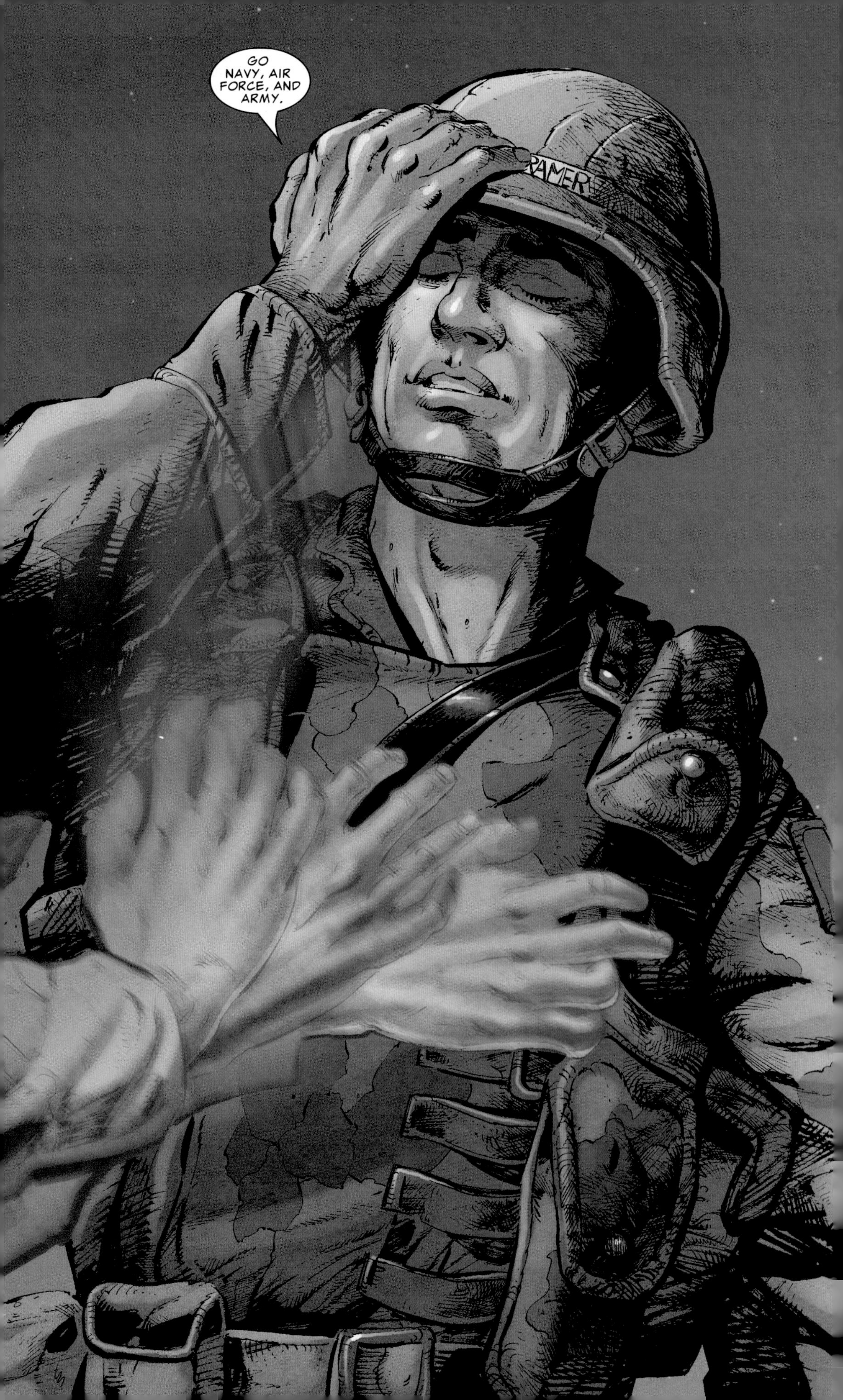
GO NAVY, AIR FORCE, AND ARMY.

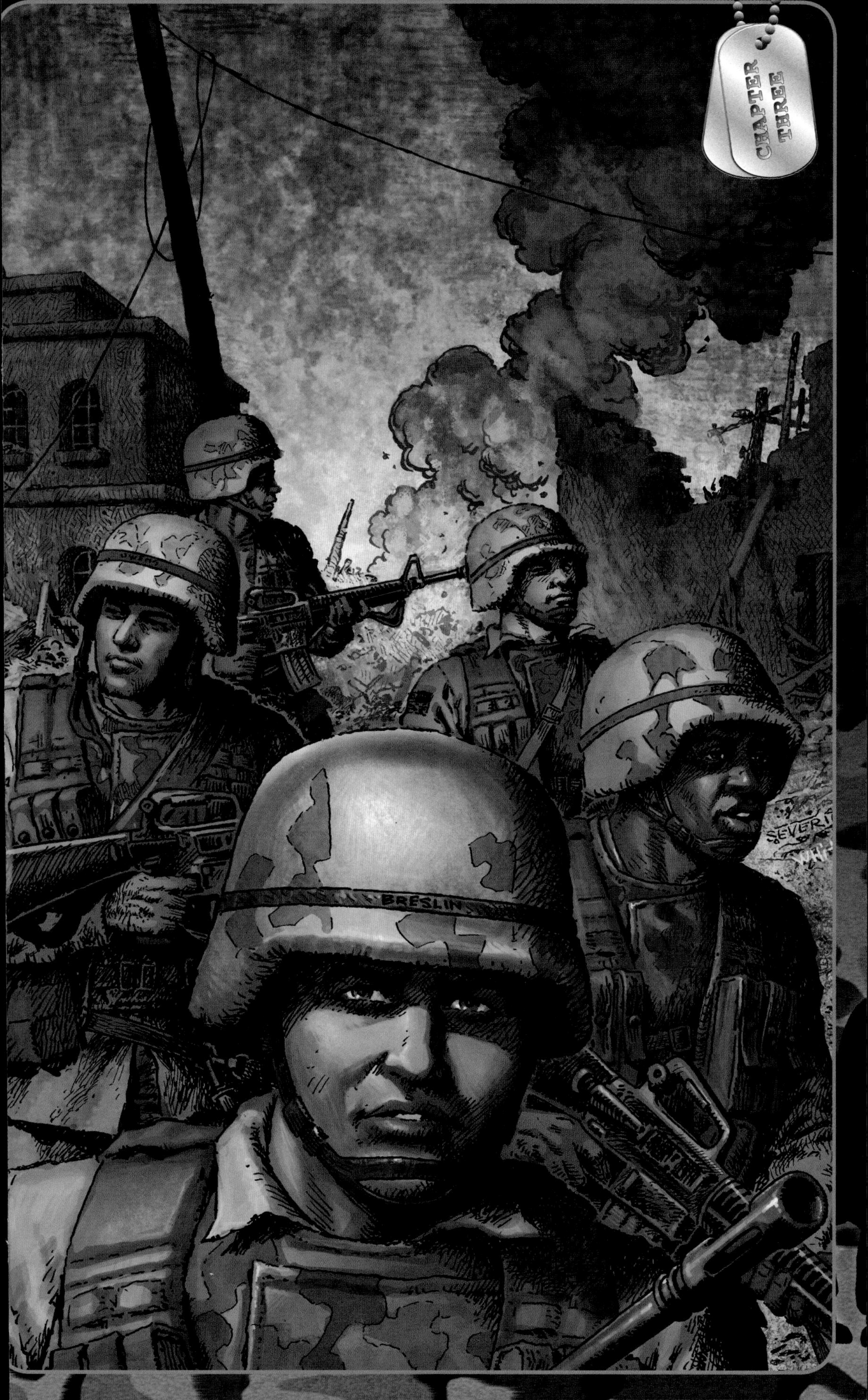
CHAPTER THREE
BRESLIN

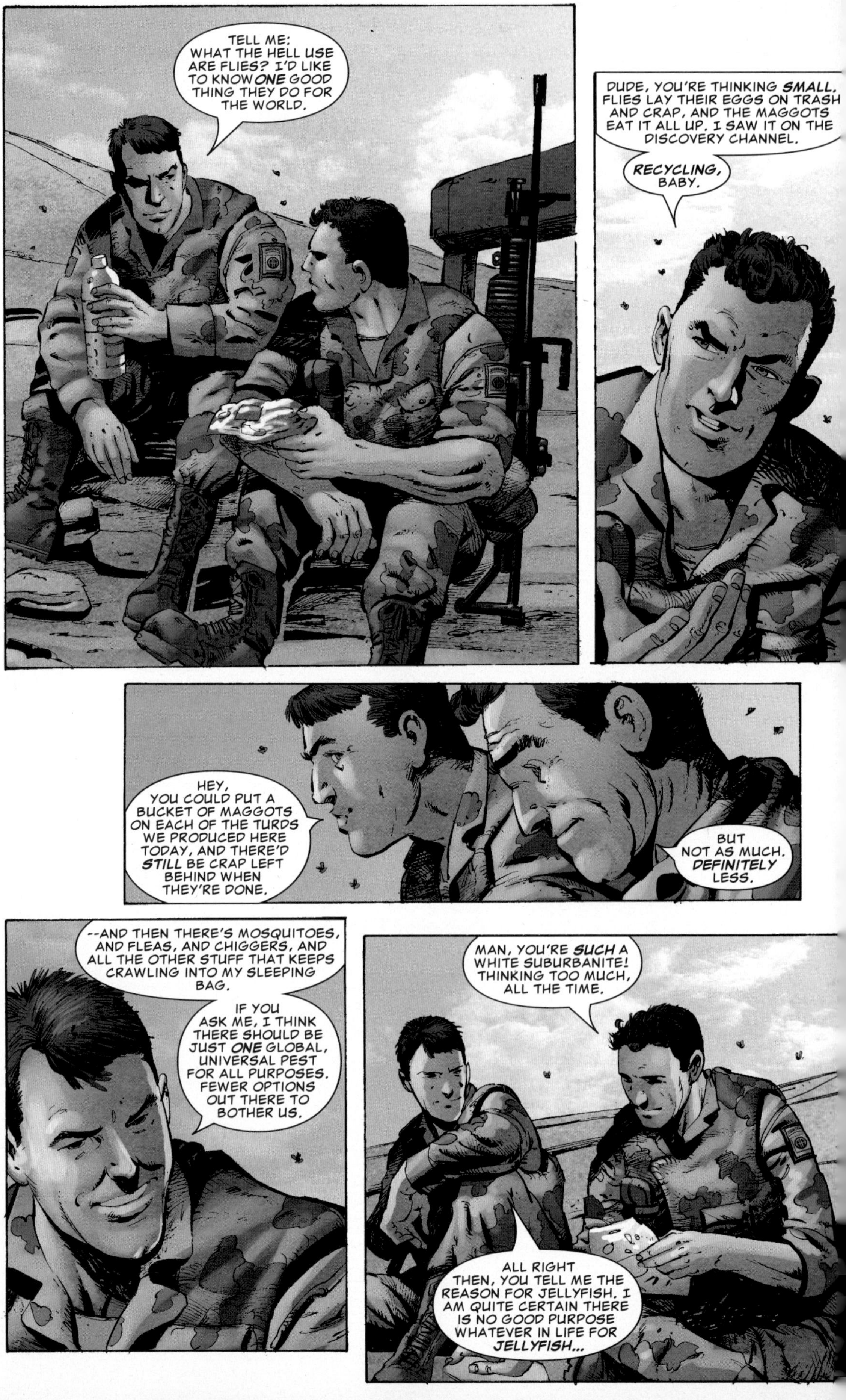
TELL ME: WHAT THE HELL USE ARE FLIES? I'D LIKE TO KNOW ONE GOOD THING THEY DO FOR THE WORLD.
DUDE, YOU'RE THINKING SMALL. FLIES LAY THEIR EGGS ON TRASH AND CRAP, AND THE MAGGOTS EAT IT ALL UP. I SAW IT ON THE DISCOVERY CHANNEL.
RECYCLING, BABY.
HEY, YOU COULD PUT A BUCKET OF MAGGOTS ON EACH OF THE TURDS WE PRODUCED HERE TODAY, AND THERE'D STILL BE CRAP LEFT BEHIND WHEN THEY'RE DONE.
BUT NOT AS MUCH. DEFINITELY LESS.
--AND THEN THERE'S MOSQUITOES, AND FLEAS, AND CHIGGERS, AND ALL THE OTHER STUFF THAT KEEPS CRAWLING INTO MY SLEEPING BAG.
IF YOU ASK ME, I THINK THERE SHOULD BE JUST ONE GLOBAL, UNIVERSAL PEST FOR ALL PURPOSES. FEWER OPTIONS OUT THERE TO BOTHER US.
MAN, YOU'RE SUCH A WHITE SUBURBANITE! THINKING TOO MUCH, ALL THE TIME.
ALL RIGHT THEN, YOU TELL ME THE REASON FOR JELLYFISH. I AM QUITE CERTAIN THERE IS NO GOOD PURPOSE WHATEVER IN LIFE FOR JELLYFISH...

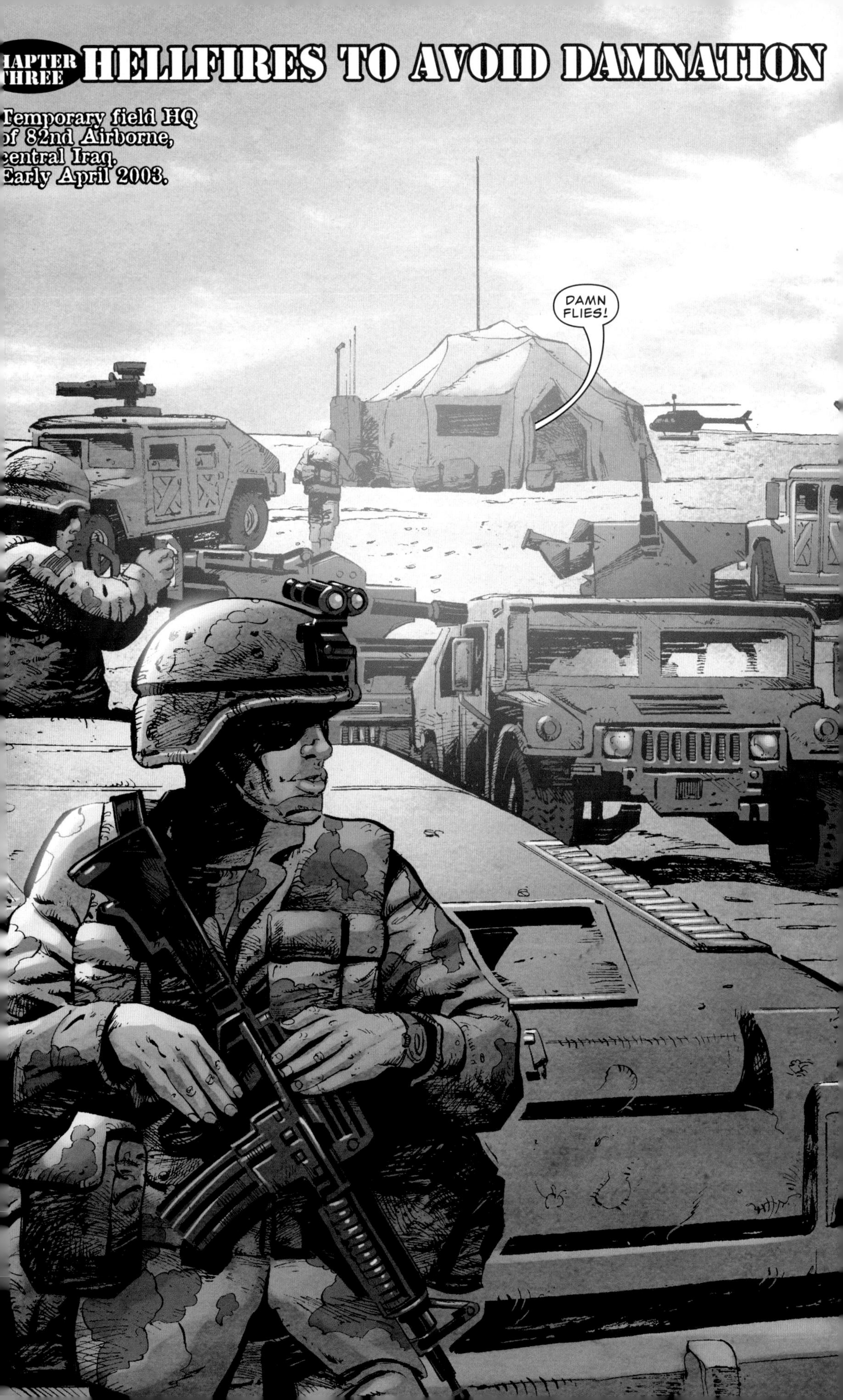
HAPTER THREE HELLFIRES TO AVOID DAMNATION
Temporary field HQ of 82nd Airborne, central Iraq. Early April 2003.
DAMN FLIES!

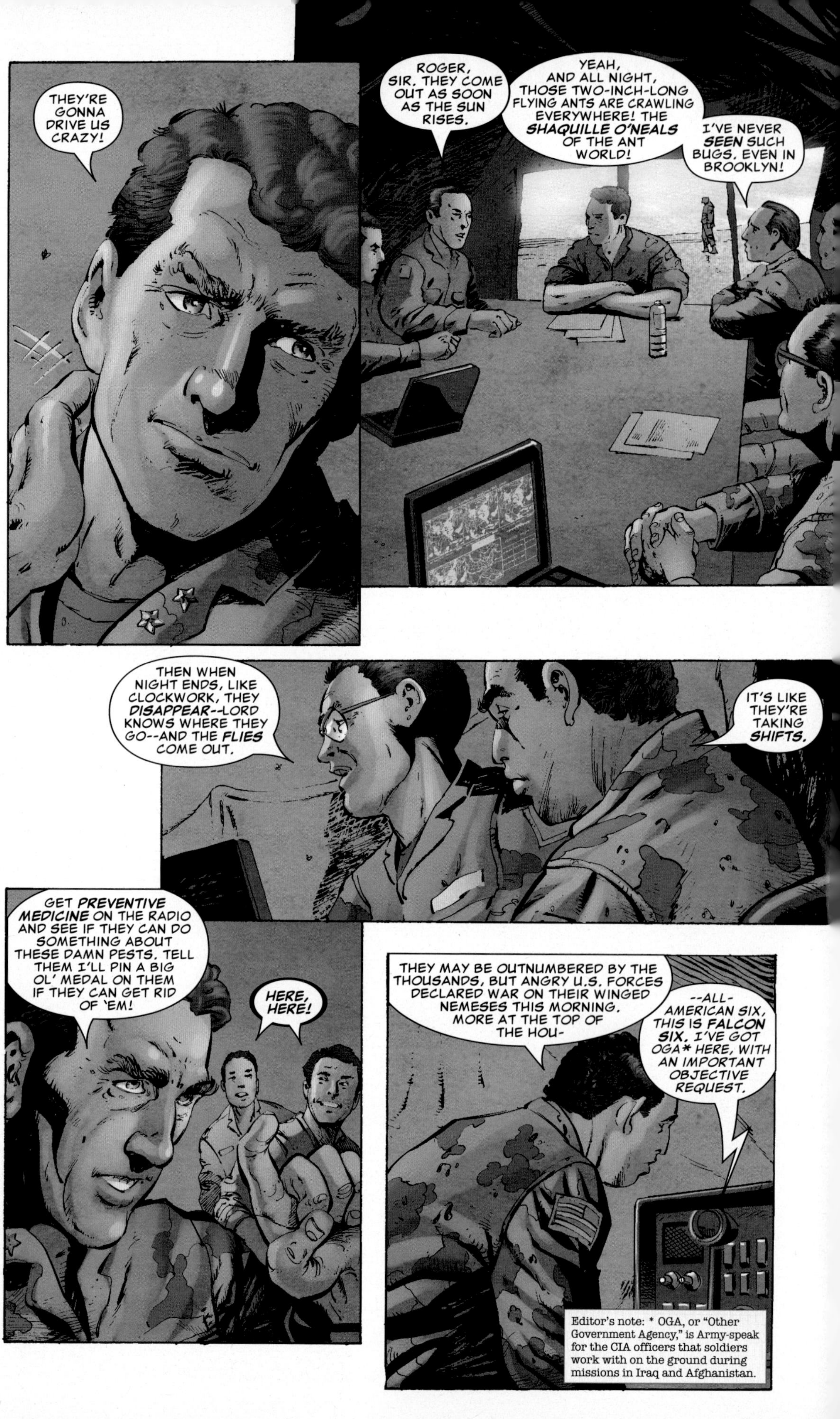
THEY'RE GONNA DRIVE US CRAZY!
ROGER, SIR. THEY COME OUT AS SOON AS THE SUN RISES.
YEAH, AND ALL NIGHT, THOSE TWO-INCH-LONG FLYING ANTS ARE CRAWLING EVERYWHERE! THE SHAQUILLE O'NEALS OF THE ANT WORLD!
I'VE NEVER SEEN SUCH BUGS, EVEN IN BROOKLYN!
THEN WHEN NIGHT ENDS, LIKE CLOCKWORK, THEY DISAPPEAR--LORD KNOWS WHERE THEY GO--AND THE FLIES COME OUT.
IT'S LIKE THEY'RE TAKING SHIFTS.
GET PREVENTIVE MEDICINE ON THE RADIO AND SEE IF THEY CAN DO SOMETHING ABOUT THESE DAMN PESTS. TELL THEM I'LL PIN A BIG OL' MEDAL ON THEM IF THEY CAN GET RID OF 'EM!
HERE, HERE!
THEY MAY BE OUTNUMBERED BY THE THOUSANDS, BUT ANGRY U.S. FORCES DECLARED WAR ON THEIR WINGED NEMESES THIS MORNING. MORE AT THE TOP OF THE HOU-
--ALL-AMERICAN SIX, THIS IS FALCON SIX. I'VE GOT OGA* HERE, WITH AN IMPORTANT OBJECTIVE REQUEST.

Editor's note: * OGA, or "Other Government Agency," is Army-speak for the CIA officers that soldiers work with on the ground during missions in Iraq and Afghanistan.

THIS IS ALL-AMERICAN SIX, OVER.

OGA HERE, SIR. WE'VE GOT **IRONCLAD** INTEL THAT A HIGH-LEVEL MEETING IS TAKING PLACE RIGHT NOW IN A BUILDING IN CENTER-CITY, TWO OF THE HIGHEST BAATH PARTY OFFICIALS IN THIS REGION.

I'VE GOT THE BUILDING UNDER VISUAL SURVEILLANCE FROM MY POSITION HERE. REQUEST IMMEDIATE AIR **STRIKE** TO TAKE IT OUT.

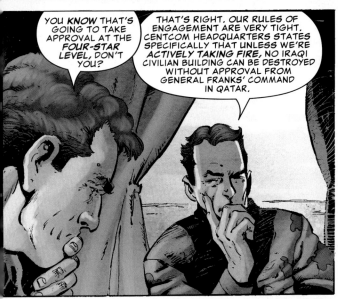

YOU **KNOW** THAT'S GOING TO TAKE APPROVAL AT THE **FOUR-STAR** LEVEL, DON'T YOU?

THAT'S RIGHT. OUR RULES OF ENGAGEMENT ARE VERY TIGHT. CENTCOM HEADQUARTERS STATES SPECIFICALLY THAT UNLESS WE'RE **ACTIVELY TAKING FIRE**, NO IRAQI CIVILIAN BUILDING CAN BE DESTROYED WITHOUT APPROVAL FROM GENERAL FRANKS' COMMAND IN QATAR.

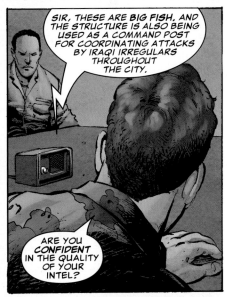

SIR, THESE ARE BIG FISH, AND THE STRUCTURE IS ALSO BEING USED AS A COMMAND POST FOR COORDINATING ATTACKS BY IRAQI IRREGULARS THROUGHOUT THE CITY.

ARE YOU **CONFIDENT** IN THE QUALITY OF YOUR INTEL?

ROGER, IT'S **DIRECT HUMINT.** * OUR SOURCE ON THIS HAS GIVEN US OUR VERY BEST INFORMATION OVER THE LAST TEN DAYS. HE'S BEEN THE SOURCE FOR MOST OF OUR IMPORTANT RAIDS AND AERIAL BOMBING.

*Humint refers to human intelligence from an informant.

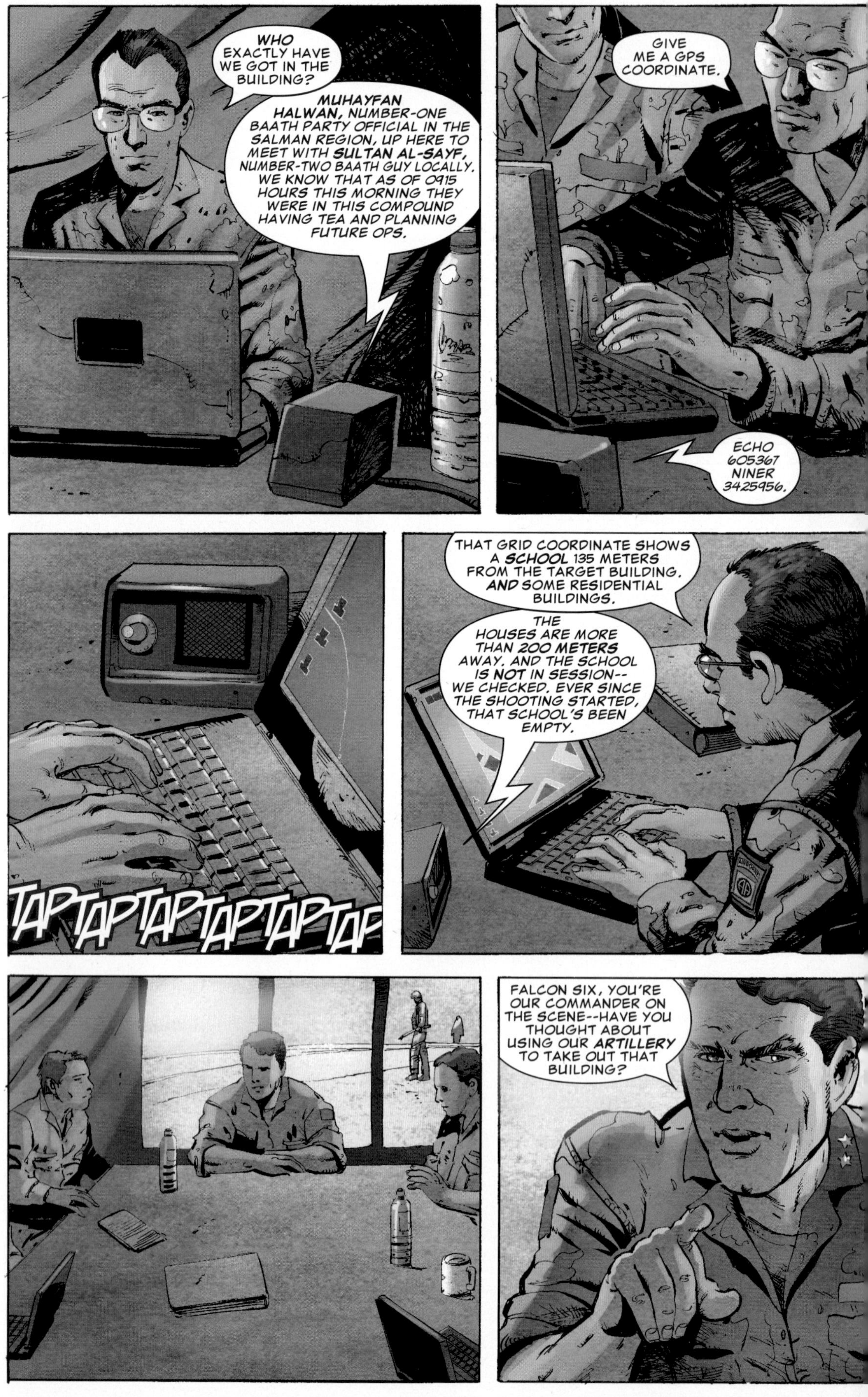
WHO EXACTLY HAVE WE GOT IN THE BUILDING?
MUHAYFAN HALWAN, NUMBER-ONE BAATH PARTY OFFICIAL IN THE SALMAN REGION, UP HERE TO MEET WITH SULTAN AL-SAYF, NUMBER-TWO BAATH GUY LOCALLY. WE KNOW THAT AS OF 0915 HOURS THIS MORNING THEY WERE IN THIS COMPOUND HAVING TEA AND PLANNING FUTURE OPS.
GIVE ME A GPS COORDINATE.
ECHO 605367 NINER 3425956.
TAPTAPTAPTAPTAPTAPTAP
THAT GRID COORDINATE SHOWS A SCHOOL 135 METERS FROM THE TARGET BUILDING. AND SOME RESIDENTIAL BUILDINGS.
THE HOUSES ARE MORE THAN 200 METERS AWAY. AND THE SCHOOL IS NOT IN SESSION-- WE CHECKED. EVER SINCE THE SHOOTING STARTED, THAT SCHOOL'S BEEN EMPTY.
FALCON SIX, YOU'RE OUR COMMANDER ON THE SCENE--HAVE YOU THOUGHT ABOUT USING OUR ARTILLERY TO TAKE OUT THAT BUILDING?

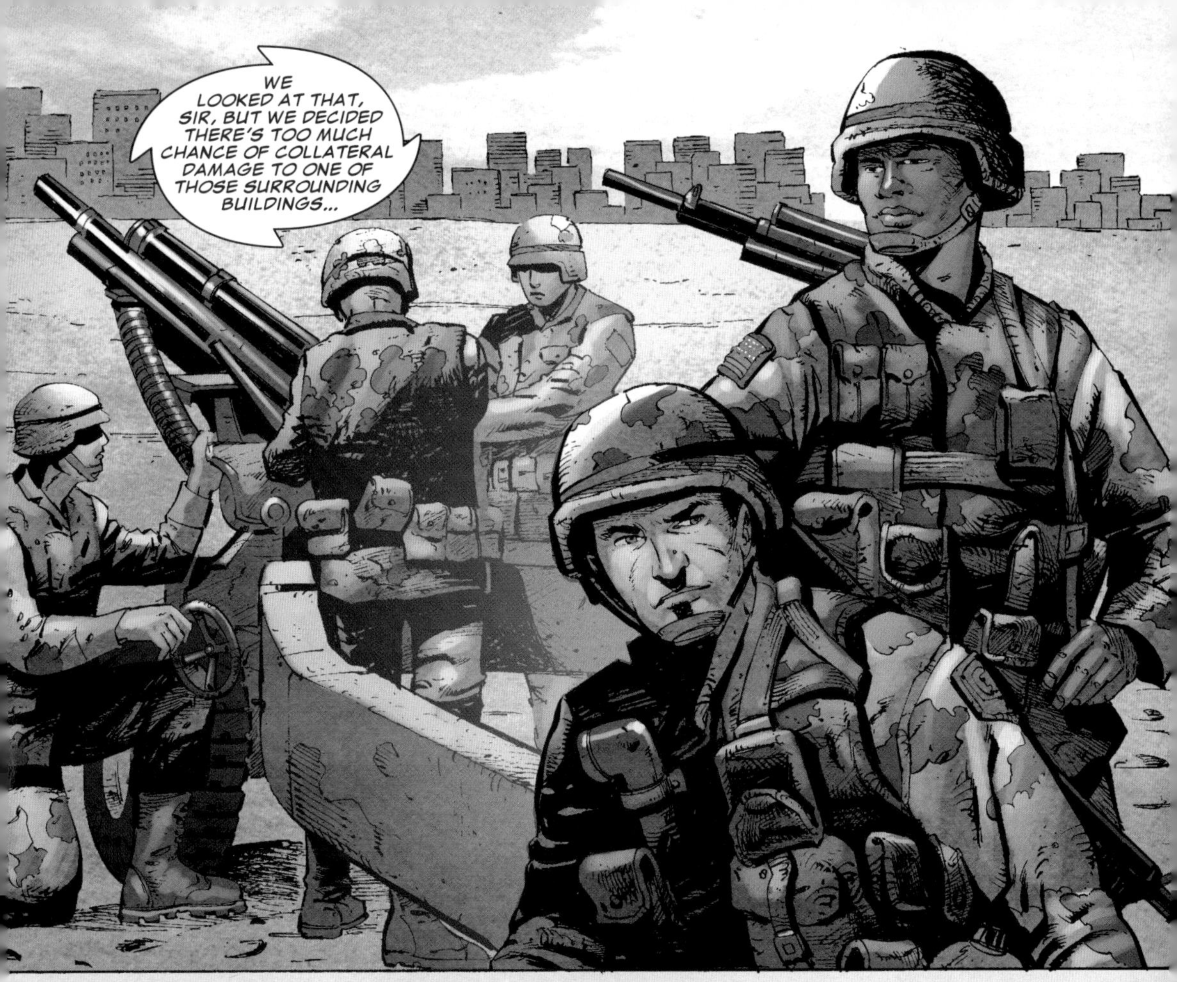
WE LOOKED AT THAT, SIR, BUT WE DECIDED THERE'S TOO MUCH CHANCE OF COLLATERAL DAMAGE TO ONE OF THOSE SURROUNDING BUILDINGS...

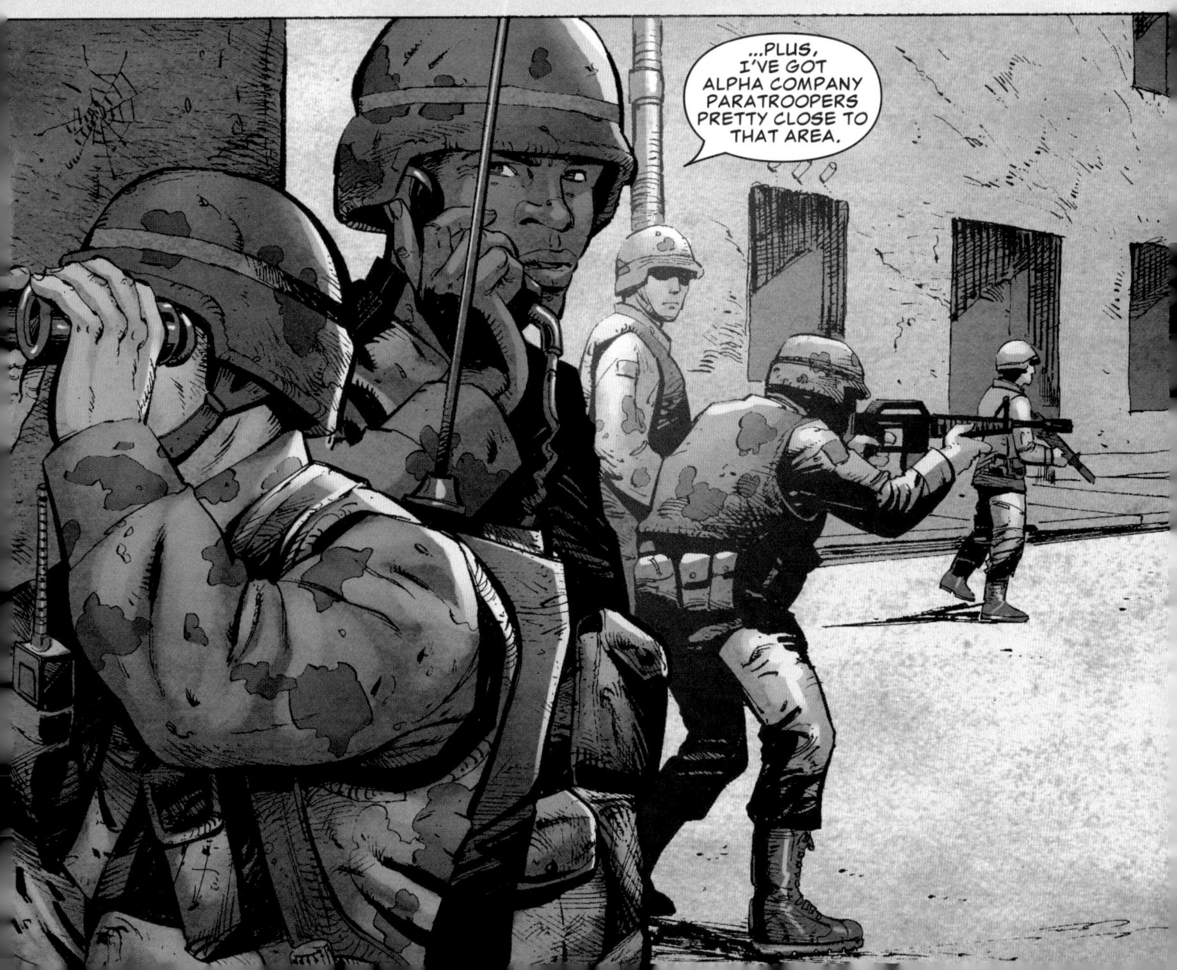
...PLUS, I'VE GOT ALPHA COMPANY PARATROOPERS PRETTY CLOSE TO THAT AREA.

OGA?
THOUGHTS?

...WE'RE GOING TO NEED A *PRECISION AIR STRIKE* ON THIS ONE, GENERAL.

GENERAL, IF *TWO HEADS* OF THE *BAATH PARTY* CAN BE TAKEN OUT HERE THIS MORNING, THAT SENDS A POWERFUL SIGNAL TO THE ENEMY.

THEN, YOUR INFANTRY PUSH PROCEEDS TO THE BRIDGES TONIGHT, AS PLANNED, AND VERY QUICKLY, RESISTANCE STARTS TO LOOK FUTILE TO THESE GUYS.

TAKING OUT THESE TWO COULD DEFINITELY HASTEN THE LIBERATION OF THE CITY WITHIN THE NEXT 48 HOURS.

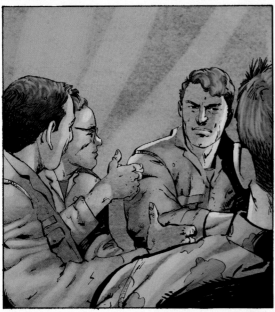

ALRIGHT.

GIVE ME A LITTLE WHILE, AND I'LL GET BACK TO YOU...

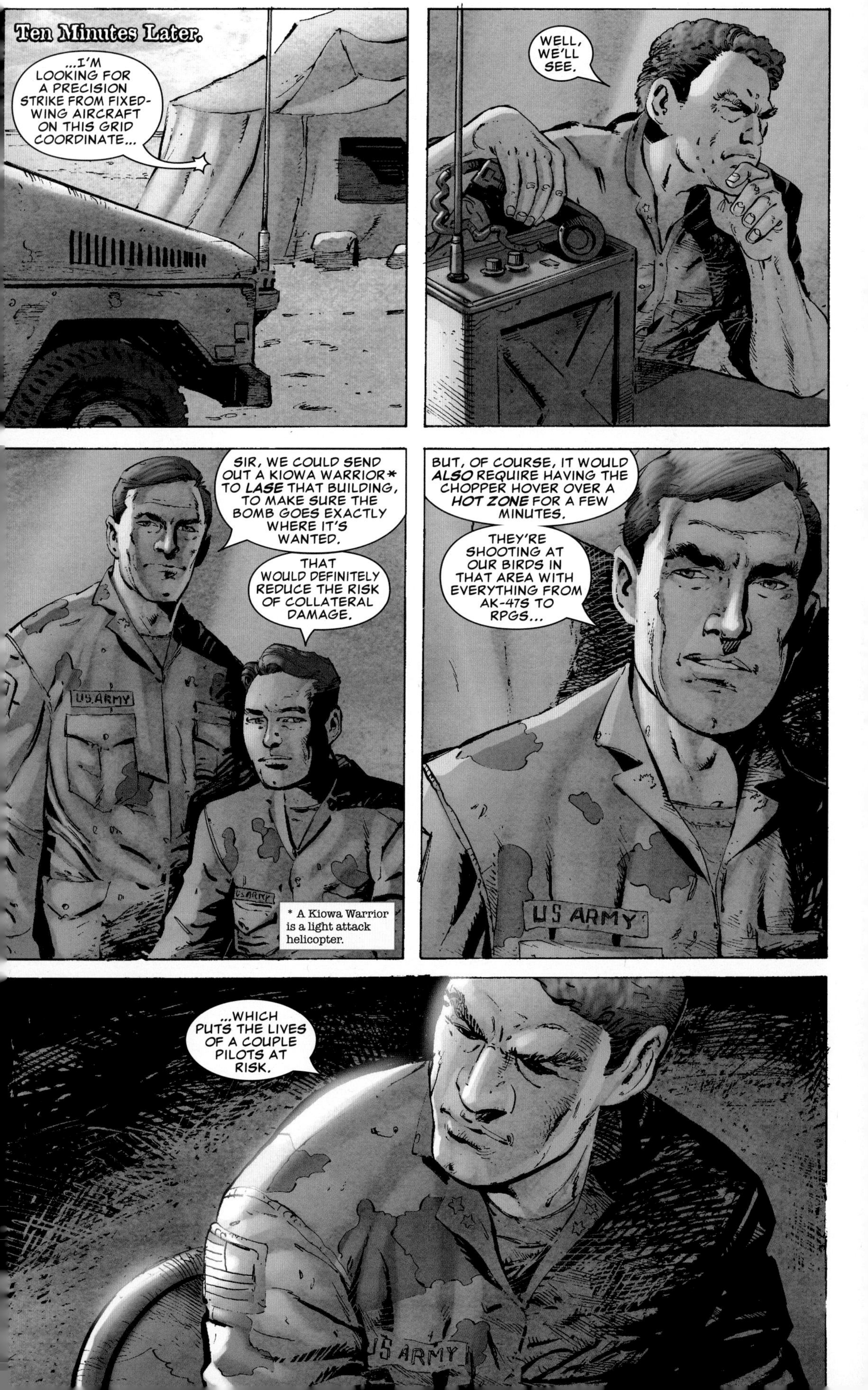
Ten Minutes Later.
...I'M LOOKING FOR A PRECISION STRIKE FROM FIXED-WING AIRCRAFT ON THIS GRID COORDINATE...
WELL, WE'LL SEE.
SIR, WE COULD SEND OUT A KIOWA WARRIOR* TO LASE THAT BUILDING, TO MAKE SURE THE BOMB GOES EXACTLY WHERE IT'S WANTED.
THAT WOULD DEFINITELY REDUCE THE RISK OF COLLATERAL DAMAGE.
U.S. ARMY
U.S. ARMY
* A Kiowa Warrior is a light attack helicopter.
BUT, OF COURSE, IT WOULD ALSO REQUIRE HAVING THE CHOPPER HOVER OVER A HOT ZONE FOR A FEW MINUTES.
THEY'RE SHOOTING AT OUR BIRDS IN THAT AREA WITH EVERYTHING FROM AK-47S TO RPGS...
US ARMY
...WHICH PUTS THE LIVES OF A COUPLE PILOTS AT RISK.
US ARMY

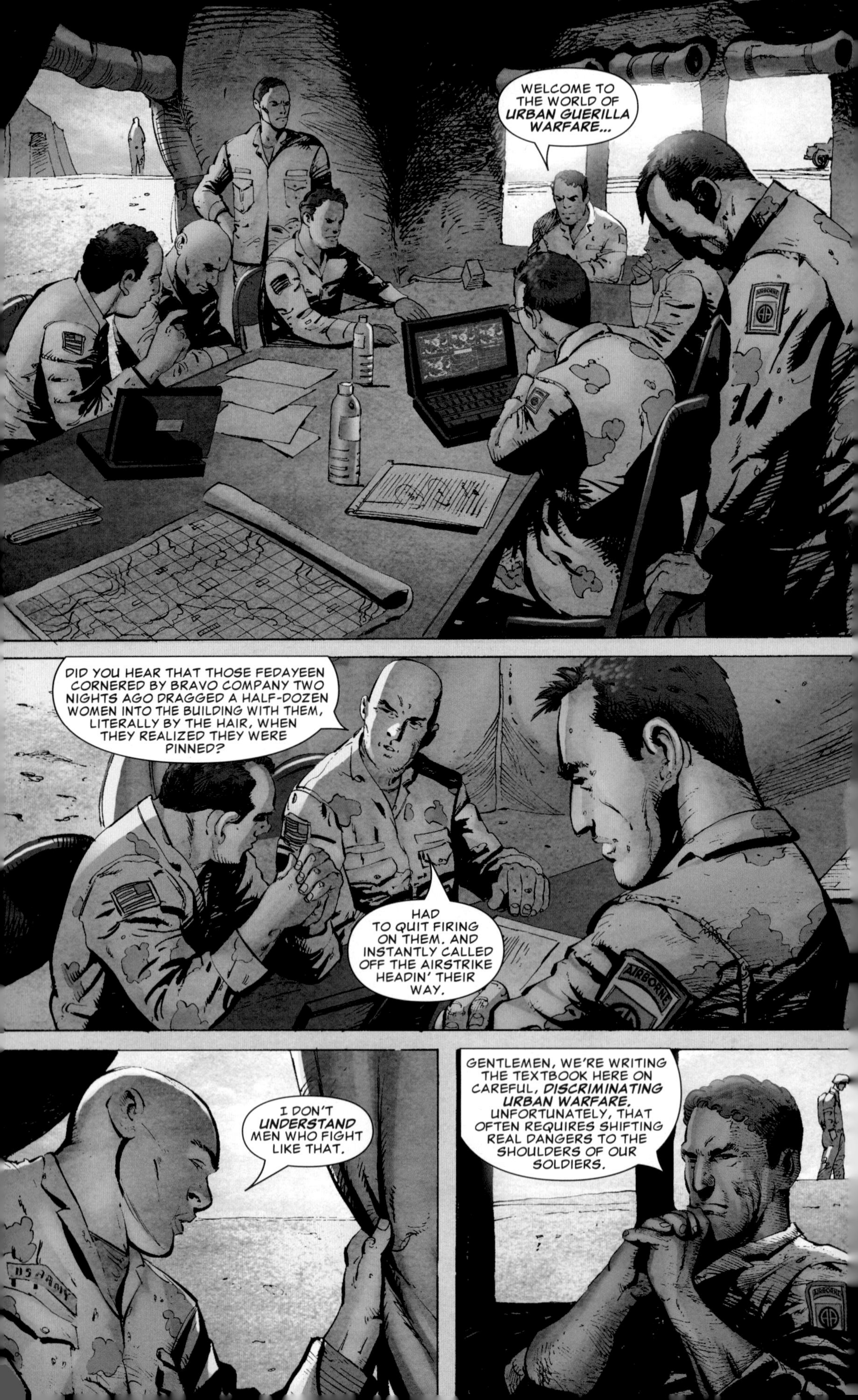

WELCOME TO THE WORLD OF *URBAN GUERILLA WARFARE...*
DID YOU HEAR THAT THOSE FEDAYEEN CORNERED BY BRAVO COMPANY TWO NIGHTS AGO DRAGGED A HALF-DOZEN WOMEN INTO THE BUILDING WITH THEM, LITERALLY BY THE HAIR, WHEN THEY REALIZED THEY WERE PINNED?
HAD TO QUIT FIRING ON THEM. AND INSTANTLY CALLED OFF THE AIRSTRIKE HEADIN' THEIR WAY.
AIRBORNE
I DON'T *UNDERSTAND* MEN WHO FIGHT LIKE THAT.
GENTLEMEN, WE'RE WRITING THE TEXTBOOK HERE ON CAREFUL, *DISCRIMINATING URBAN WARFARE.* UNFORTUNATELY, THAT OFTEN REQUIRES SHIFTING REAL DANGERS TO THE SHOULDERS OF OUR SOLDIERS.

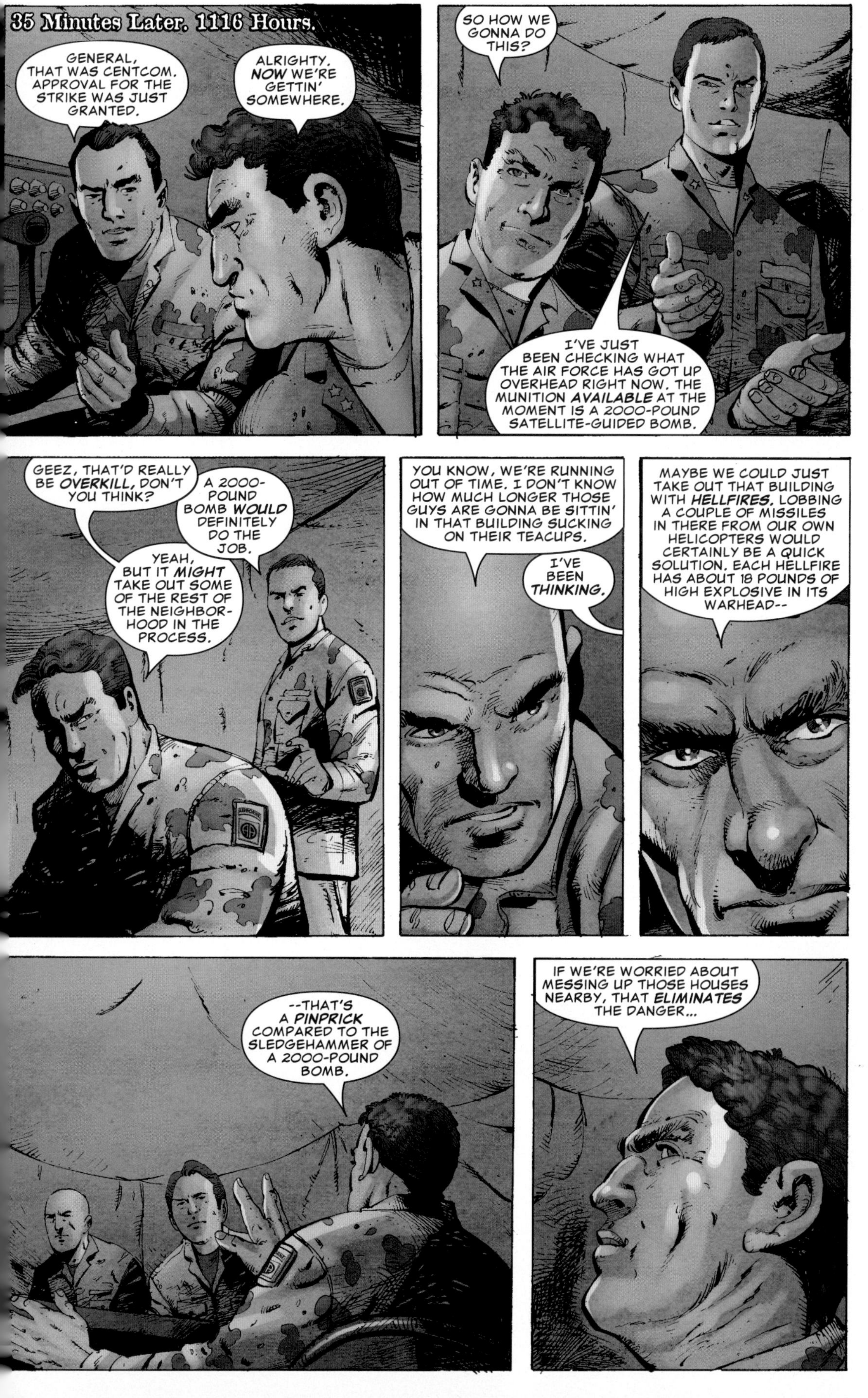
35 Minutes Later. 1116 Hours.
GENERAL, THAT WAS CENTCOM. APPROVAL FOR THE STRIKE WAS JUST GRANTED.
ALRIGHTY. NOW WE'RE GETTIN' SOMEWHERE.
SO HOW WE GONNA DO THIS?
I'VE JUST BEEN CHECKING WHAT THE AIR FORCE HAS GOT UP OVERHEAD RIGHT NOW. THE MUNITION AVAILABLE AT THE MOMENT IS A 2000-POUND SATELLITE-GUIDED BOMB.
GEEZ, THAT'D REALLY BE OVERKILL, DON'T YOU THINK?
A 2000-POUND BOMB WOULD DEFINITELY DO THE JOB.
YEAH, BUT IT MIGHT TAKE OUT SOME OF THE REST OF THE NEIGHBORHOOD IN THE PROCESS.
YOU KNOW, WE'RE RUNNING OUT OF TIME. I DON'T KNOW HOW MUCH LONGER THOSE GUYS ARE GONNA BE SITTIN' IN THAT BUILDING SUCKING ON THEIR TEACUPS.
I'VE BEEN THINKING.
MAYBE WE COULD JUST TAKE OUT THAT BUILDING WITH HELLFIRES. LOBBING A COUPLE OF MISSILES IN THERE FROM OUR OWN HELICOPTERS WOULD CERTAINLY BE A QUICK SOLUTION. EACH HELLFIRE HAS ABOUT 18 POUNDS OF HIGH EXPLOSIVE IN ITS WARHEAD--
--THAT'S A PINPRICK COMPARED TO THE SLEDGEHAMMER OF A 2000-POUND BOMB.
IF WE'RE WORRIED ABOUT MESSING UP THOSE HOUSES NEARBY, THAT ELIMINATES THE DANGER...

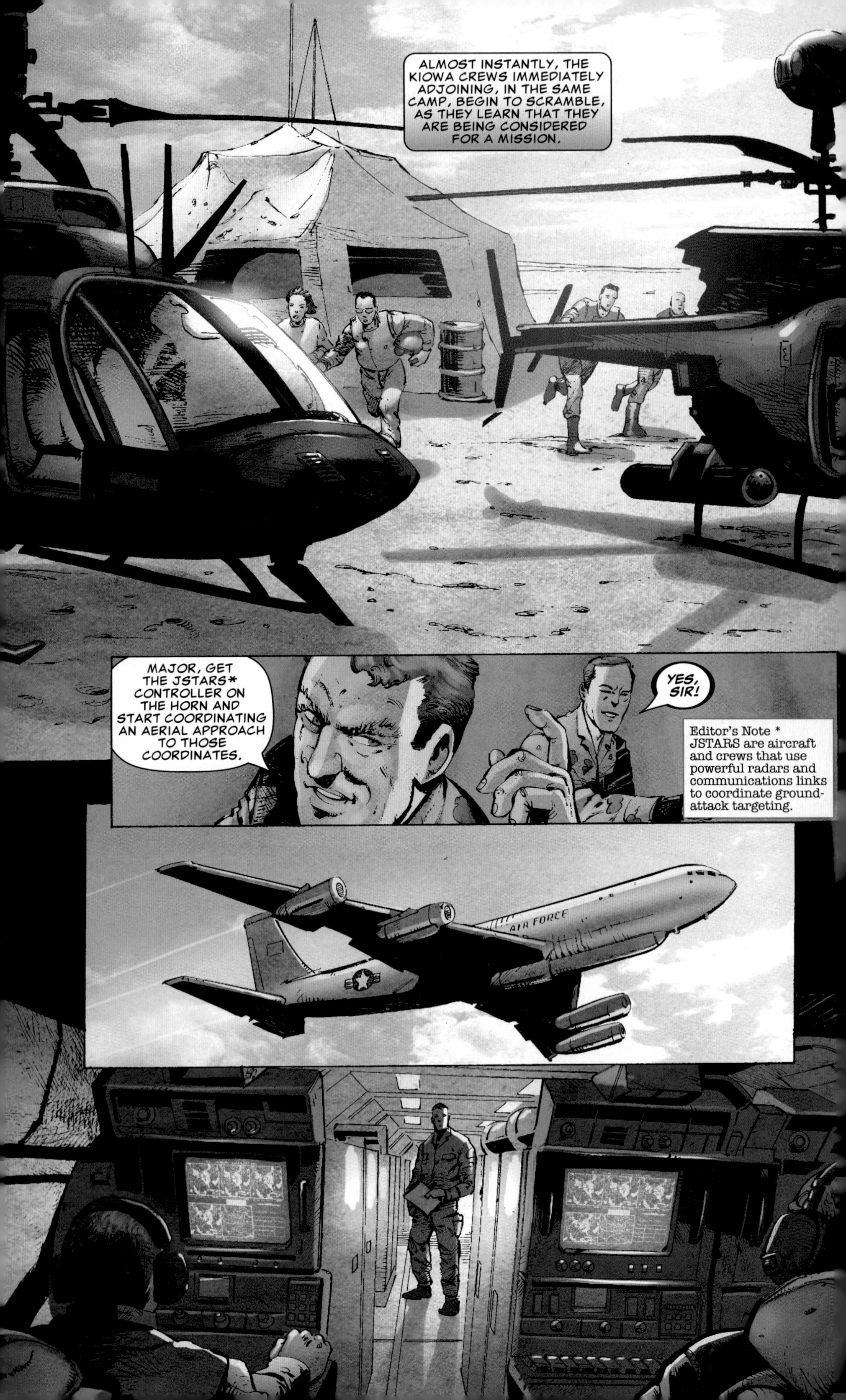
ALMOST INSTANTLY, THE KIOWA CREWS IMMEDIATELY ADJOINING, IN THE SAME CAMP, BEGIN TO SCRAMBLE, AS THEY LEARN THAT THEY ARE BEING CONSIDERED FOR A MISSION.
MAJOR, GET THE JSTARS* CONTROLLER ON THE HORN AND START COORDINATING AN AERIAL APPROACH TO THOSE COORDINATES.
YES, SIR!
Editor's Note * JSTARS are aircraft and crews that use powerful radars and communications links to coordinate ground-attack targeting.
AIR FORCE

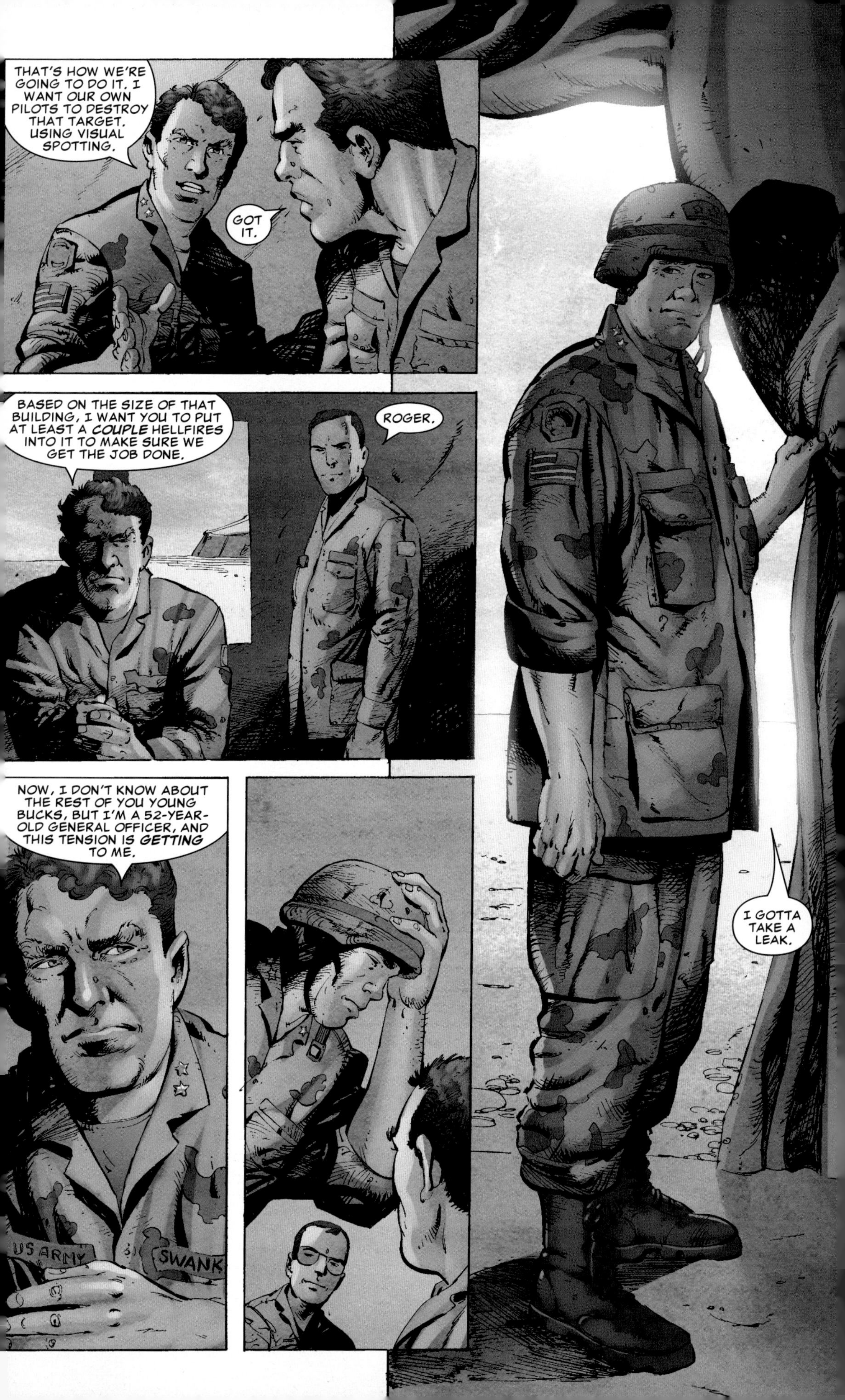
THAT'S HOW WE'RE GOING TO DO IT. I WANT OUR OWN PILOTS TO DESTROY THAT TARGET. USING VISUAL SPOTTING.
GOT IT.
BASED ON THE SIZE OF THAT BUILDING, I WANT YOU TO PUT AT LEAST A COUPLE HELLFIRES INTO IT TO MAKE SURE WE GET THE JOB DONE.
ROGER.
NOW, I DON'T KNOW ABOUT THE REST OF YOU YOUNG BUCKS, BUT I'M A 52-YEAR-OLD GENERAL OFFICER, AND THIS TENSION IS GETTING TO ME.
US ARMY
SWANK
I GOTTA TAKE A LEAK.

FORTY YARDS AWAY, THE CAVALRY CREW GUARDING THE GENERAL'S COMMAND POST DISCUSSES THE MORNING'S EVENTS.

...SMITTY WAS JUST ON THE RADIO TALKING TO THE REFUELING AND REARMING POINT FOR THE KIOWAS. HE SAYS THEY'RE LAUNCHING TWO BIRDS TO GO HIT A TARGET IN THE CITY WITH FOUR HELLFIRES.

WOAH. THAT'S A BIG SHOOT FOR THOSE FLIERS.

YUP. THEY RARELY GET TO PULL THE TRIGGER ON EVEN ONE LIVE HELLFIRE AT THE TRAINING RANGE BACK AT FORT BRAGG.

YEAH, 'CUZ EACH OF THOSE MISSILES COSTS ABOUT AS MUCH AS A MERCEDES.

AND FOR ALL THAT MONEY, THEY GET EVEN WORSE GAS MILEAGE THAN A BENZ.

AND STILL COME IN ON ONE COLOR BLACK.

TALK ABOUT A RIP-OFF.

LOOKS LIKE THE GROUND CREW SENT A LITTLE MESSAGE.

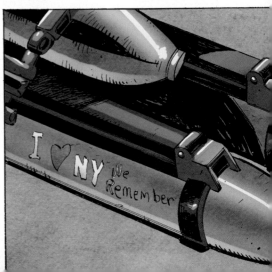

I ♥ NY We Remember

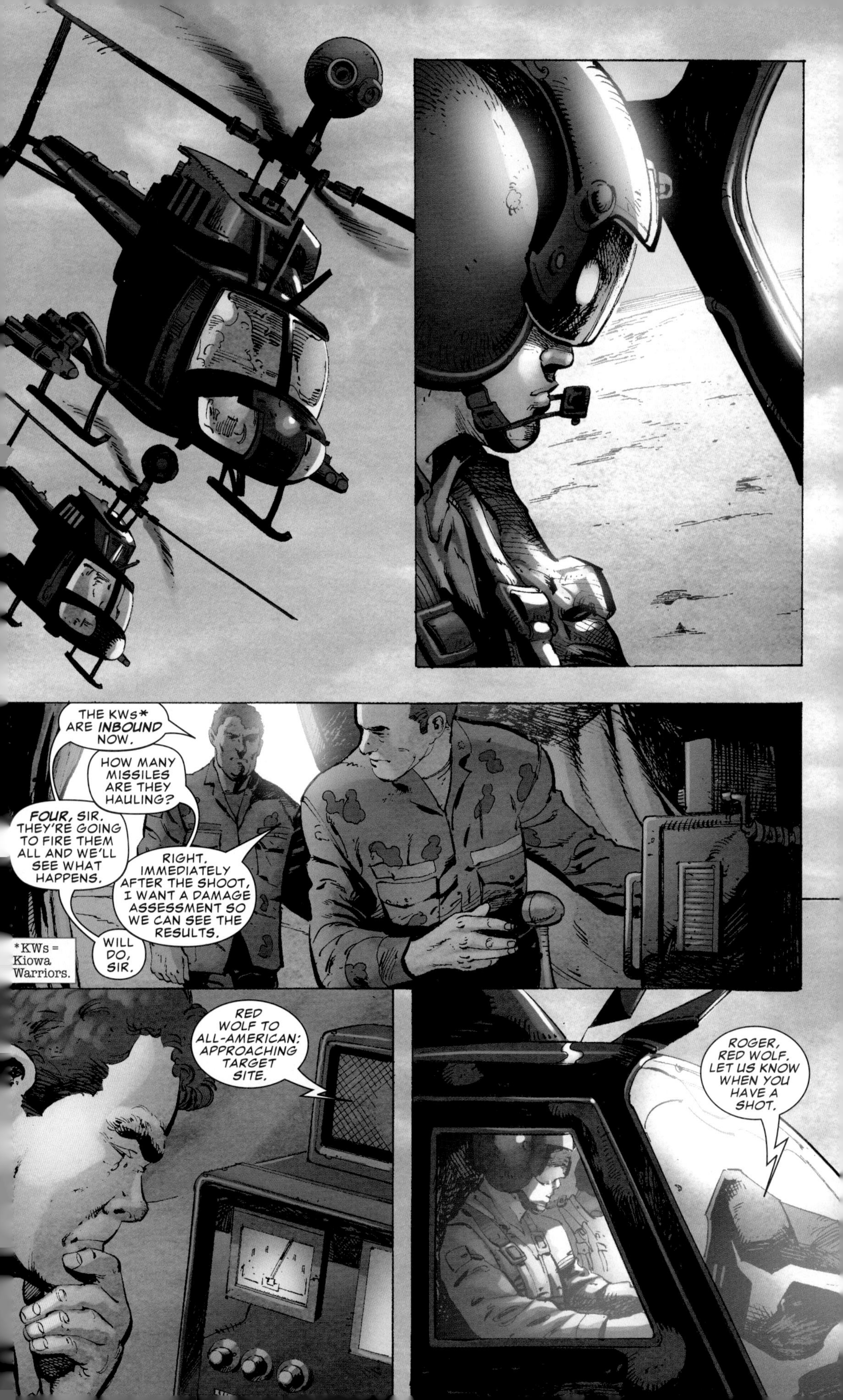

THE KWs* ARE INBOUND NOW.
HOW MANY MISSILES ARE THEY HAULING?
FOUR, SIR. THEY'RE GOING TO FIRE THEM ALL AND WE'LL SEE WHAT HAPPENS.
RIGHT. IMMEDIATELY AFTER THE SHOOT, I WANT A DAMAGE ASSESSMENT SO WE CAN SEE THE RESULTS.
WILL DO, SIR.
*KWs = Kiowa Warriors.
RED WOLF TO ALL-AMERICAN: APPROACHING TARGET SITE.
ROGER, RED WOLF. LET US KNOW WHEN YOU HAVE A SHOT.

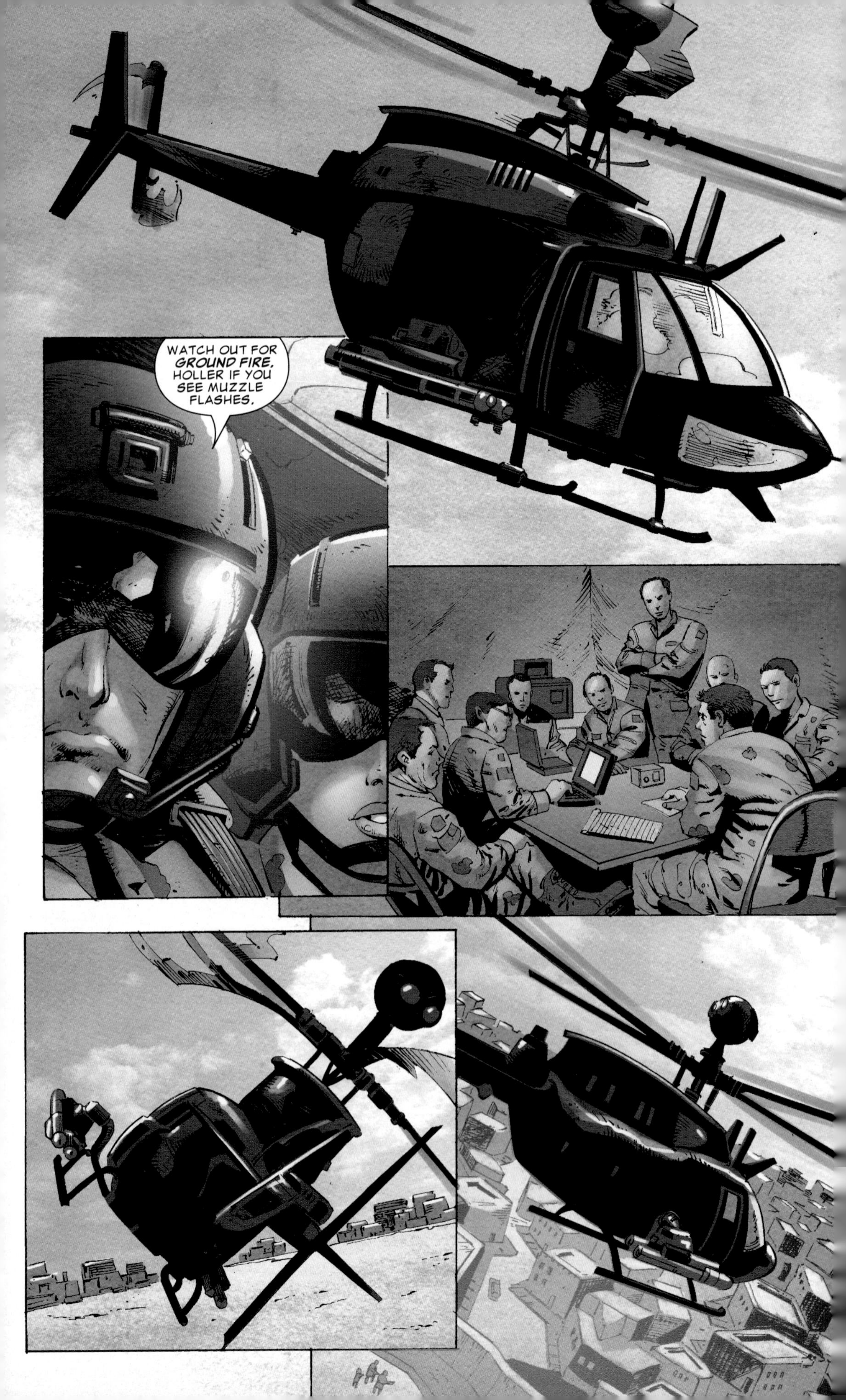
WATCH OUT FOR *GROUND FIRE.* HOLLER IF YOU SEE MUZZLE FLASHES.

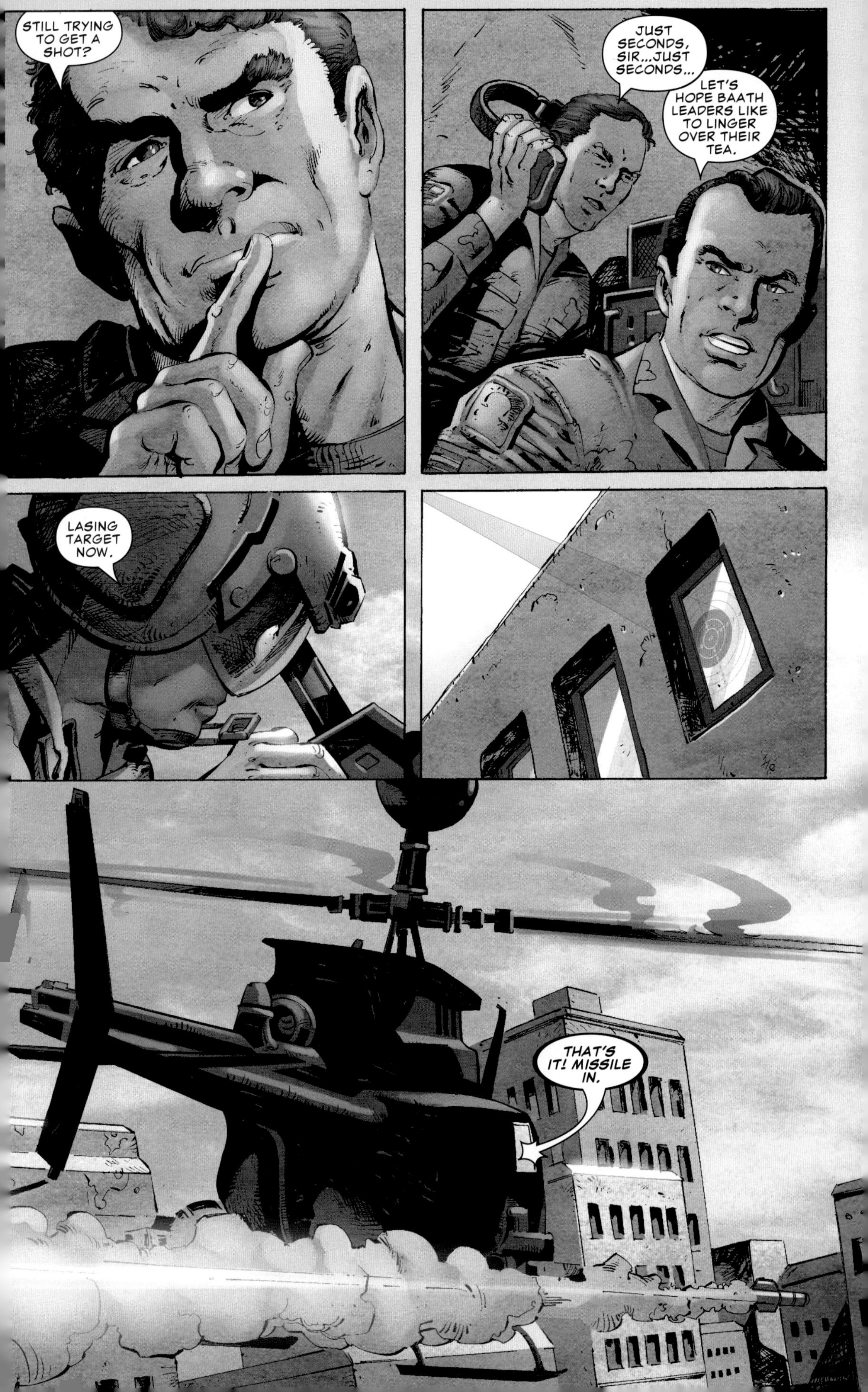
STILL TRYING TO GET A SHOT?
JUST SECONDS, SIR...JUST SECONDS...
LET'S HOPE BAATH LEADERS LIKE TO LINGER OVER THEIR TEA.
LASING TARGET NOW.
THAT'S IT! MISSILE IN.

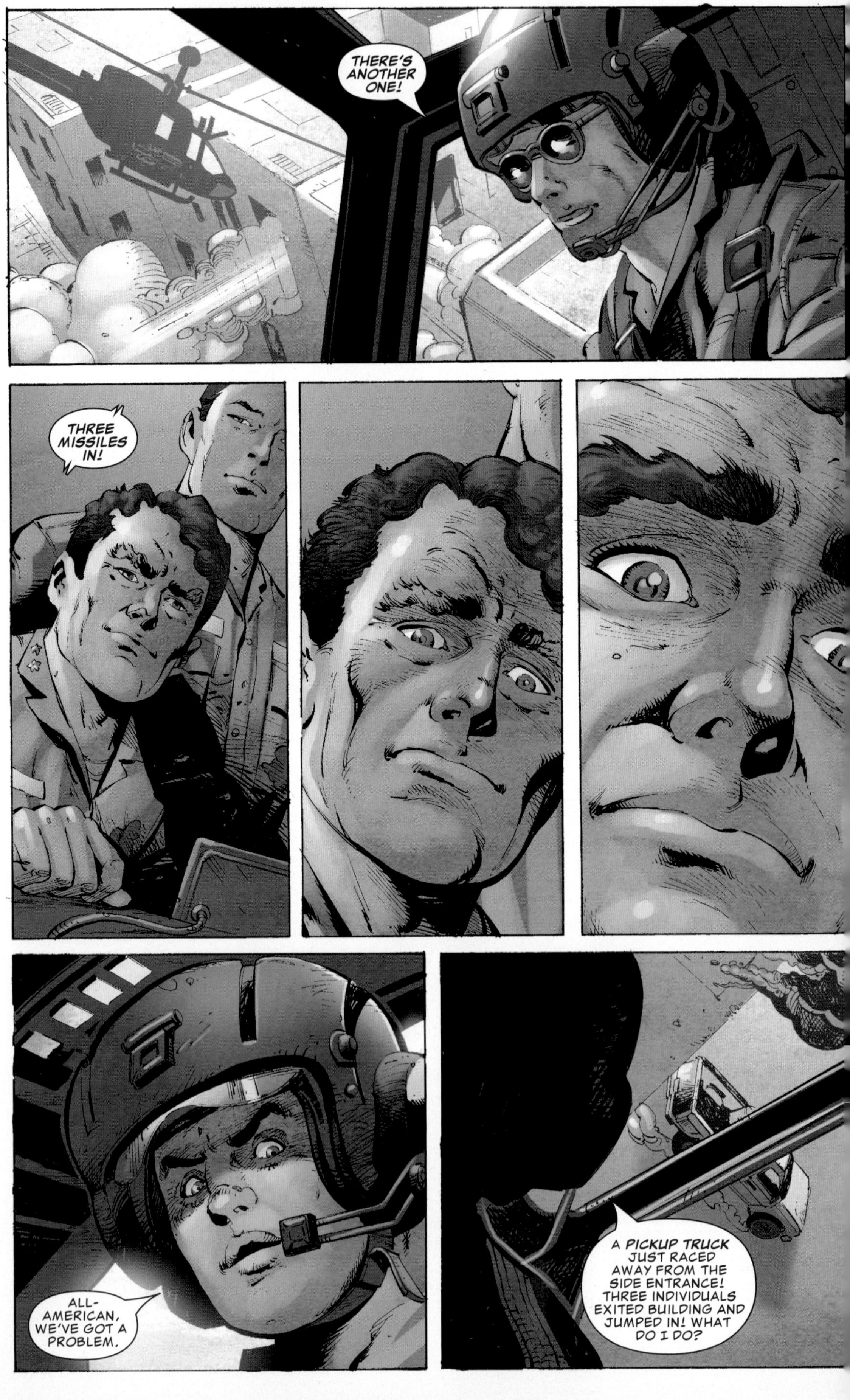
THERE'S ANOTHER ONE!
THREE MISSILES IN!
ALL-AMERICAN, WE'VE GOT A PROBLEM.
A PICKUP TRUCK JUST RACED AWAY FROM THE SIDE ENTRANCE! THREE INDIVIDUALS EXITED BUILDING AND JUMPED IN! WHAT DO I DO?

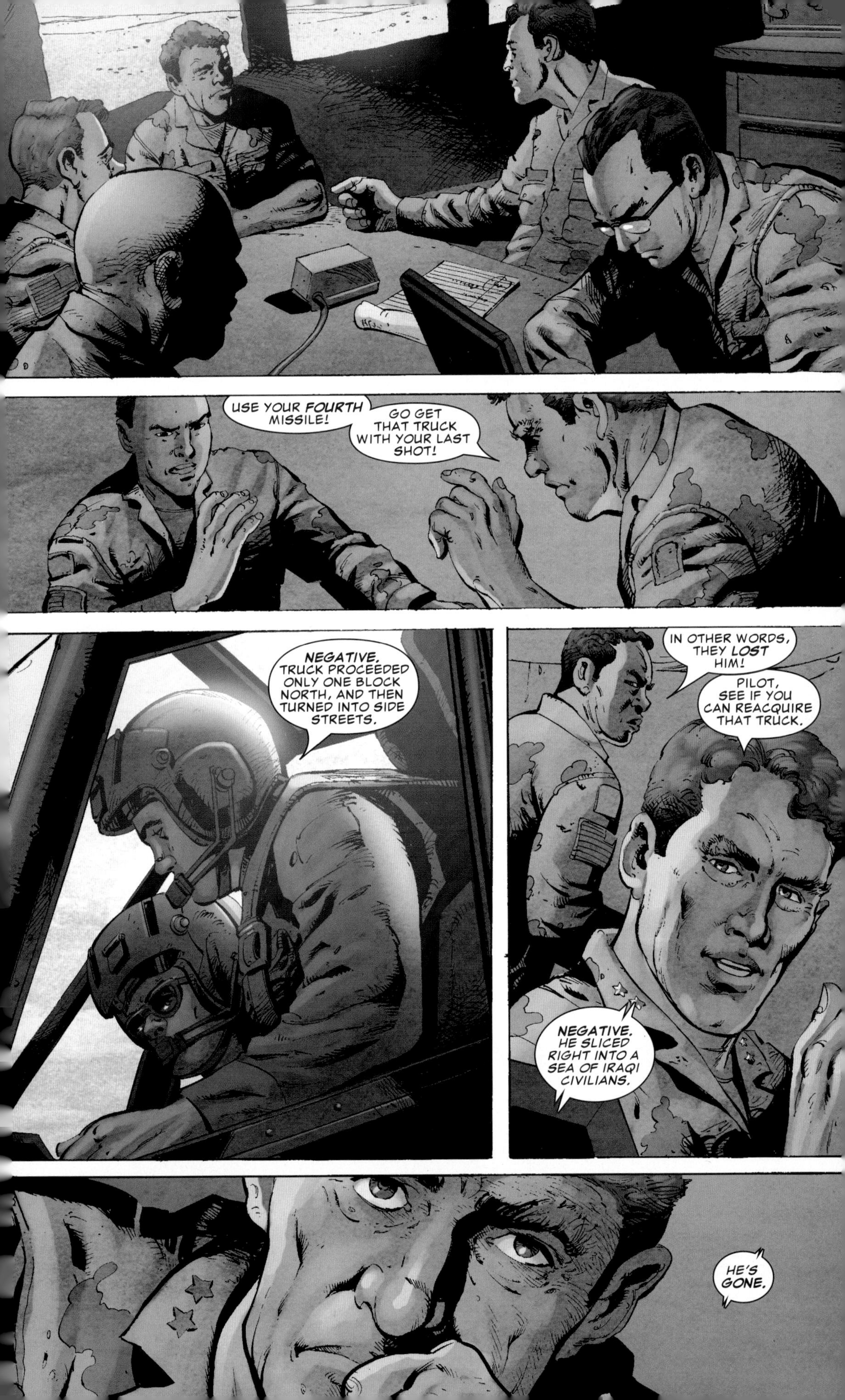
USE YOUR FOURTH MISSILE!
GO GET THAT TRUCK WITH YOUR LAST SHOT!
NEGATIVE. TRUCK PROCEEDED ONLY ONE BLOCK NORTH, AND THEN TURNED INTO SIDE STREETS.
IN OTHER WORDS, THEY LOST HIM!
PILOT, SEE IF YOU CAN REACQUIRE THAT TRUCK.
NEGATIVE. HE SLICED RIGHT INTO A SEA OF IRAQI CIVILIANS.
HE'S GONE.

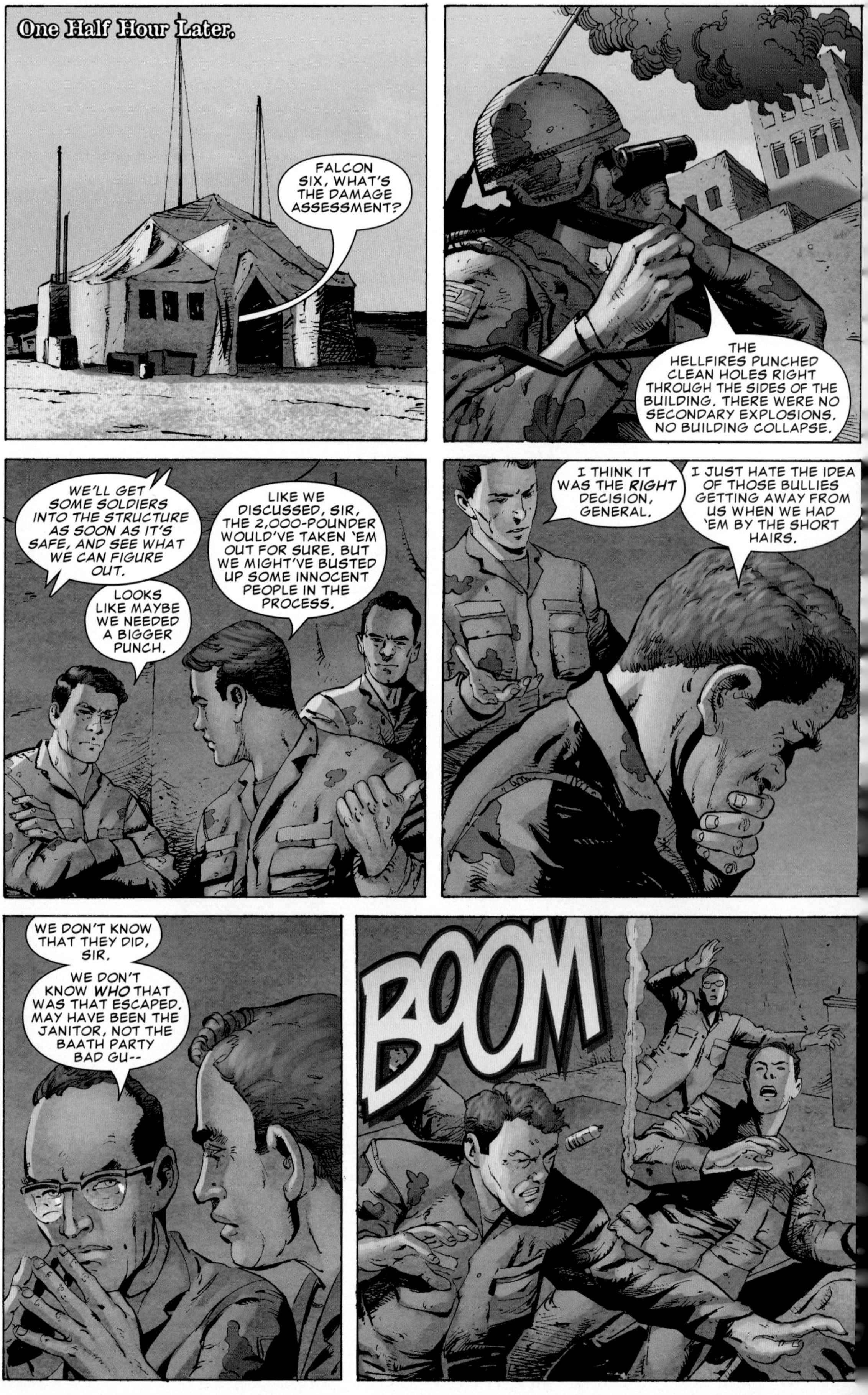
One Half Hour Later.
FALCON SIX, WHAT'S THE DAMAGE ASSESSMENT?
THE HELLFIRES PUNCHED CLEAN HOLES RIGHT THROUGH THE SIDES OF THE BUILDING. THERE WERE NO SECONDARY EXPLOSIONS. NO BUILDING COLLAPSE.
WE'LL GET SOME SOLDIERS INTO THE STRUCTURE AS SOON AS IT'S SAFE, AND SEE WHAT WE CAN FIGURE OUT.
LOOKS LIKE MAYBE WE NEEDED A BIGGER PUNCH.
LIKE WE DISCUSSED, SIR, THE 2,000-POUNDER WOULD'VE TAKEN 'EM OUT FOR SURE. BUT WE MIGHT'VE BUSTED UP SOME INNOCENT PEOPLE IN THE PROCESS.
I THINK IT WAS THE RIGHT DECISION, GENERAL.
I JUST HATE THE IDEA OF THOSE BULLIES GETTING AWAY FROM US WHEN WE HAD 'EM BY THE SHORT HAIRS.
WE DON'T KNOW THAT THEY DID, SIR.
WE DON'T KNOW WHO THAT WAS THAT ESCAPED. MAY HAVE BEEN THE JANITOR, NOT THE BAATH PARTY BAD GU--
BOOM

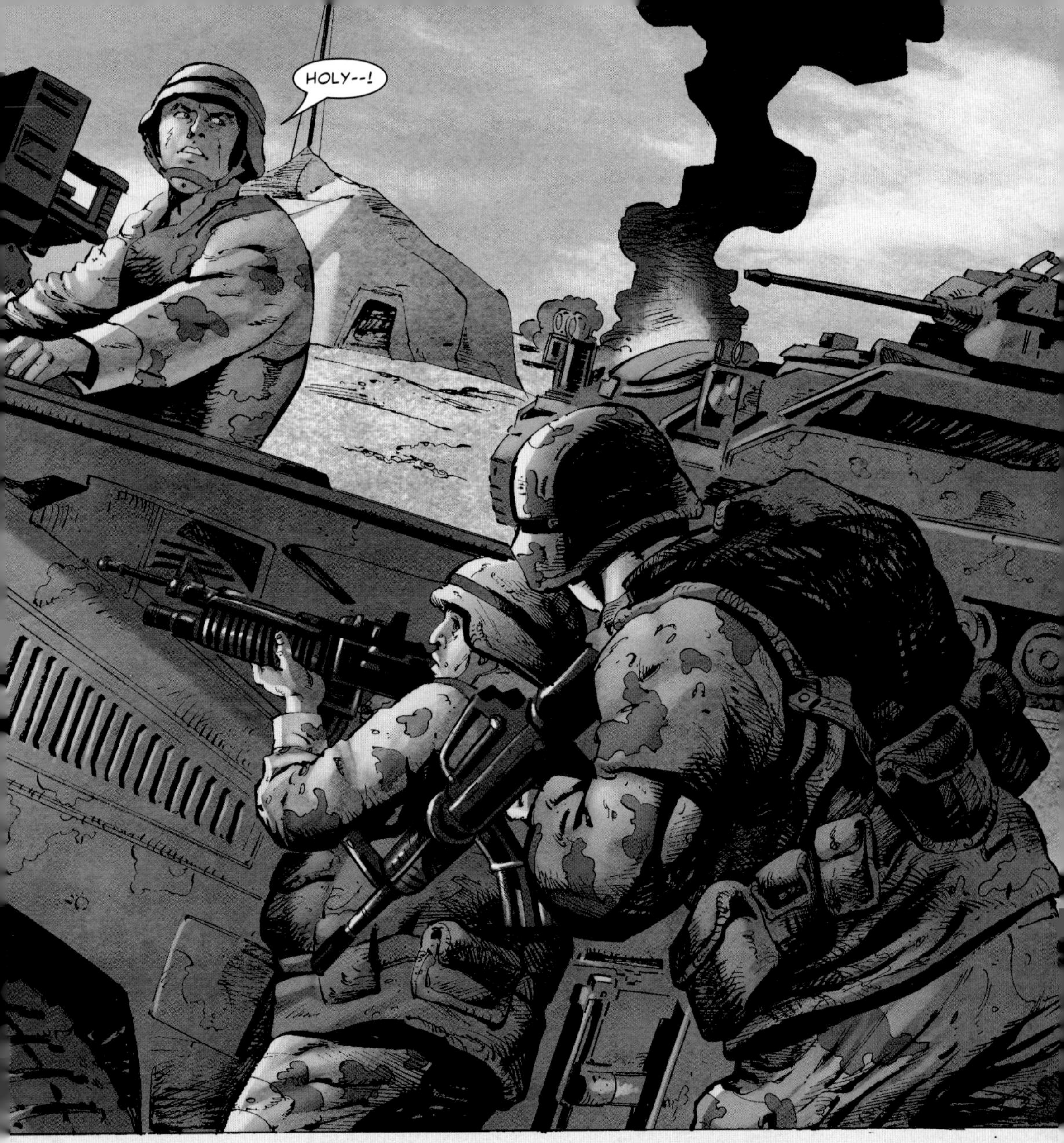
HOLY--!

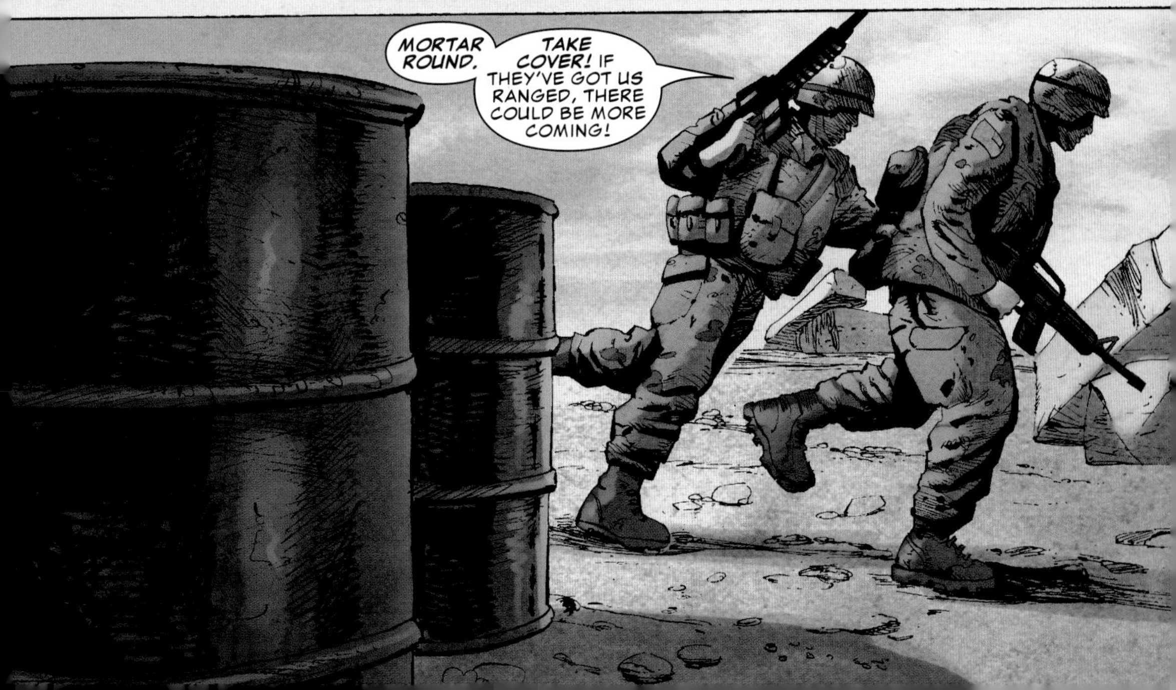
MORTAR ROUND.
TAKE COVER! IF THEY'VE GOT US RANGED, THERE COULD BE MORE COMING!

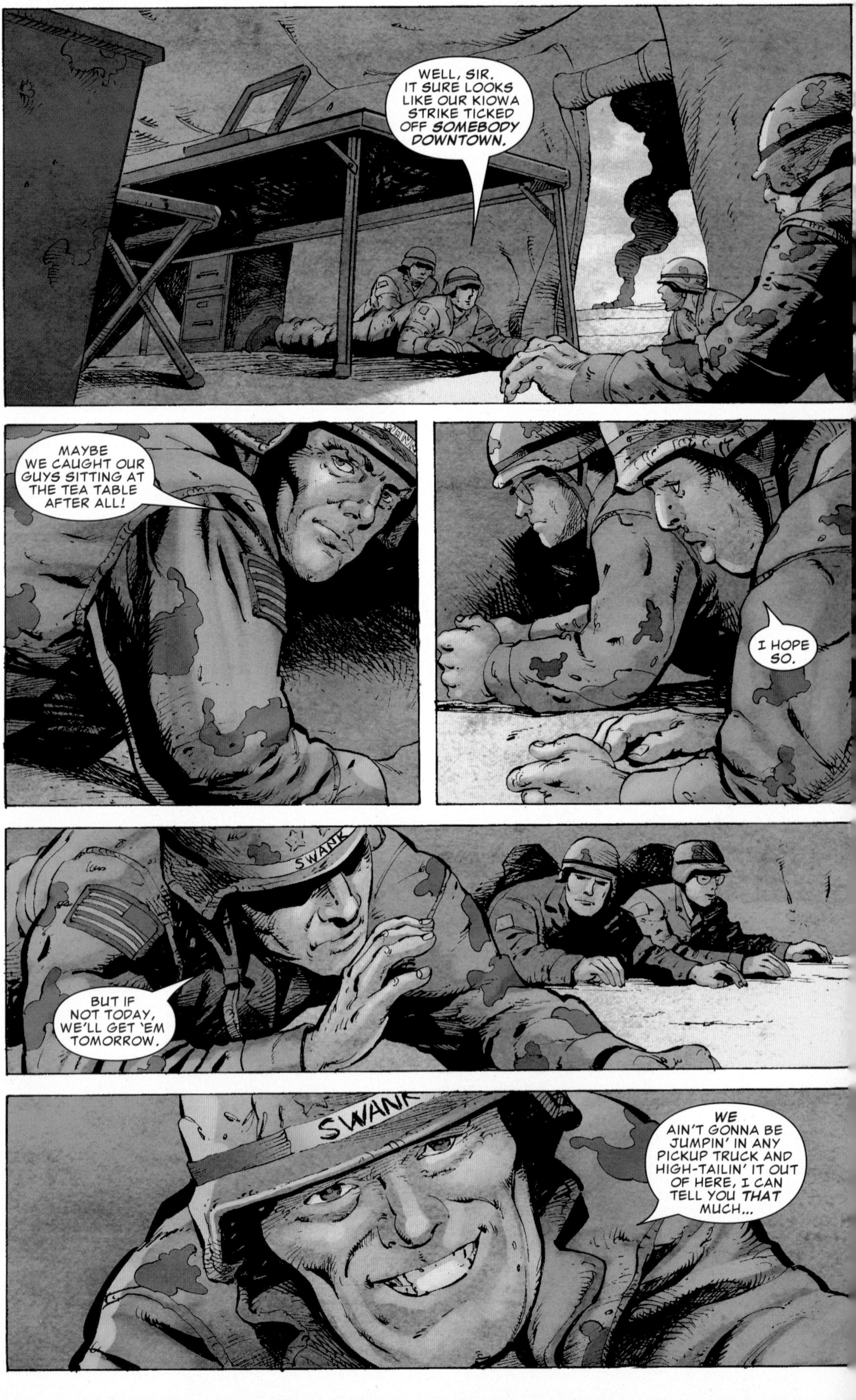

WELL, SIR. IT SURE LOOKS LIKE OUR KIOWA STRIKE TICKED OFF SOMEBODY DOWNTOWN.
MAYBE WE CAUGHT OUR GUYS SITTING AT THE TEA TABLE AFTER ALL!
I HOPE SO.
SWANK
BUT IF NOT TODAY, WE'LL GET 'EM TOMORROW.
SWANK
WE AIN'T GONNA BE JUMPIN' IN ANY PICKUP TRUCK AND HIGH-TAILIN' IT OUT OF HERE, I CAN TELL YOU THAT MUCH...

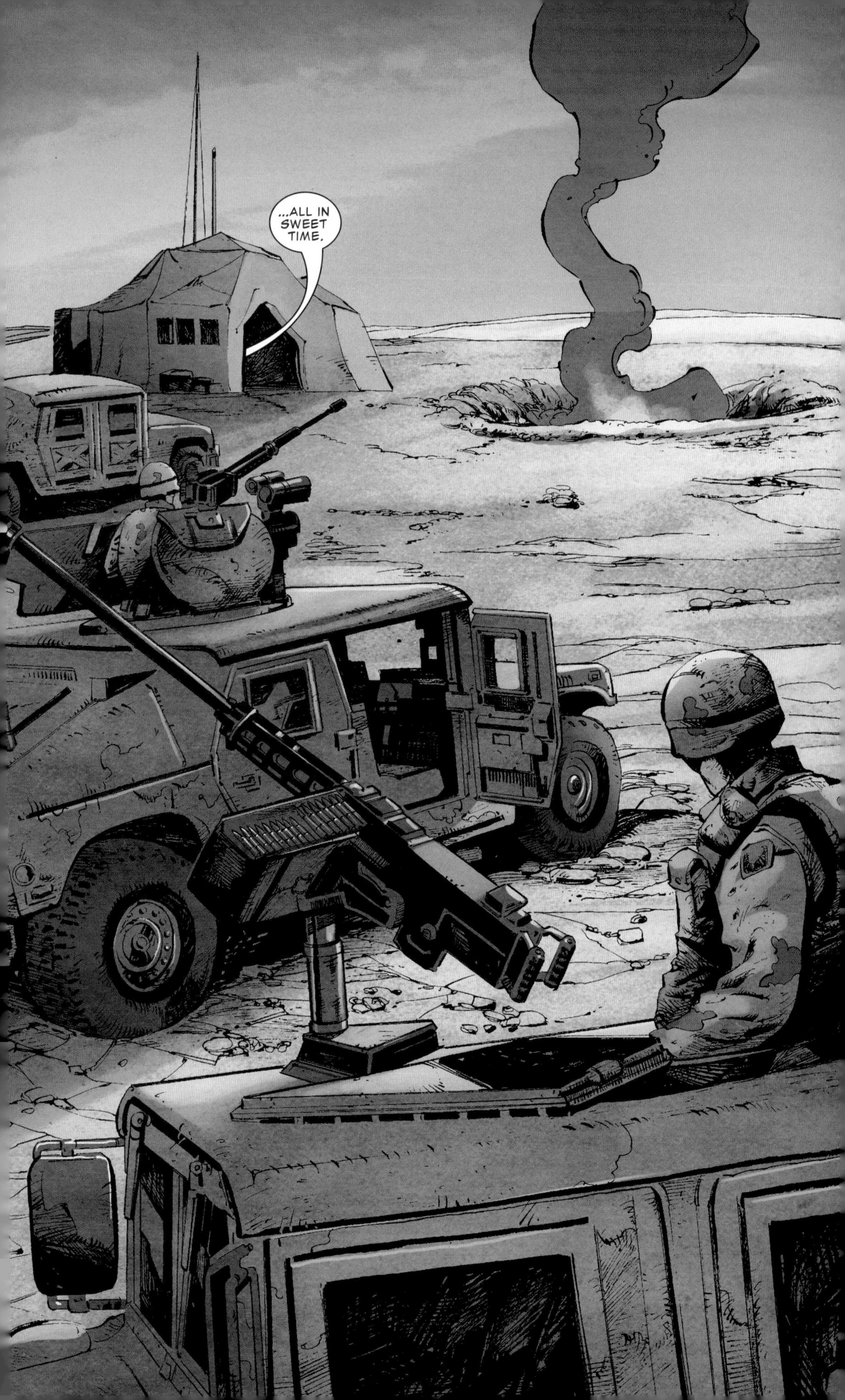
...ALL IN SWEET TIME.

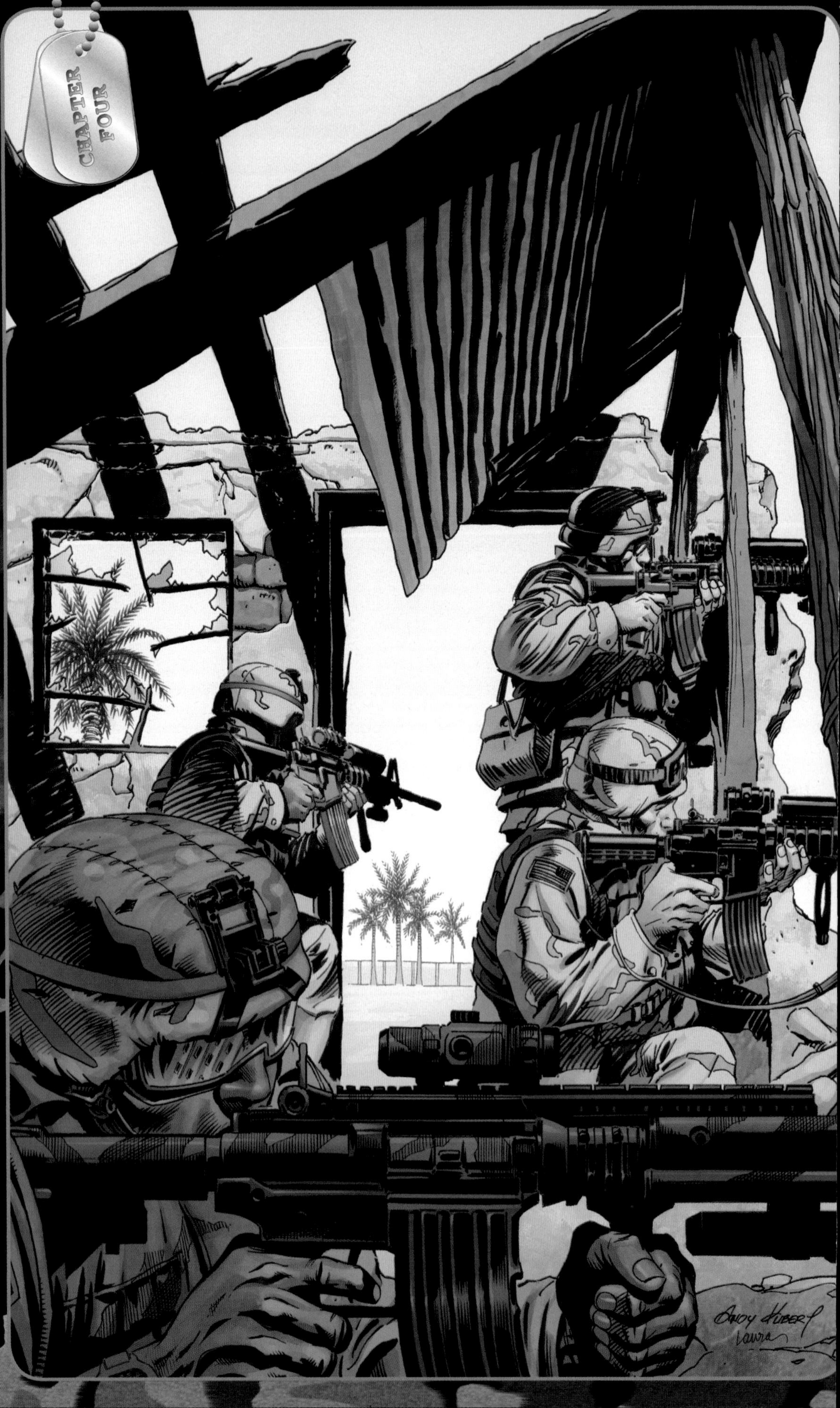
CHAPTER
FOUR

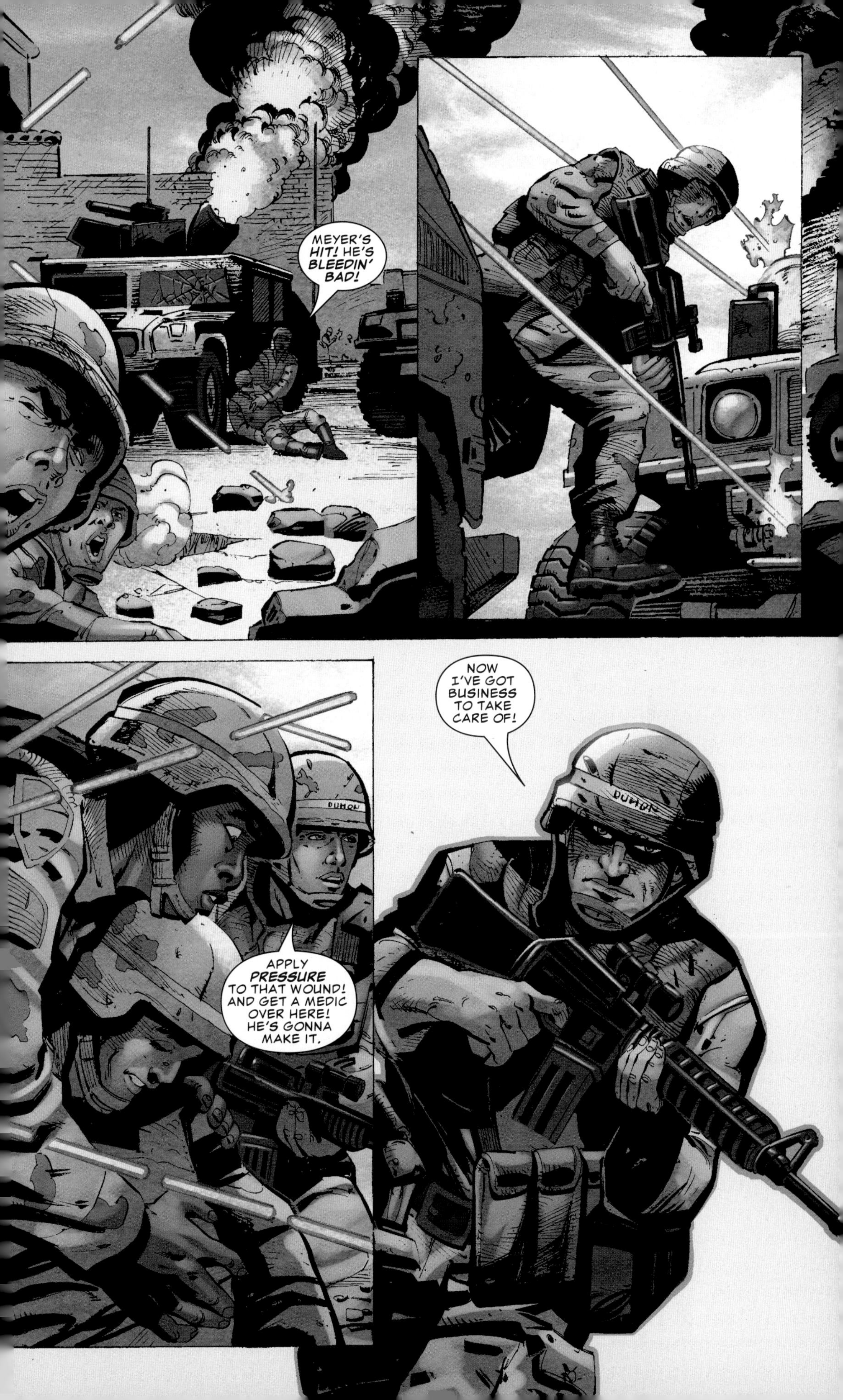
MEYER'S HIT! HE'S BLEEDIN' BAD!
DUHON
APPLY PRESSURE TO THAT WOUND! AND GET A MEDIC OVER HERE! HE'S GONNA MAKE IT.
NOW I'VE GOT BUSINESS TO TAKE CARE OF!
DUHON

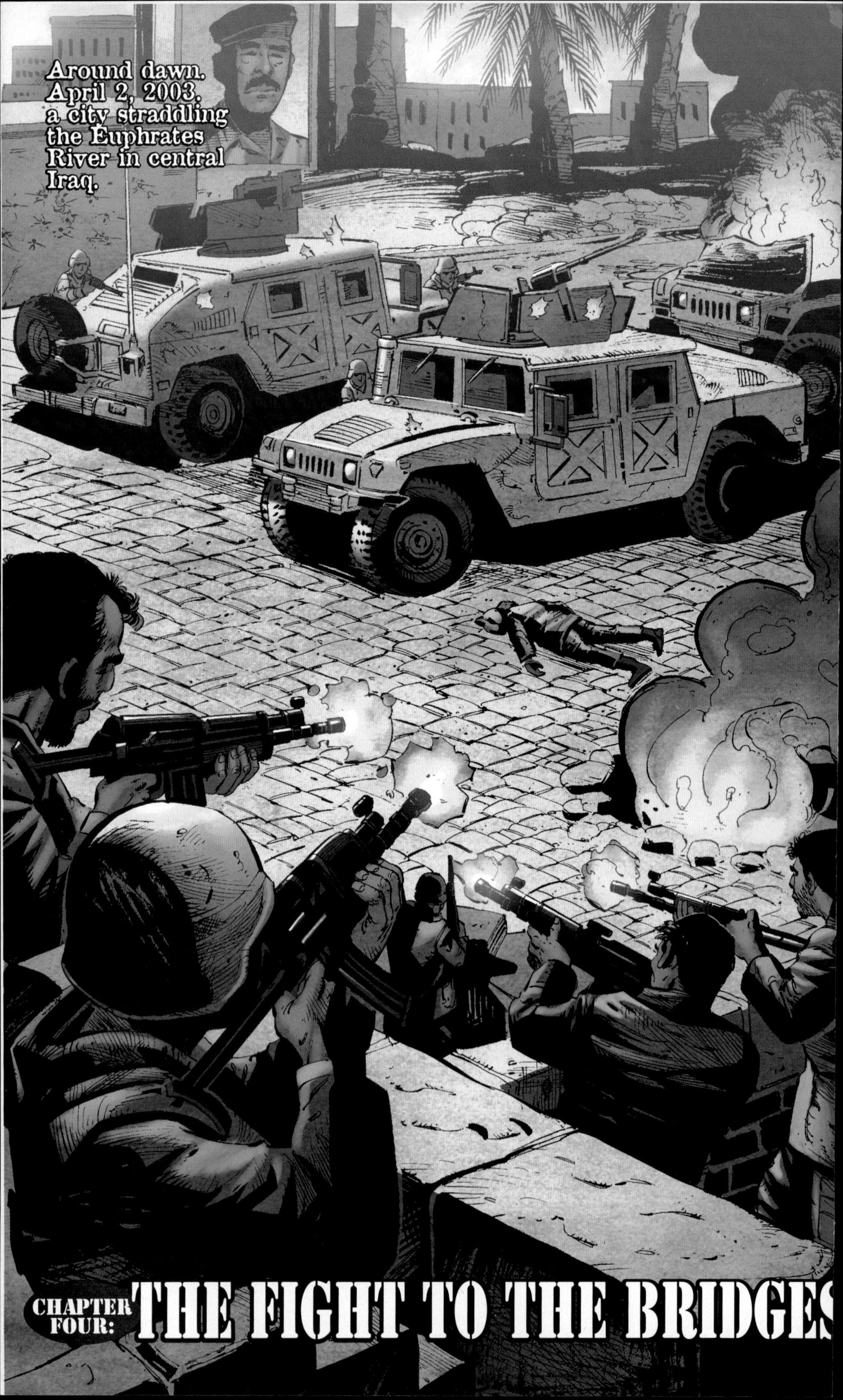
Around dawn. April 2, 2003. a city straddling the Euphrates River in central Iraq.
CHAPTER FOUR: THE FIGHT TO THE BRIDGES

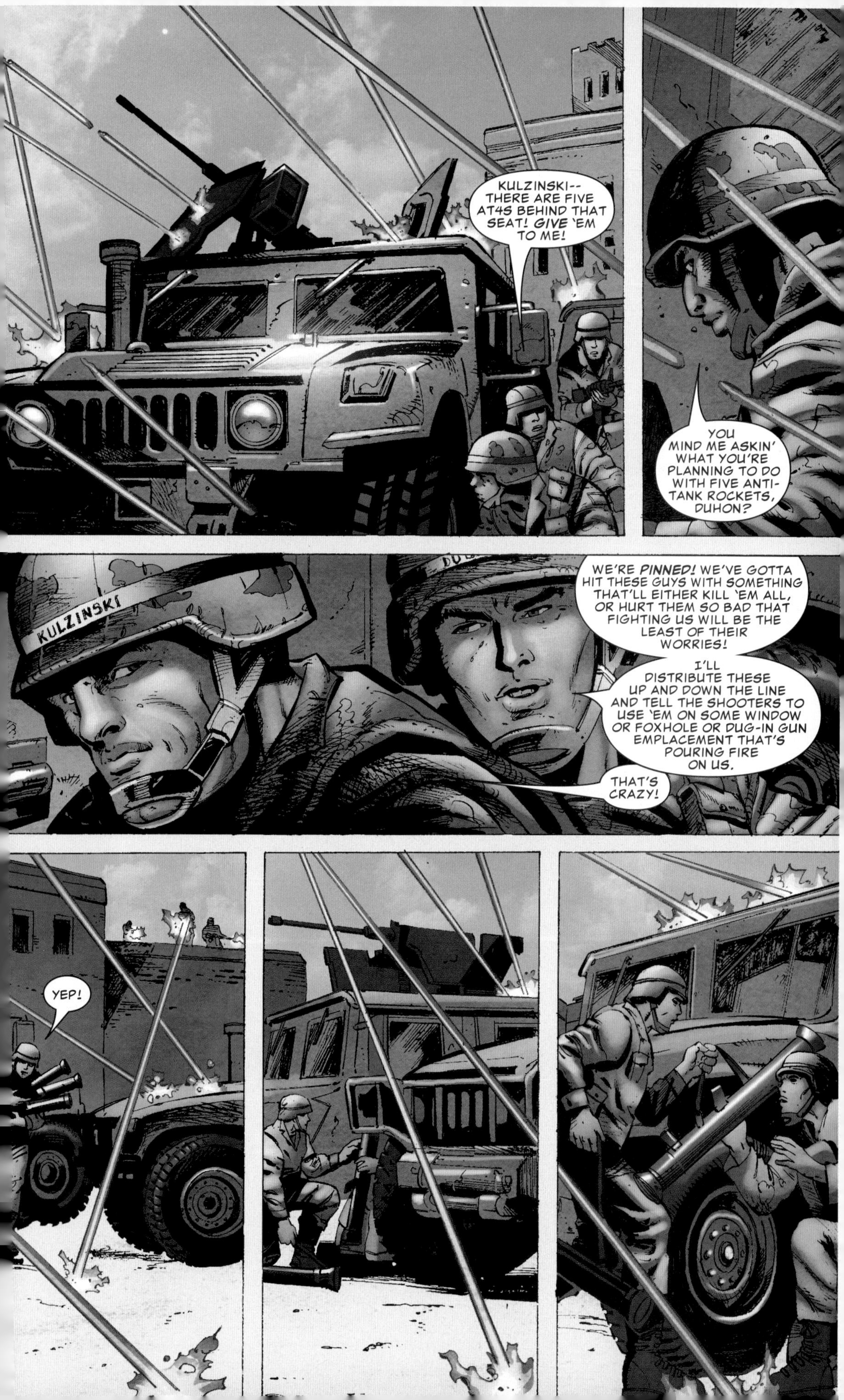
KULZINSKI-- THERE ARE FIVE AT4S BEHIND THAT SEAT! *GIVE* 'EM TO ME!
YOU MIND ME ASKIN' WHAT YOU'RE PLANNING TO DO WITH FIVE ANTI-TANK ROCKETS, DUHON?
KULZINSKI
WE'RE *PINNED!* WE'VE GOTTA HIT THESE GUYS WITH SOMETHING THAT'LL EITHER KILL 'EM ALL, OR HURT THEM SO BAD THAT FIGHTING US WILL BE THE LEAST OF THEIR WORRIES!
I'LL DISTRIBUTE THESE UP AND DOWN THE LINE AND TELL THE SHOOTERS TO USE 'EM ON SOME WINDOW OR FOXHOLE OR DUG-IN GUN EMPLACEMENT THAT'S POURING FIRE ON US.
THAT'S CRAZY!
YEP!

MISS ME?

NOT REALLY.

BUT I DID *LEARN* SOMETHING WATCHING YOUR MAD SPRINT BETWEEN OUR VEHICLES.

EACH TIME YOU EXPOSED YOURSELF, AUTOMATIC FIRE WOULD POUR OUT OF THE SAME POINTS ACROSS THE PLAZA.

WATCH THIS.

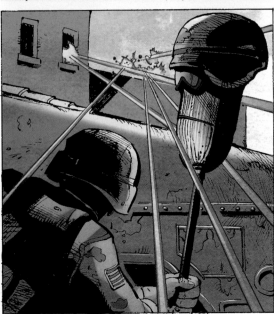

SEE THAT? THEY'RE GIVING AWAY THEIR *POSITIONS.*

I'VE GOT A LITTLE *PROPOSAL* FOR YOU:

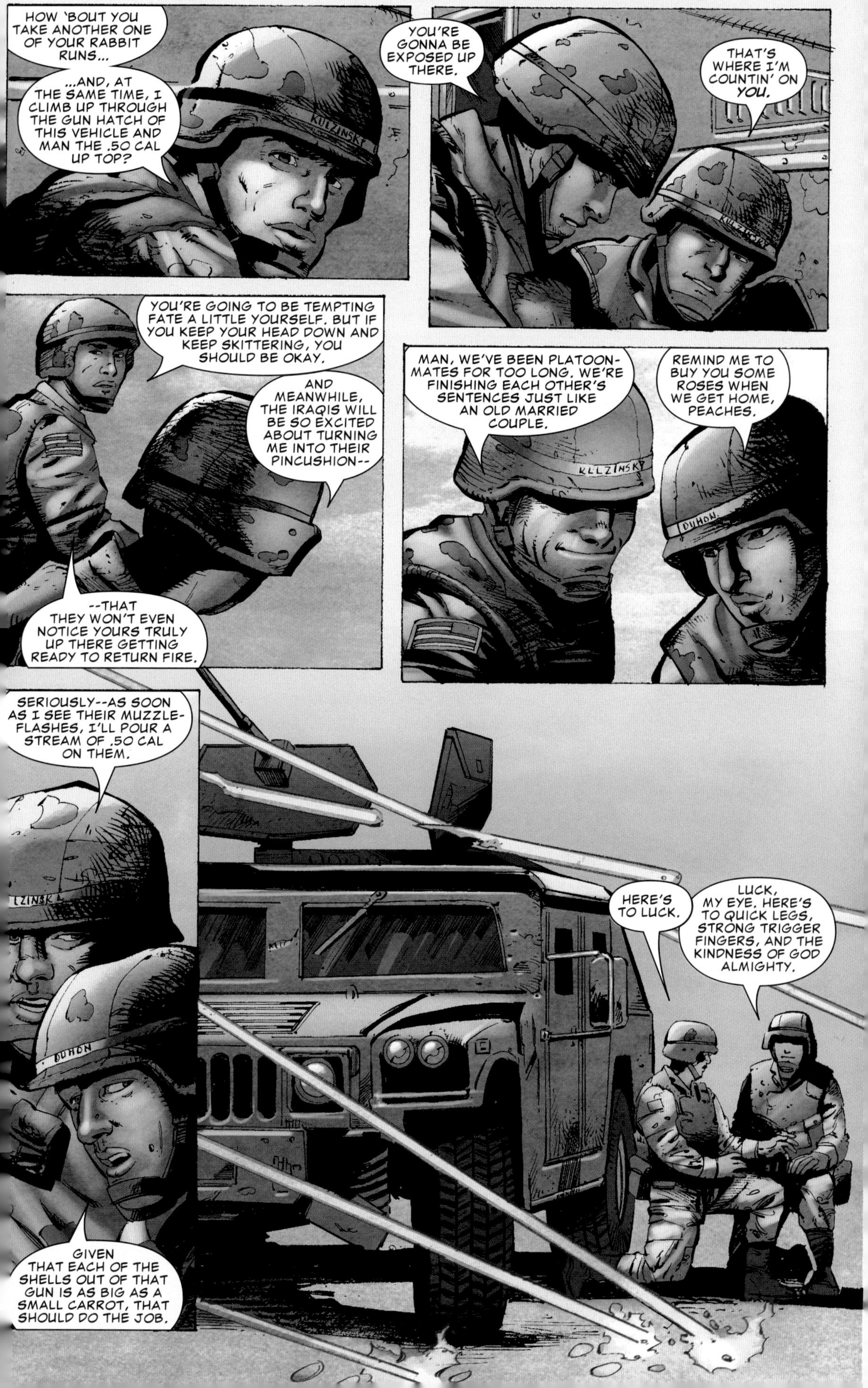
HOW 'BOUT YOU TAKE ANOTHER ONE OF YOUR RABBIT RUNS...
...AND, AT THE SAME TIME, I CLIMB UP THROUGH THE GUN HATCH OF THIS VEHICLE AND MAN THE .50 CAL UP TOP?
KULZINSKY
YOU'RE GONNA BE EXPOSED UP THERE.
THAT'S WHERE I'M COUNTIN' ON *YOU.*
KULZINSKY
YOU'RE GOING TO BE TEMPTING FATE A LITTLE YOURSELF. BUT IF YOU KEEP YOUR HEAD DOWN AND KEEP SKITTERING, YOU SHOULD BE OKAY.
AND MEANWHILE, THE IRAQIS WILL BE SO EXCITED ABOUT TURNING ME INTO THEIR PINCUSHION--
--THAT THEY WON'T EVEN NOTICE YOURS TRULY UP THERE GETTING READY TO RETURN FIRE.
MAN, WE'VE BEEN PLATOON-MATES FOR TOO LONG. WE'RE FINISHING EACH OTHER'S SENTENCES JUST LIKE AN OLD MARRIED COUPLE.
REMIND ME TO BUY YOU SOME ROSES WHEN WE GET HOME, PEACHES.
KULZINSKY
DUHON
SERIOUSLY--AS SOON AS I SEE THEIR MUZZLE-FLASHES, I'LL POUR A STREAM OF .50 CAL ON THEM.
GIVEN THAT EACH OF THE SHELLS OUT OF THAT GUN IS AS BIG AS A SMALL CARROT, THAT SHOULD DO THE JOB.
HERE'S TO LUCK.
LUCK, MY EYE. HERE'S TO QUICK LEGS, STRONG TRIGGER FINGERS, AND THE KINDNESS OF GOD ALMIGHTY.

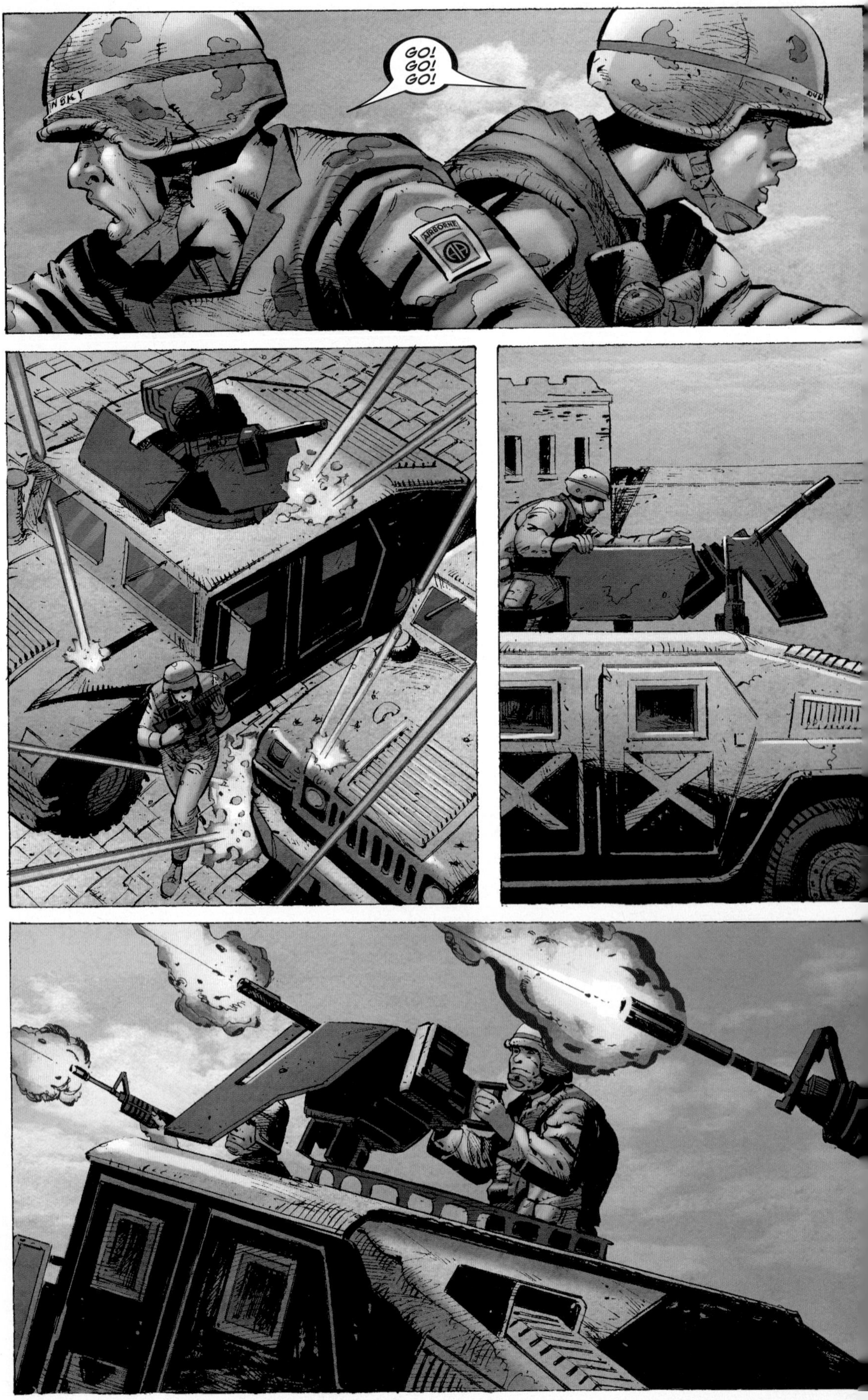
GO!
GO!
GO!
AIRBORNE

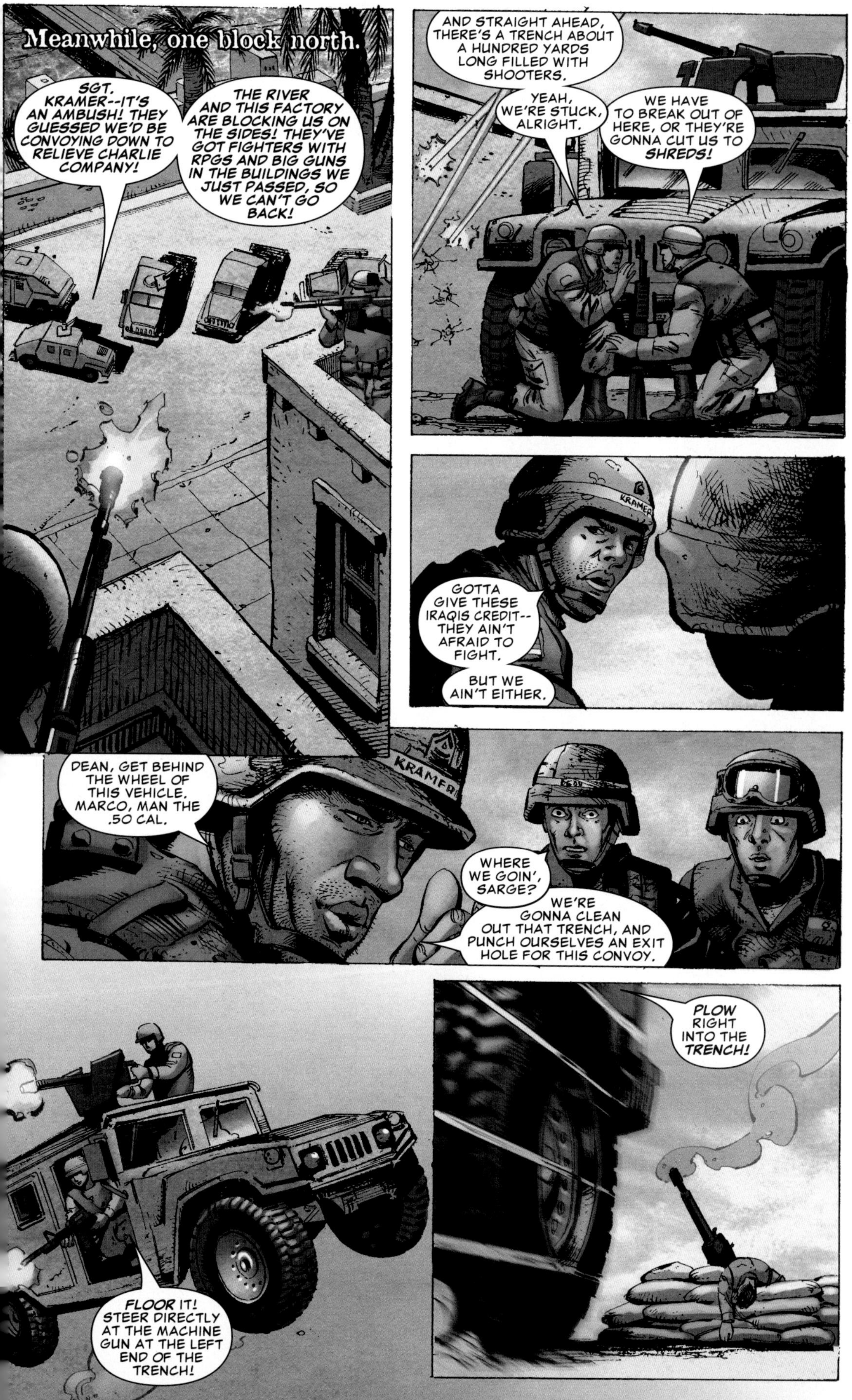
Meanwhile, one block north.
SGT. KRAMER--IT'S AN AMBUSH! THEY GUESSED WE'D BE CONVOYING DOWN TO RELIEVE CHARLIE COMPANY!
THE RIVER AND THIS FACTORY ARE BLOCKING US ON THE SIDES! THEY'VE GOT FIGHTERS WITH RPGS AND BIG GUNS IN THE BUILDINGS WE JUST PASSED, SO WE CAN'T GO BACK!
AND STRAIGHT AHEAD, THERE'S A TRENCH ABOUT A HUNDRED YARDS LONG FILLED WITH SHOOTERS.
YEAH, WE'RE STUCK, ALRIGHT.
WE HAVE TO BREAK OUT OF HERE, OR THEY'RE GONNA CUT US TO SHREDS!
KRAMER
GOTTA GIVE THESE IRAQIS CREDIT--THEY AIN'T AFRAID TO FIGHT.
BUT WE AIN'T EITHER.
KRAMER
DEAN, GET BEHIND THE WHEEL OF THIS VEHICLE. MARCO, MAN THE .50 CAL.
WHERE WE GOIN', SARGE?
WE'RE GONNA CLEAN OUT THAT TRENCH, AND PUNCH OURSELVES AN EXIT HOLE FOR THIS CONVOY.
FLOOR IT! STEER DIRECTLY AT THE MACHINE GUN AT THE LEFT END OF THE TRENCH!
PLOW RIGHT INTO THE TRENCH!

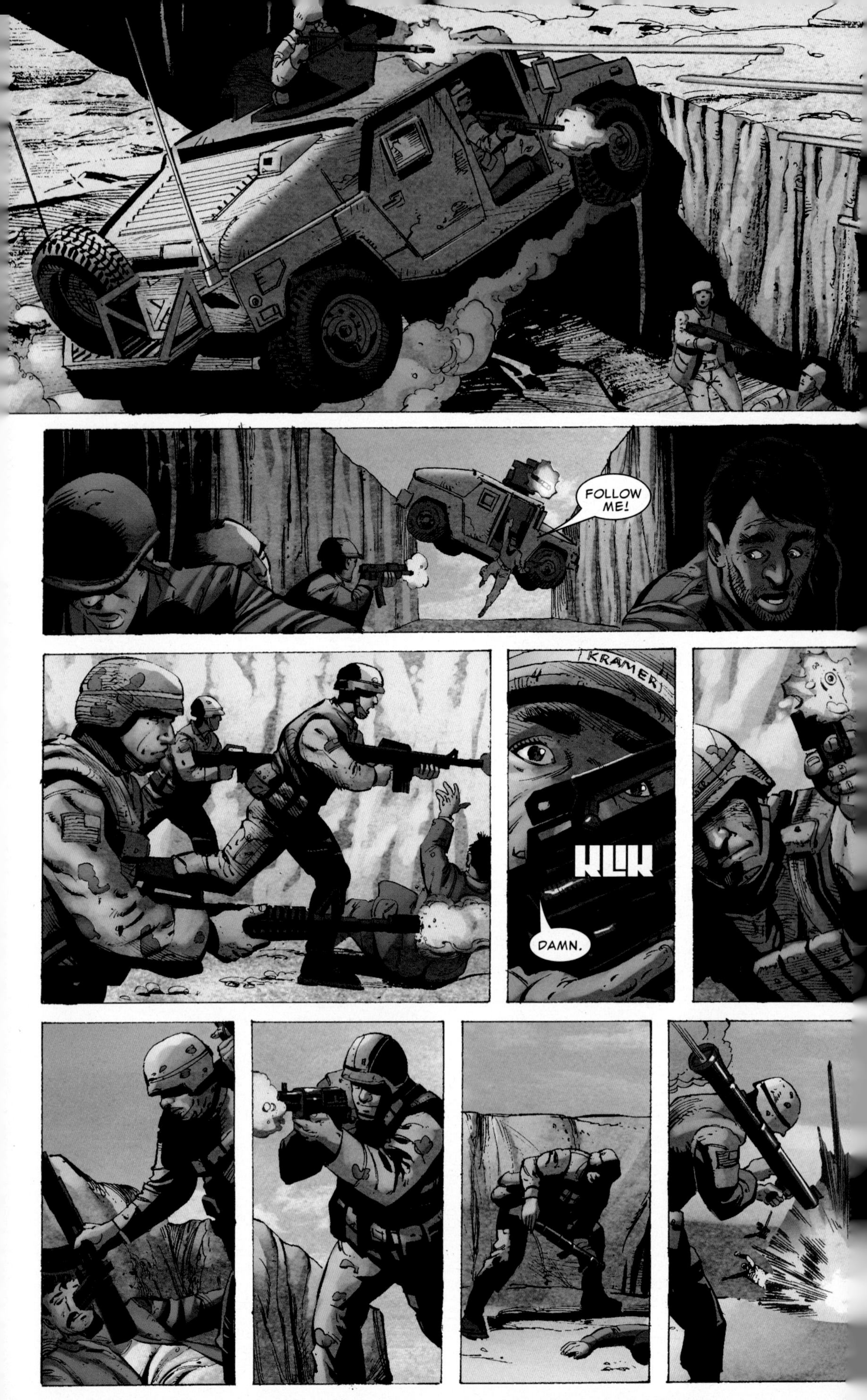
FOLLOW ME!
KRAMER
KLIK
DAMN.

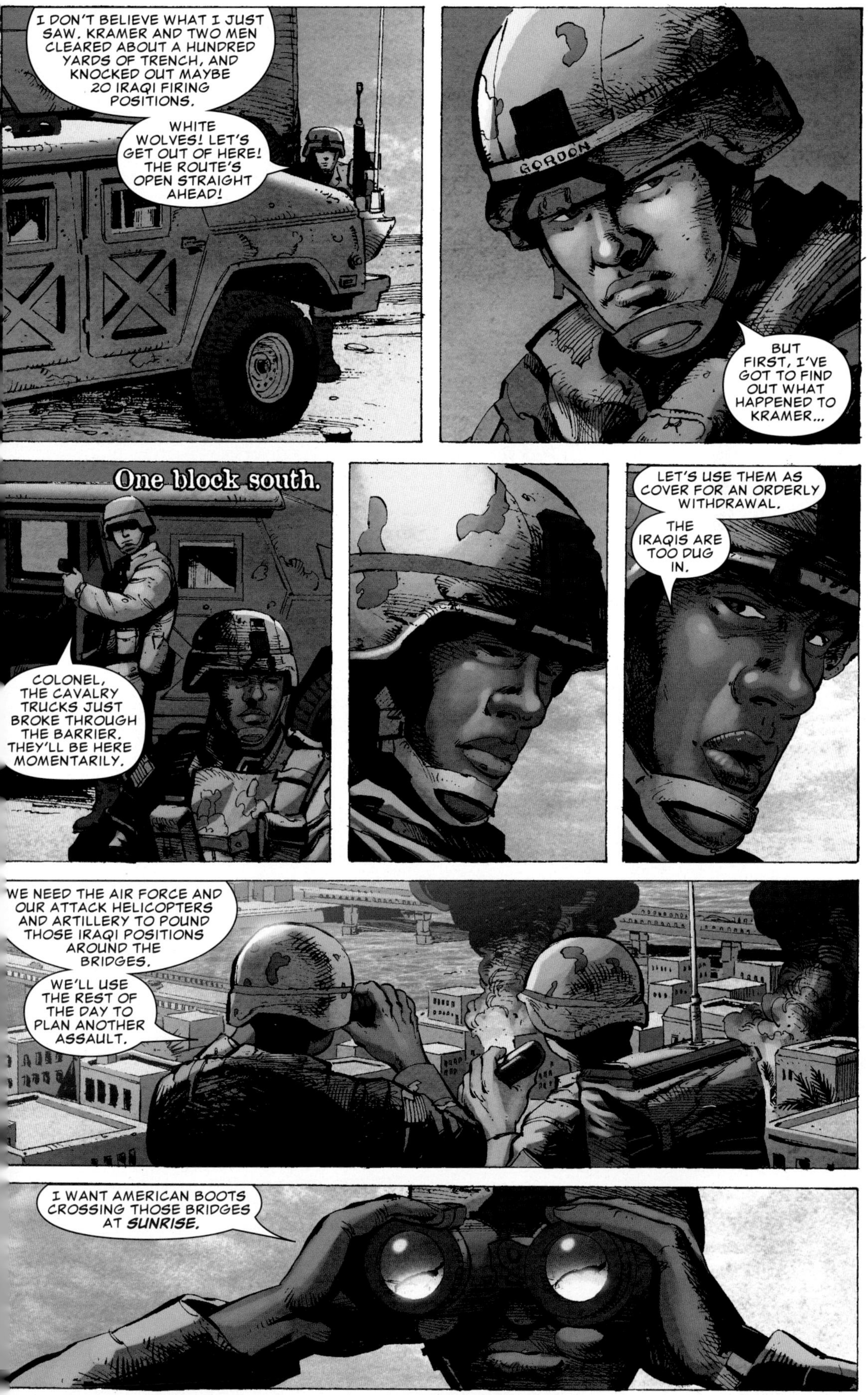

I DON'T BELIEVE WHAT I JUST SAW. KRAMER AND TWO MEN CLEARED ABOUT A HUNDRED YARDS OF TRENCH, AND KNOCKED OUT MAYBE 20 IRAQI FIRING POSITIONS.
WHITE WOLVES! LET'S GET OUT OF HERE! THE ROUTE'S OPEN STRAIGHT AHEAD!
GORDON
BUT FIRST, I'VE GOT TO FIND OUT WHAT HAPPENED TO KRAMER...
One block south.
COLONEL, THE CAVALRY TRUCKS JUST BROKE THROUGH THE BARRIER. THEY'LL BE HERE MOMENTARILY.
LET'S USE THEM AS COVER FOR AN ORDERLY WITHDRAWAL.
THE IRAQIS ARE TOO DUG IN.
WE NEED THE AIR FORCE AND OUR ATTACK HELICOPTERS AND ARTILLERY TO POUND THOSE IRAQI POSITIONS AROUND THE BRIDGES.
WE'LL USE THE REST OF THE DAY TO PLAN ANOTHER ASSAULT.
I WANT AMERICAN BOOTS CROSSING THOSE BRIDGES AT SUNRISE.

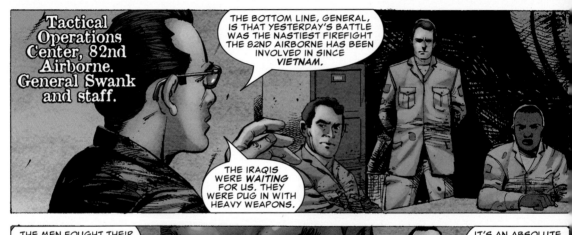

Tactical Operations Center, 82nd Airborne. General Swank and staff.

THE BOTTOM LINE, GENERAL, IS THAT YESTERDAY'S BATTLE WAS THE NASTIEST FIREFIGHT THE 82ND AIRBORNE HAS BEEN INVOLVED IN SINCE *VIETNAM.*

THE IRAQIS WERE *WAITING* FOR US. THEY WERE DUG IN WITH HEAVY WEAPONS.

THE MEN FOUGHT THEIR WAY RIGHT UP TO THE RIVER, BUT THE ENEMY HAD FORTIFIED ALL THE KEY POINTS AT EACH OF THE BRIDGES CROSSING THE EUPHRATES.

AFTER A COUPLE HOURS, WE REALIZED WE WERE GOING TO HAVE TO COME BACK ANOTHER DAY.

IT'S AN ABSOLUTE MIRACLE WE DIDN'T HAVE ANYONE *KILLED* YESTERDAY.

WHAT KIND OF CASUALTIES *DID* WE HAVE?

TWENTY WOUNDED, SIR. THE WORST IS SGT. KRAMER, WITH THE CAVALRY. REMEMBER HIM-- DID TOUGH DUTY IN THE FIRST GULF WAR? WELL, YESTERDAY HE PROBABLY EARNED HIMSELF A DSC*.

SPRUNG HIS ENTIRE COMPANY FROM A KILLING ZONE BY TAKING OUT A DOZEN ENTRENCHED IRAQIS SINGLE-HANDEDLY.

*D.S.C. is the Distinguished Service Cross, the second highest award for combat heroism the nation can bestow.

SGT. KRAMER WAS SHOT IN THE CHEST. BULLET JUST MISSED THE HARD SHIELD IN HIS FLAK JACKET, BUT FORTUNATELY THE KEVLAR VEST SLOWED IT DOWN, AND THE DOCS SAY IT RICOCHETED OFF ONE OF HIS RIBS.

THAT TOOK A LOT OF DESTRUCTIVE ENERGY OUT OF THE ROUND. THE BULLET JUST MISSED HIS AORTA. WE'VE FLOWN HIM OUT TO LANDSTUHL MEDICAL CENTER IN GERMANY. HE'S CRITICAL BUT STABLE.

I'M GLAD TO HEAR THAT.

SO.

WHAT NEXT?

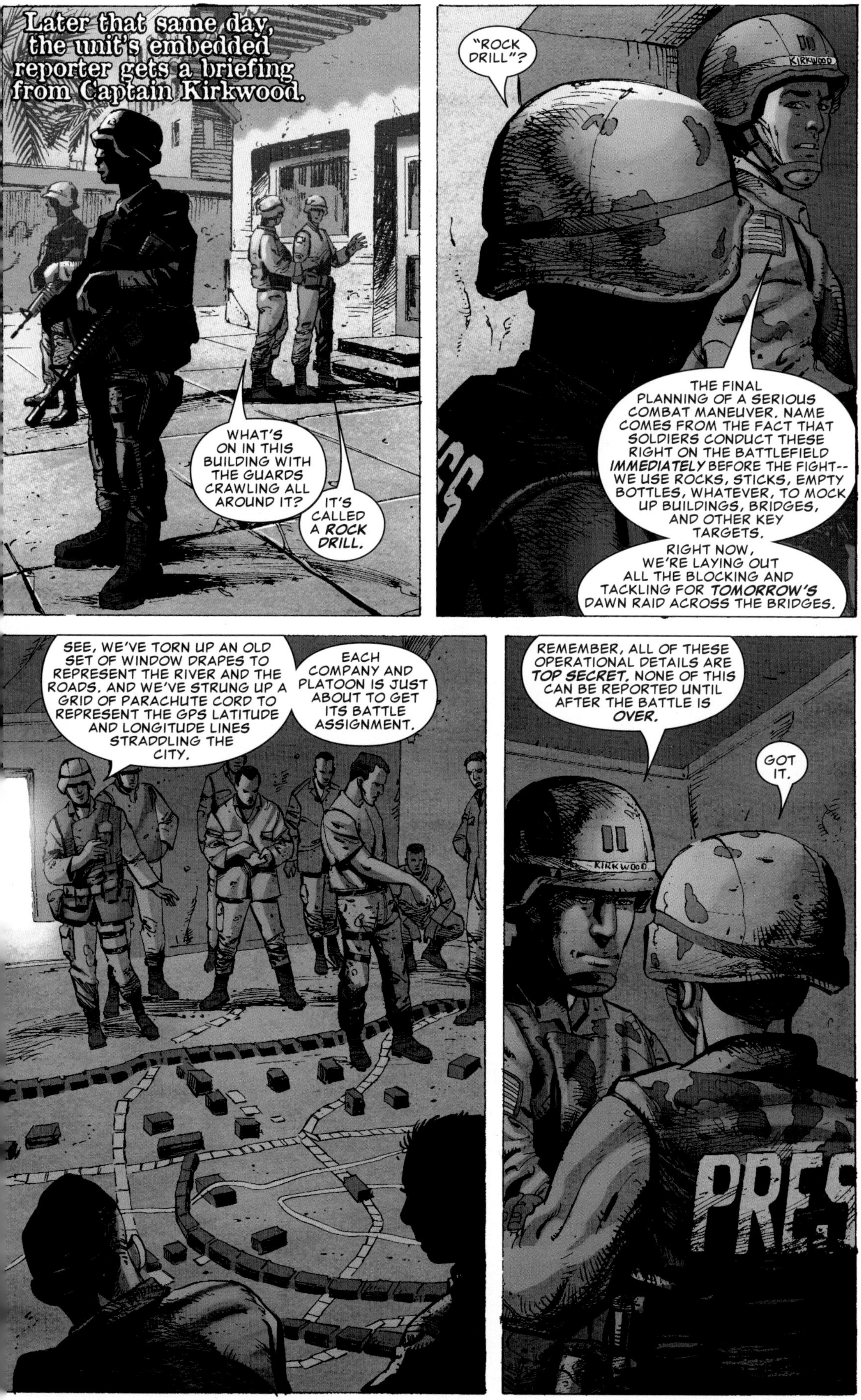

Later that same day, the unit's embedded reporter gets a briefing from Captain Kirkwood.
WHAT'S ON IN THIS BUILDING WITH THE GUARDS CRAWLING ALL AROUND IT?
IT'S CALLED A ROCK DRILL.
"ROCK DRILL"?
KIRKWOOD
THE FINAL PLANNING OF A SERIOUS COMBAT MANEUVER. NAME COMES FROM THE FACT THAT SOLDIERS CONDUCT THESE RIGHT ON THE BATTLEFIELD IMMEDIATELY BEFORE THE FIGHT--WE USE ROCKS, STICKS, EMPTY BOTTLES, WHATEVER, TO MOCK UP BUILDINGS, BRIDGES, AND OTHER KEY TARGETS.
RIGHT NOW, WE'RE LAYING OUT ALL THE BLOCKING AND TACKLING FOR TOMORROW'S DAWN RAID ACROSS THE BRIDGES.
SEE, WE'VE TORN UP AN OLD SET OF WINDOW DRAPES TO REPRESENT THE RIVER AND THE ROADS, AND WE'VE STRUNG UP A GRID OF PARACHUTE CORD TO REPRESENT THE GPS LATITUDE AND LONGITUDE LINES STRADDLING THE CITY.
EACH COMPANY AND PLATOON IS JUST ABOUT TO GET ITS BATTLE ASSIGNMENT.
REMEMBER, ALL OF THESE OPERATIONAL DETAILS ARE TOP SECRET. NONE OF THIS CAN BE REPORTED UNTIL AFTER THE BATTLE IS OVER.
GOT IT.
KIRKWOOD
PRES

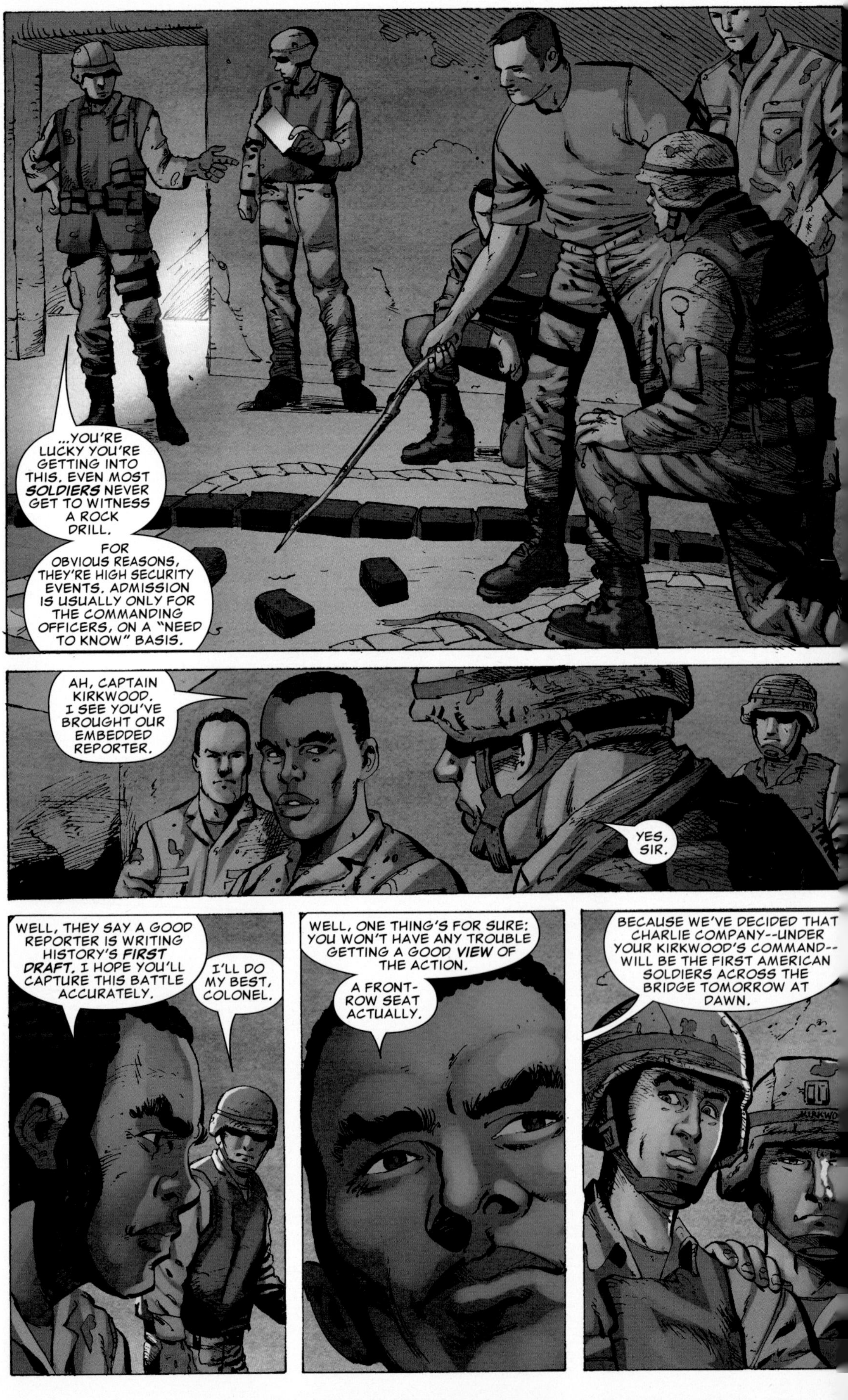

...YOU'RE LUCKY YOU'RE GETTING INTO THIS. EVEN MOST SOLDIERS NEVER GET TO WITNESS A ROCK DRILL.
FOR OBVIOUS REASONS, THEY'RE HIGH SECURITY EVENTS. ADMISSION IS USUALLY ONLY FOR THE COMMANDING OFFICERS, ON A "NEED TO KNOW" BASIS.
AH, CAPTAIN KIRKWOOD. I SEE YOU'VE BROUGHT OUR EMBEDDED REPORTER.
YES, SIR.
WELL, THEY SAY A GOOD REPORTER IS WRITING HISTORY'S FIRST DRAFT. I HOPE YOU'LL CAPTURE THIS BATTLE ACCURATELY.
I'LL DO MY BEST, COLONEL.
WELL, ONE THING'S FOR SURE: YOU WON'T HAVE ANY TROUBLE GETTING A GOOD VIEW OF THE ACTION.
A FRONT-ROW SEAT ACTUALLY.
BECAUSE WE'VE DECIDED THAT CHARLIE COMPANY--UNDER YOUR KIRKWOOD'S COMMAND--WILL BE THE FIRST AMERICAN SOLDIERS ACROSS THE BRIDGE TOMORROW AT DAWN.

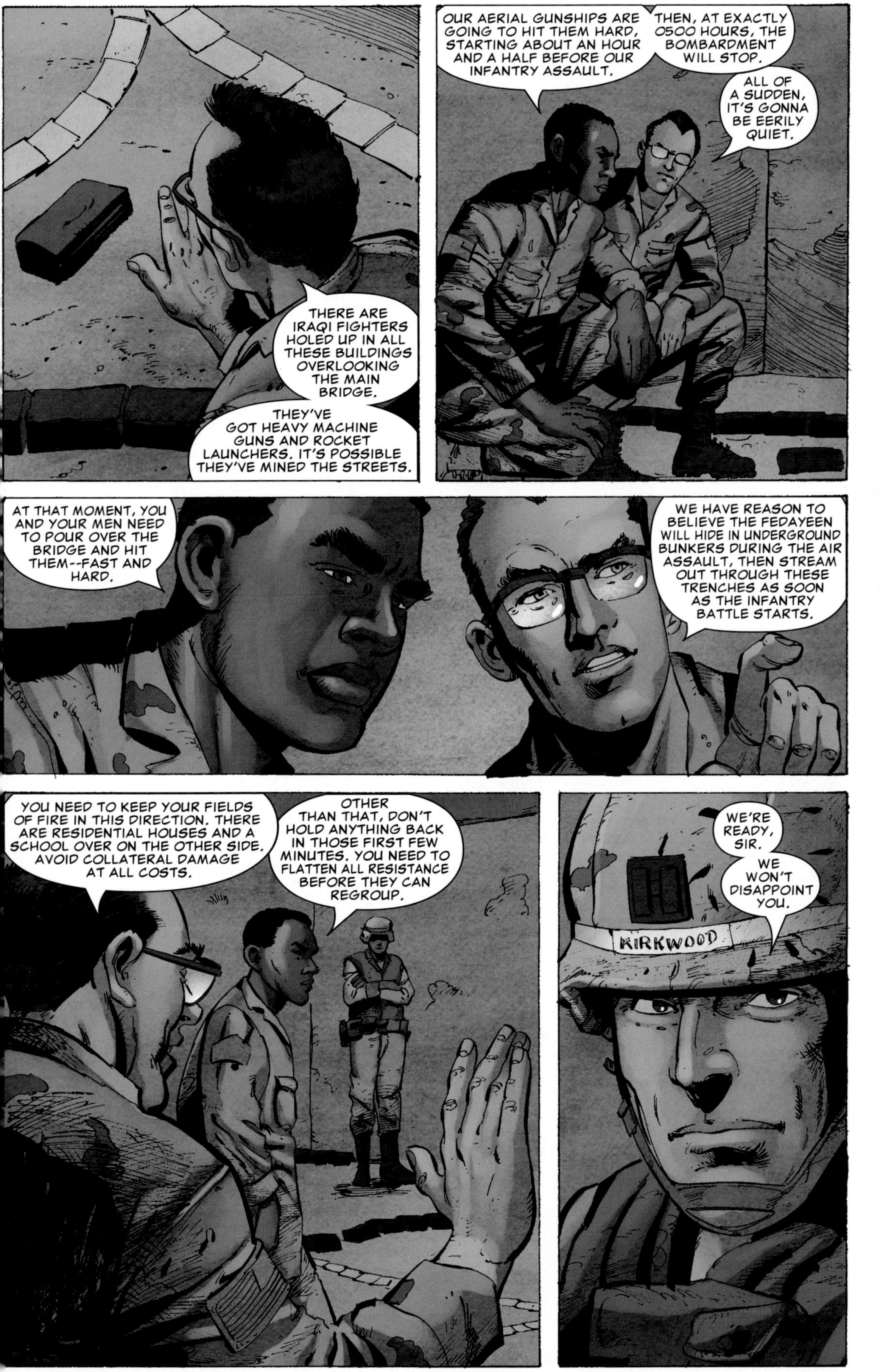
THERE ARE IRAQI FIGHTERS HOLED UP IN ALL THESE BUILDINGS OVERLOOKING THE MAIN BRIDGE.
THEY'VE GOT HEAVY MACHINE GUNS AND ROCKET LAUNCHERS. IT'S POSSIBLE THEY'VE MINED THE STREETS.
OUR AERIAL GUNSHIPS ARE GOING TO HIT THEM HARD, STARTING ABOUT AN HOUR AND A HALF BEFORE OUR INFANTRY ASSAULT.
THEN, AT EXACTLY 0500 HOURS, THE BOMBARDMENT WILL STOP.
ALL OF A SUDDEN, IT'S GONNA BE EERILY QUIET.
AT THAT MOMENT, YOU AND YOUR MEN NEED TO POUR OVER THE BRIDGE AND HIT THEM--FAST AND HARD.
WE HAVE REASON TO BELIEVE THE FEDAYEEN WILL HIDE IN UNDERGROUND BUNKERS DURING THE AIR ASSAULT, THEN STREAM OUT THROUGH THESE TRENCHES AS SOON AS THE INFANTRY BATTLE STARTS.
YOU NEED TO KEEP YOUR FIELDS OF FIRE IN THIS DIRECTION. THERE ARE RESIDENTIAL HOUSES AND A SCHOOL OVER ON THE OTHER SIDE. AVOID COLLATERAL DAMAGE AT ALL COSTS.
OTHER THAN THAT, DON'T HOLD ANYTHING BACK IN THOSE FIRST FEW MINUTES. YOU NEED TO FLATTEN ALL RESISTANCE BEFORE THEY CAN REGROUP.
WE'RE READY, SIR.
WE WON'T DISAPPOINT YOU.
KIRKWOOD

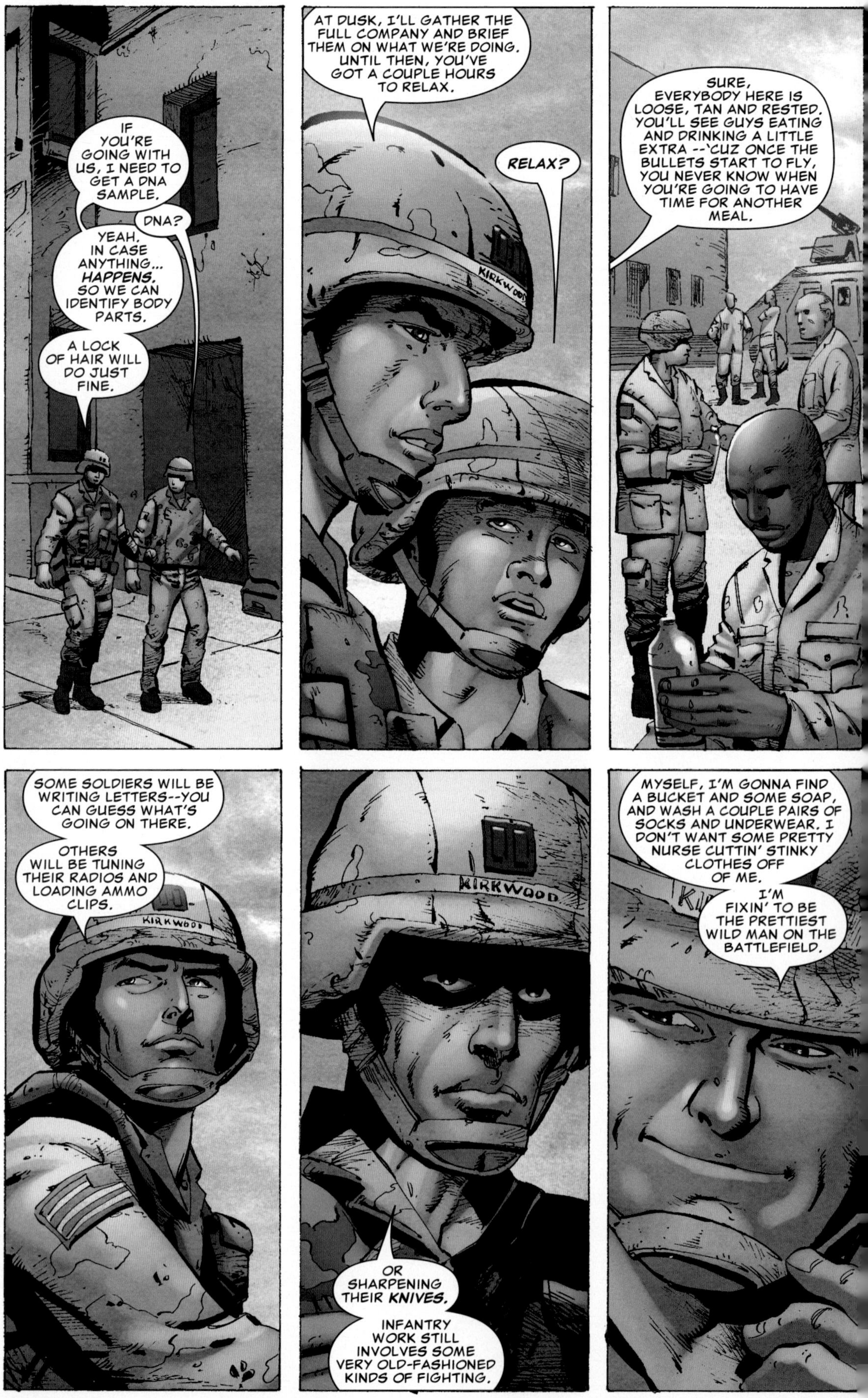
IF YOU'RE GOING WITH US, I NEED TO GET A DNA SAMPLE.
DNA?
YEAH. IN CASE ANYTHING... HAPPENS. SO WE CAN IDENTIFY BODY PARTS.
A LOCK OF HAIR WILL DO JUST FINE.
AT DUSK, I'LL GATHER THE FULL COMPANY AND BRIEF THEM ON WHAT WE'RE DOING. UNTIL THEN, YOU'VE GOT A COUPLE HOURS TO RELAX.
KIRKWOOD
RELAX?
SURE, EVERYBODY HERE IS LOOSE, TAN AND RESTED. YOU'LL SEE GUYS EATING AND DRINKING A LITTLE EXTRA --'CUZ ONCE THE BULLETS START TO FLY, YOU NEVER KNOW WHEN YOU'RE GOING TO HAVE TIME FOR ANOTHER MEAL.
SOME SOLDIERS WILL BE WRITING LETTERS--YOU CAN GUESS WHAT'S GOING ON THERE.
OTHERS WILL BE TUNING THEIR RADIOS AND LOADING AMMO CLIPS.
KIRKWOOD
KIRKWOOD
OR SHARPENING THEIR KNIVES.
INFANTRY WORK STILL INVOLVES SOME VERY OLD-FASHIONED KINDS OF FIGHTING.
MYSELF, I'M GONNA FIND A BUCKET AND SOME SOAP, AND WASH A COUPLE PAIRS OF SOCKS AND UNDERWEAR. I DON'T WANT SOME PRETTY NURSE CUTTIN' STINKY CLOTHES OFF OF ME.
I'M FIXIN' TO BE THE PRETTIEST WILD MAN ON THE BATTLEFIELD.

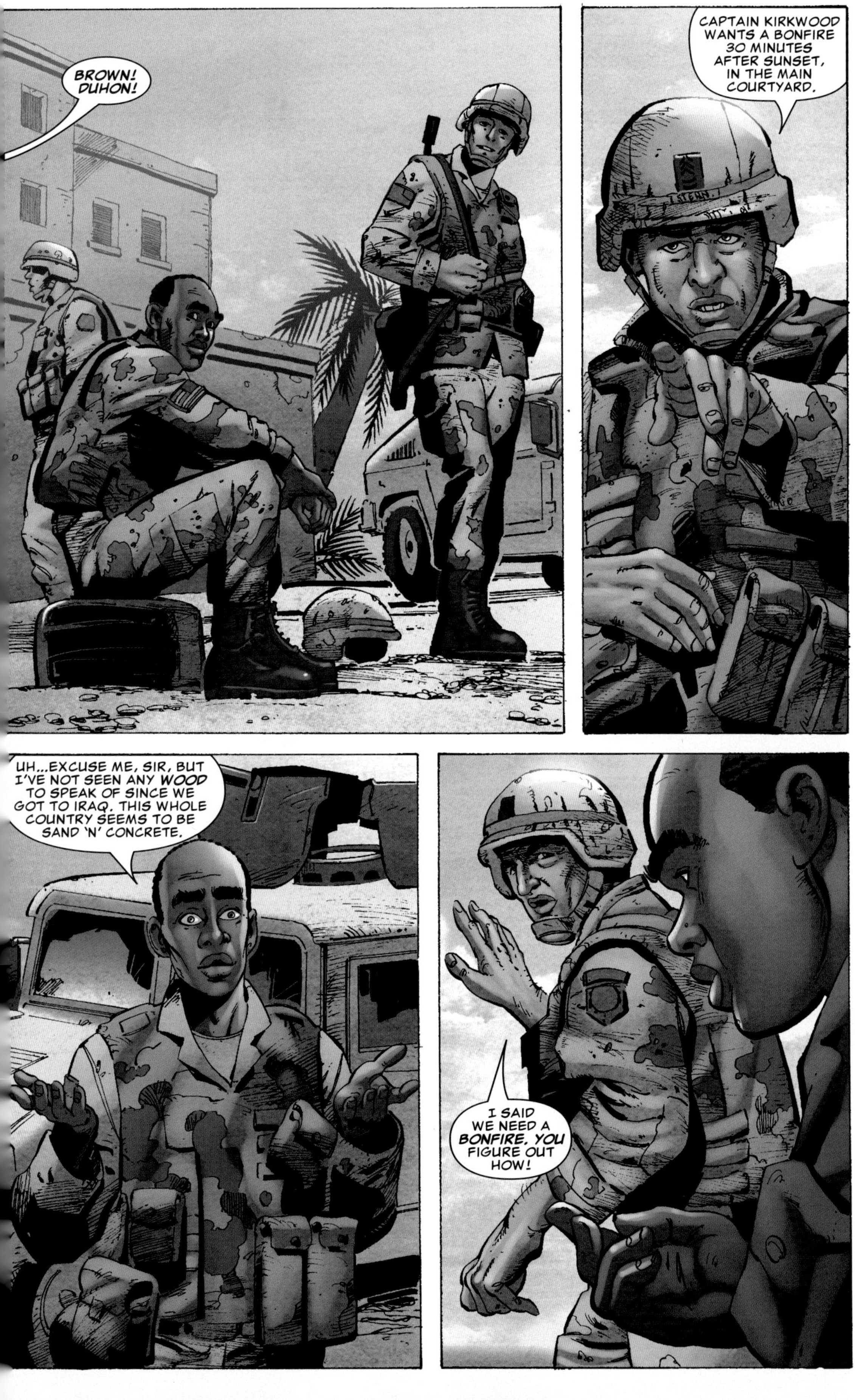
BROWN! DUHON!
CAPTAIN KIRKWOOD WANTS A BONFIRE 30 MINUTES AFTER SUNSET, IN THE MAIN COURTYARD.
UH...EXCUSE ME, SIR, BUT I'VE NOT SEEN ANY WOOD TO SPEAK OF SINCE WE GOT TO IRAQ. THIS WHOLE COUNTRY SEEMS TO BE SAND 'N' CONCRETE.
I SAID WE NEED A BONFIRE. YOU FIGURE OUT HOW!

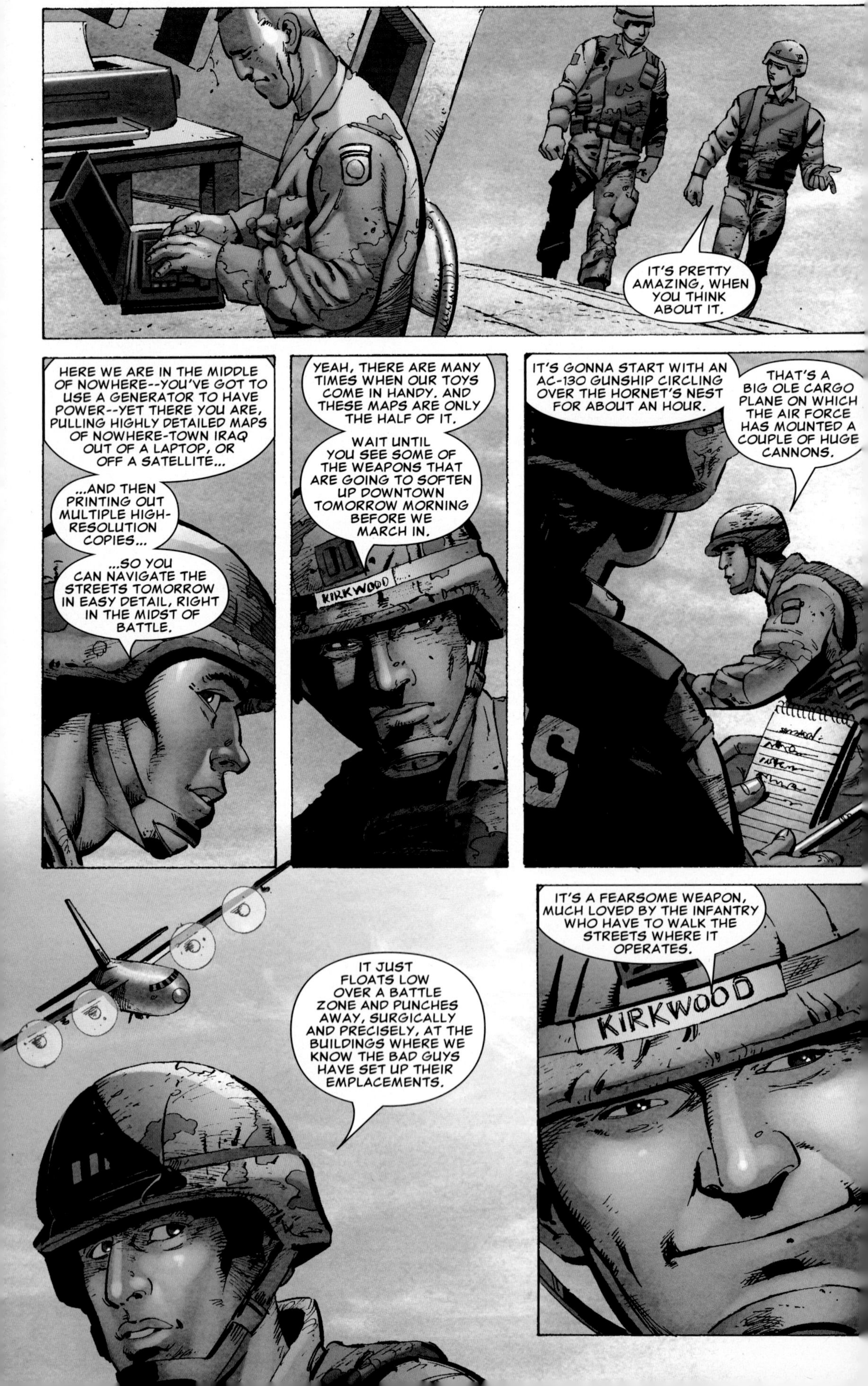
IT'S PRETTY AMAZING, WHEN YOU THINK ABOUT IT.
HERE WE ARE IN THE MIDDLE OF NOWHERE--YOU'VE GOT TO USE A GENERATOR TO HAVE POWER--YET THERE YOU ARE, PULLING HIGHLY DETAILED MAPS OF NOWHERE-TOWN IRAQ OUT OF A LAPTOP, OR OFF A SATELLITE...
...AND THEN PRINTING OUT MULTIPLE HIGH-RESOLUTION COPIES...
...SO YOU CAN NAVIGATE THE STREETS TOMORROW IN EASY DETAIL, RIGHT IN THE MIDST OF BATTLE.
YEAH, THERE ARE MANY TIMES WHEN OUR TOYS COME IN HANDY. AND THESE MAPS ARE ONLY THE HALF OF IT.
WAIT UNTIL YOU SEE SOME OF THE WEAPONS THAT ARE GOING TO SOFTEN UP DOWNTOWN TOMORROW MORNING BEFORE WE MARCH IN.
KIRKWOOD
IT'S GONNA START WITH AN AC-130 GUNSHIP CIRCLING OVER THE HORNET'S NEST FOR ABOUT AN HOUR.
THAT'S A BIG OLE CARGO PLANE ON WHICH THE AIR FORCE HAS MOUNTED A COUPLE OF HUGE CANNONS.
IT JUST FLOATS LOW OVER A BATTLE ZONE AND PUNCHES AWAY, SURGICALLY AND PRECISELY, AT THE BUILDINGS WHERE WE KNOW THE BAD GUYS HAVE SET UP THEIR EMPLACEMENTS.
IT'S A FEARSOME WEAPON, MUCH LOVED BY THE INFANTRY WHO HAVE TO WALK THE STREETS WHERE IT OPERATES.
KIRKWOOD

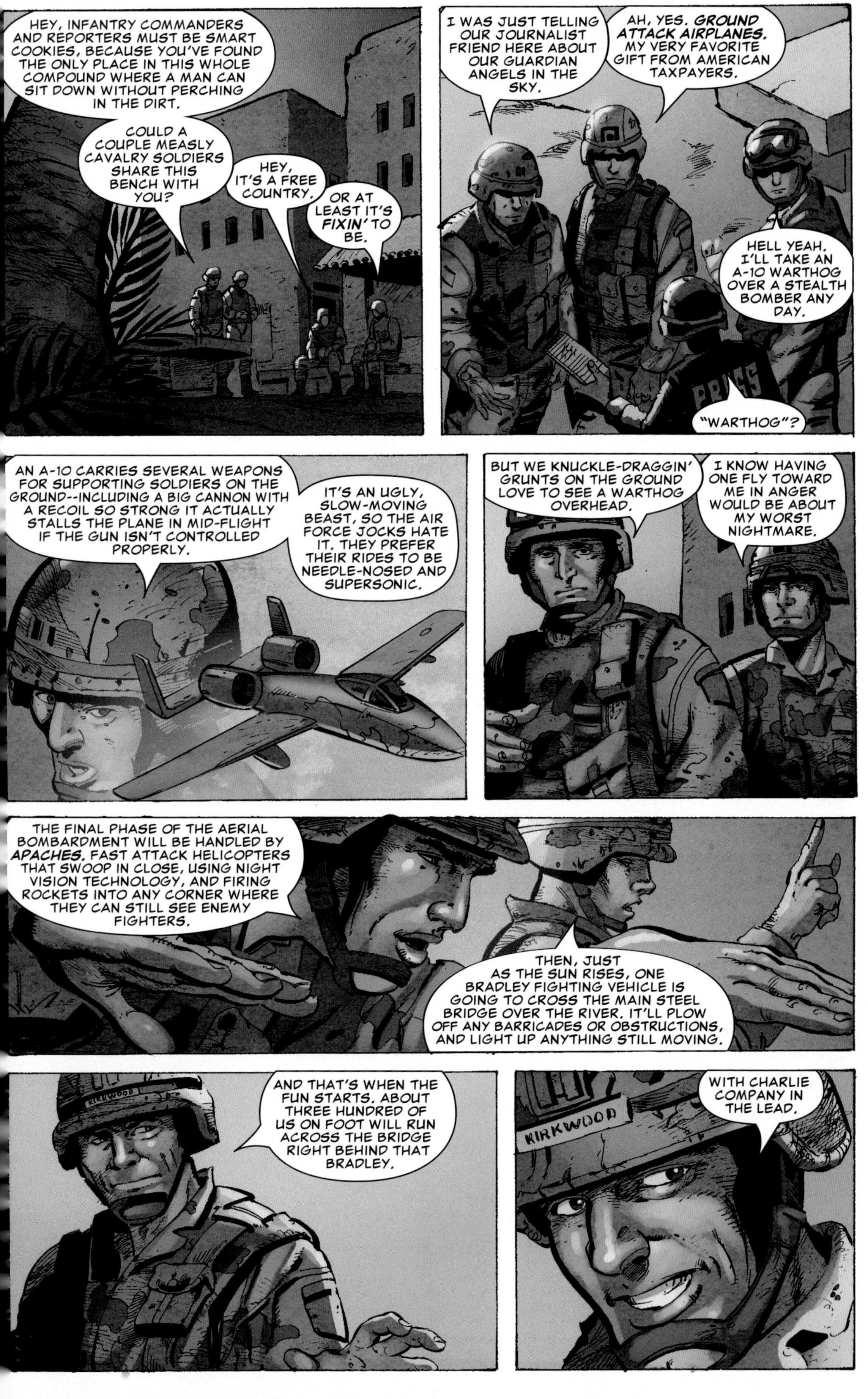
HEY, INFANTRY COMMANDERS AND REPORTERS MUST BE SMART COOKIES, BECAUSE YOU'VE FOUND THE ONLY PLACE IN THIS WHOLE COMPOUND WHERE A MAN CAN SIT DOWN WITHOUT PERCHING IN THE DIRT.
COULD A COUPLE MEASLY CAVALRY SOLDIERS SHARE THIS BENCH WITH YOU?
HEY, IT'S A FREE COUNTRY.
OR AT LEAST IT'S *FIXIN'* TO BE.
I WAS JUST TELLING OUR JOURNALIST FRIEND HERE ABOUT OUR GUARDIAN ANGELS IN THE SKY.
AH, YES. ***GROUND ATTACK AIRPLANES.*** MY VERY FAVORITE GIFT FROM AMERICAN TAXPAYERS.
HELL YEAH. I'LL TAKE AN A-10 WARTHOG OVER A STEALTH BOMBER ANY DAY.
"WARTHOG"?
AN A-10 CARRIES SEVERAL WEAPONS FOR SUPPORTING SOLDIERS ON THE GROUND--INCLUDING A BIG CANNON WITH A RECOIL SO STRONG IT ACTUALLY STALLS THE PLANE IN MID-FLIGHT IF THE GUN ISN'T CONTROLLED PROPERLY.
IT'S AN UGLY, SLOW-MOVING BEAST, SO THE AIR FORCE JOCKS HATE IT. THEY PREFER THEIR RIDES TO BE NEEDLE-NOSED AND SUPERSONIC.
BUT WE KNUCKLE-DRAGGIN' GRUNTS ON THE GROUND LOVE TO SEE A WARTHOG OVERHEAD.
I KNOW HAVING ONE FLY TOWARD ME IN ANGER WOULD BE ABOUT MY WORST NIGHTMARE.
THE FINAL PHASE OF THE AERIAL BOMBARDMENT WILL BE HANDLED BY ***APACHES.*** FAST ATTACK HELICOPTERS THAT SWOOP IN CLOSE, USING NIGHT VISION TECHNOLOGY, AND FIRING ROCKETS INTO ANY CORNER WHERE THEY CAN STILL SEE ENEMY FIGHTERS.
THEN, JUST AS THE SUN RISES, ONE BRADLEY FIGHTING VEHICLE IS GOING TO CROSS THE MAIN STEEL BRIDGE OVER THE RIVER. IT'LL PLOW OFF ANY BARRICADES OR OBSTRUCTIONS, AND LIGHT UP ANYTHING STILL MOVING.
AND THAT'S WHEN THE FUN STARTS. ABOUT THREE HUNDRED OF US ON FOOT WILL RUN ACROSS THE BRIDGE RIGHT BEHIND THAT BRADLEY.
KIRKWOOD
WITH CHARLIE COMPANY IN THE LEAD.

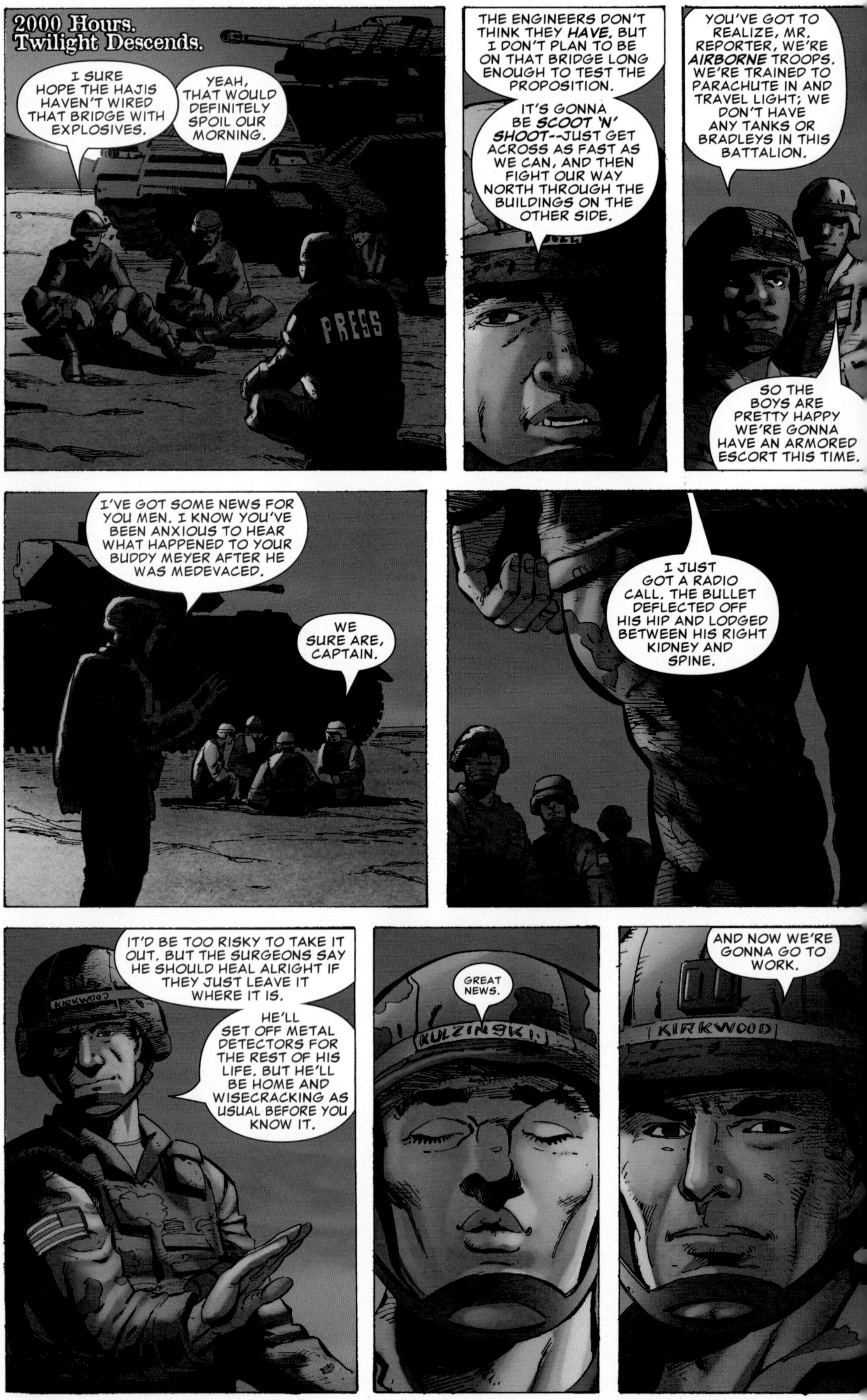

2000 Hours. Twilight Descends.
I SURE HOPE THE HAJIS HAVEN'T WIRED THAT BRIDGE WITH EXPLOSIVES.
YEAH, THAT WOULD DEFINITELY SPOIL OUR MORNING.
PRESS
THE ENGINEERS DON'T THINK THEY HAVE, BUT I DON'T PLAN TO BE ON THAT BRIDGE LONG ENOUGH TO TEST THE PROPOSITION.
IT'S GONNA BE SCOOT 'N' SHOOT--JUST GET ACROSS AS FAST AS WE CAN, AND THEN FIGHT OUR WAY NORTH THROUGH THE BUILDINGS ON THE OTHER SIDE.
YOU'VE GOT TO REALIZE, MR. REPORTER, WE'RE AIRBORNE TROOPS. WE'RE TRAINED TO PARACHUTE IN AND TRAVEL LIGHT; WE DON'T HAVE ANY TANKS OR BRADLEYS IN THIS BATTALION.
SO THE BOYS ARE PRETTY HAPPY WE'RE GONNA HAVE AN ARMORED ESCORT THIS TIME.
I'VE GOT SOME NEWS FOR YOU MEN. I KNOW YOU'VE BEEN ANXIOUS TO HEAR WHAT HAPPENED TO YOUR BUDDY MEYER AFTER HE WAS MEDEVACED.
WE SURE ARE, CAPTAIN.
I JUST GOT A RADIO CALL. THE BULLET DEFLECTED OFF HIS HIP AND LODGED BETWEEN HIS RIGHT KIDNEY AND SPINE.
IT'D BE TOO RISKY TO TAKE IT OUT. BUT THE SURGEONS SAY HE SHOULD HEAL ALRIGHT IF THEY JUST LEAVE IT WHERE IT IS.
HE'LL SET OFF METAL DETECTORS FOR THE REST OF HIS LIFE, BUT HE'LL BE HOME AND WISECRACKING AS USUAL BEFORE YOU KNOW IT.
KIRKWOOD
GREAT NEWS.
KULZINSKI
AND NOW WE'RE GONNA GO TO WORK.
KIRKWOOD

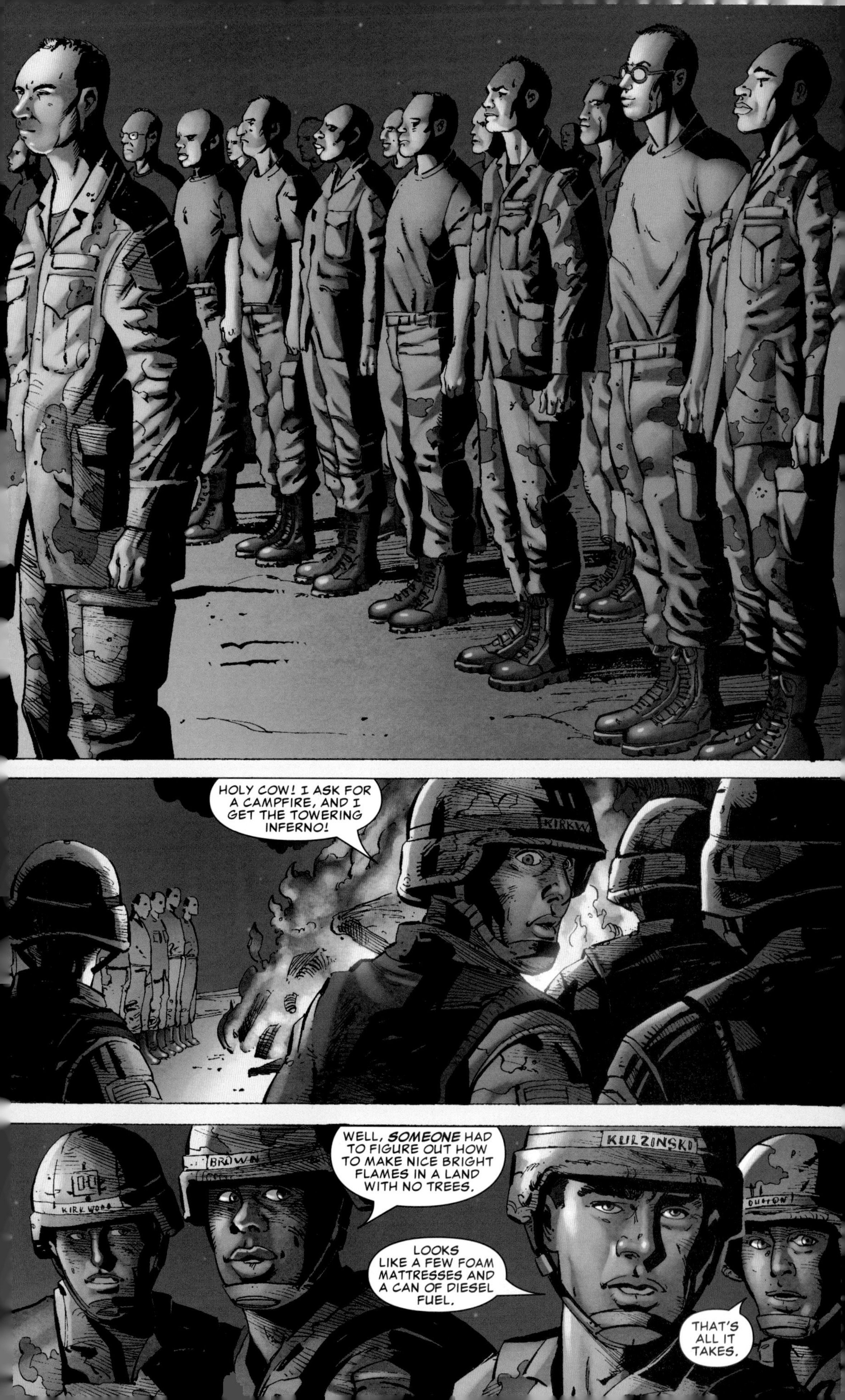

HOLY COW! I ASK FOR A CAMPFIRE, AND I GET THE TOWERING INFERNO!
WELL, *SOMEONE* HAD TO FIGURE OUT HOW TO MAKE NICE BRIGHT FLAMES IN A LAND WITH NO TREES.
LOOKS LIKE A FEW FOAM MATTRESSES AND A CAN OF DIESEL FUEL.
THAT'S ALL IT TAKES.

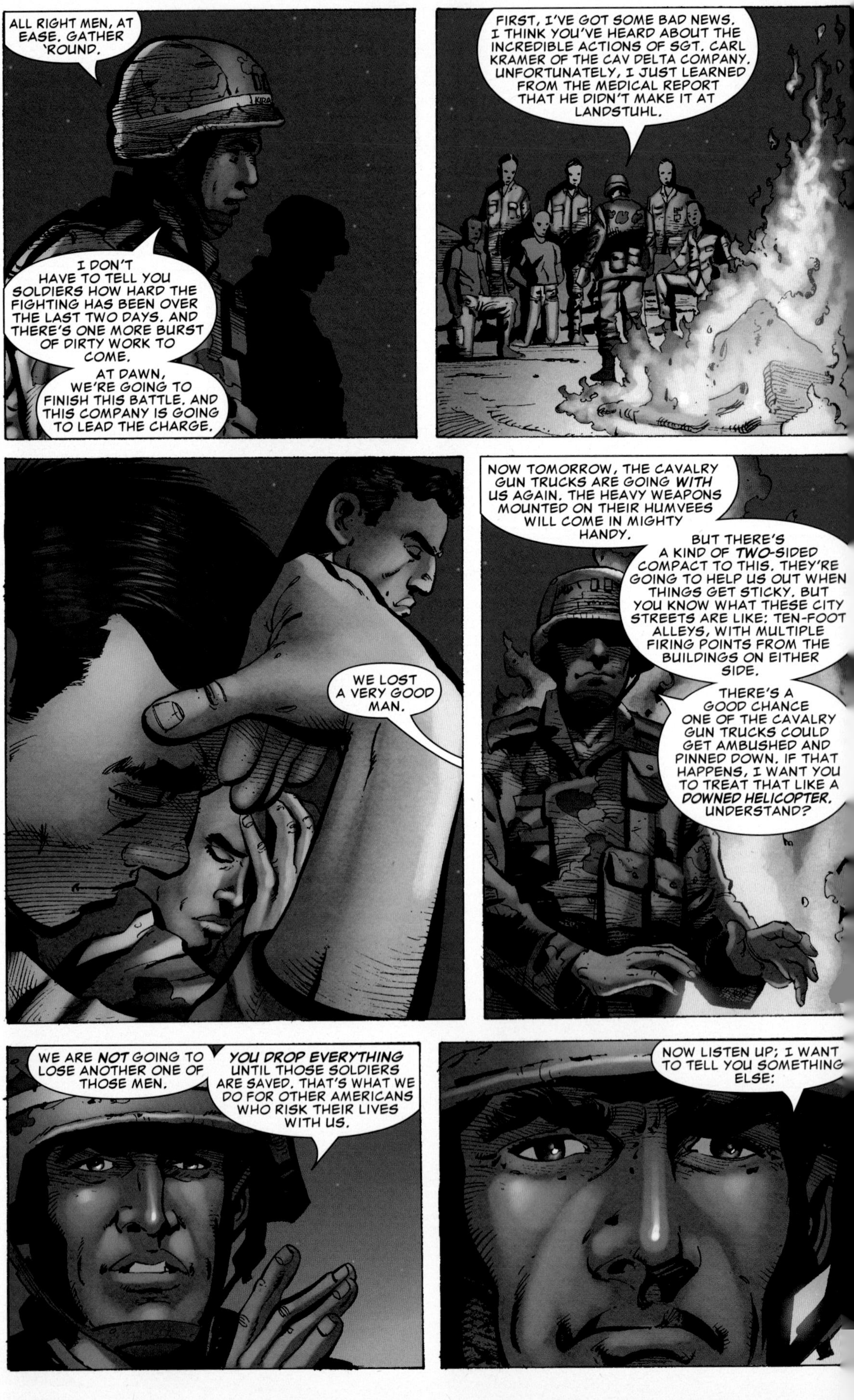
ALL RIGHT MEN, AT EASE. GATHER 'ROUND.
I DON'T HAVE TO TELL YOU SOLDIERS HOW HARD THE FIGHTING HAS BEEN OVER THE LAST TWO DAYS. AND THERE'S ONE MORE BURST OF DIRTY WORK TO COME.
AT DAWN, WE'RE GOING TO FINISH THIS BATTLE. AND THIS COMPANY IS GOING TO LEAD THE CHARGE.
FIRST, I'VE GOT SOME BAD NEWS. I THINK YOU'VE HEARD ABOUT THE INCREDIBLE ACTIONS OF SGT. CARL KRAMER OF THE CAV DELTA COMPANY. UNFORTUNATELY, I JUST LEARNED FROM THE MEDICAL REPORT THAT HE DIDN'T MAKE IT AT LANDSTUHL.
WE LOST A VERY GOOD MAN.
NOW TOMORROW, THE CAVALRY GUN TRUCKS ARE GOING *WITH* US AGAIN. THE HEAVY WEAPONS MOUNTED ON THEIR HUMVEES WILL COME IN MIGHTY HANDY.
BUT THERE'S A KIND OF ***TWO***-SIDED COMPACT TO THIS. THEY'RE GOING TO HELP US OUT WHEN THINGS GET STICKY. BUT YOU KNOW WHAT THESE CITY STREETS ARE LIKE: TEN-FOOT ALLEYS, WITH MULTIPLE FIRING POINTS FROM THE BUILDINGS ON EITHER SIDE.
THERE'S A GOOD CHANCE ONE OF THE CAVALRY GUN TRUCKS COULD GET AMBUSHED AND PINNED DOWN. IF THAT HAPPENS, I WANT YOU TO TREAT THAT LIKE A *DOWNED HELICOPTER.* UNDERSTAND?
WE ARE ***NOT*** GOING TO LOSE ANOTHER ONE OF THOSE MEN.
YOU DROP EVERYTHING UNTIL THOSE SOLDIERS ARE SAVED. THAT'S WHAT WE DO FOR OTHER AMERICANS WHO RISK THEIR LIVES WITH US.
NOW LISTEN UP; I WANT TO TELL YOU SOMETHING ELSE:

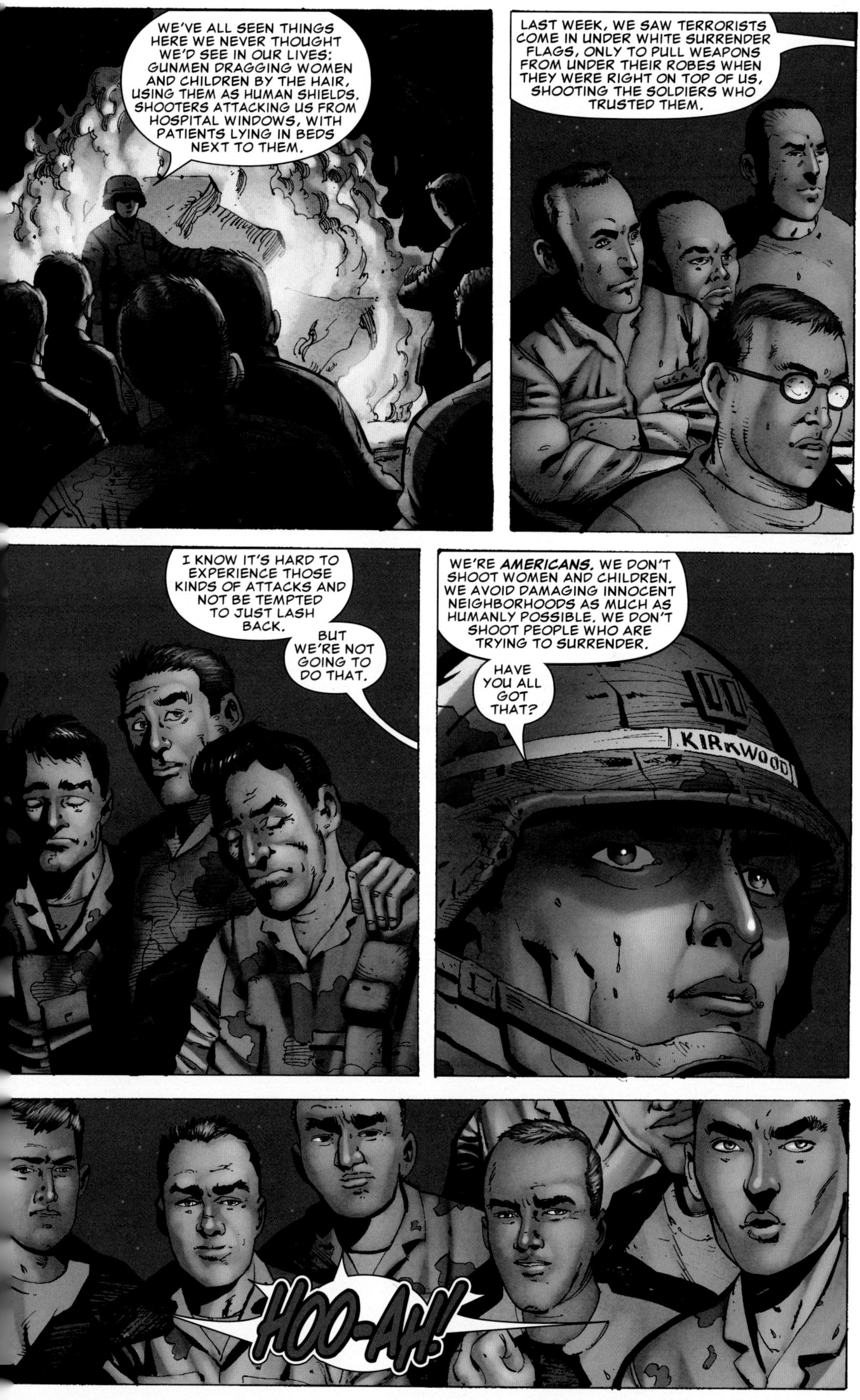
WE'VE ALL SEEN THINGS HERE WE NEVER THOUGHT WE'D SEE IN OUR LIVES: GUNMEN DRAGGING WOMEN AND CHILDREN BY THE HAIR, USING THEM AS HUMAN SHIELDS. SHOOTERS ATTACKING US FROM HOSPITAL WINDOWS, WITH PATIENTS LYING IN BEDS NEXT TO THEM.
LAST WEEK, WE SAW TERRORISTS COME IN UNDER WHITE SURRENDER FLAGS, ONLY TO PULL WEAPONS FROM UNDER THEIR ROBES WHEN THEY WERE RIGHT ON TOP OF US, SHOOTING THE SOLDIERS WHO TRUSTED THEM.
USA
I KNOW IT'S HARD TO EXPERIENCE THOSE KINDS OF ATTACKS AND NOT BE TEMPTED TO JUST LASH BACK.
BUT WE'RE NOT GOING TO DO THAT.
WE'RE AMERICANS. WE DON'T SHOOT WOMEN AND CHILDREN. WE AVOID DAMAGING INNOCENT NEIGHBORHOODS AS MUCH AS HUMANLY POSSIBLE. WE DON'T SHOOT PEOPLE WHO ARE TRYING TO SURRENDER.
HAVE YOU ALL GOT THAT?
KIRKWOOD
HOO-AH!

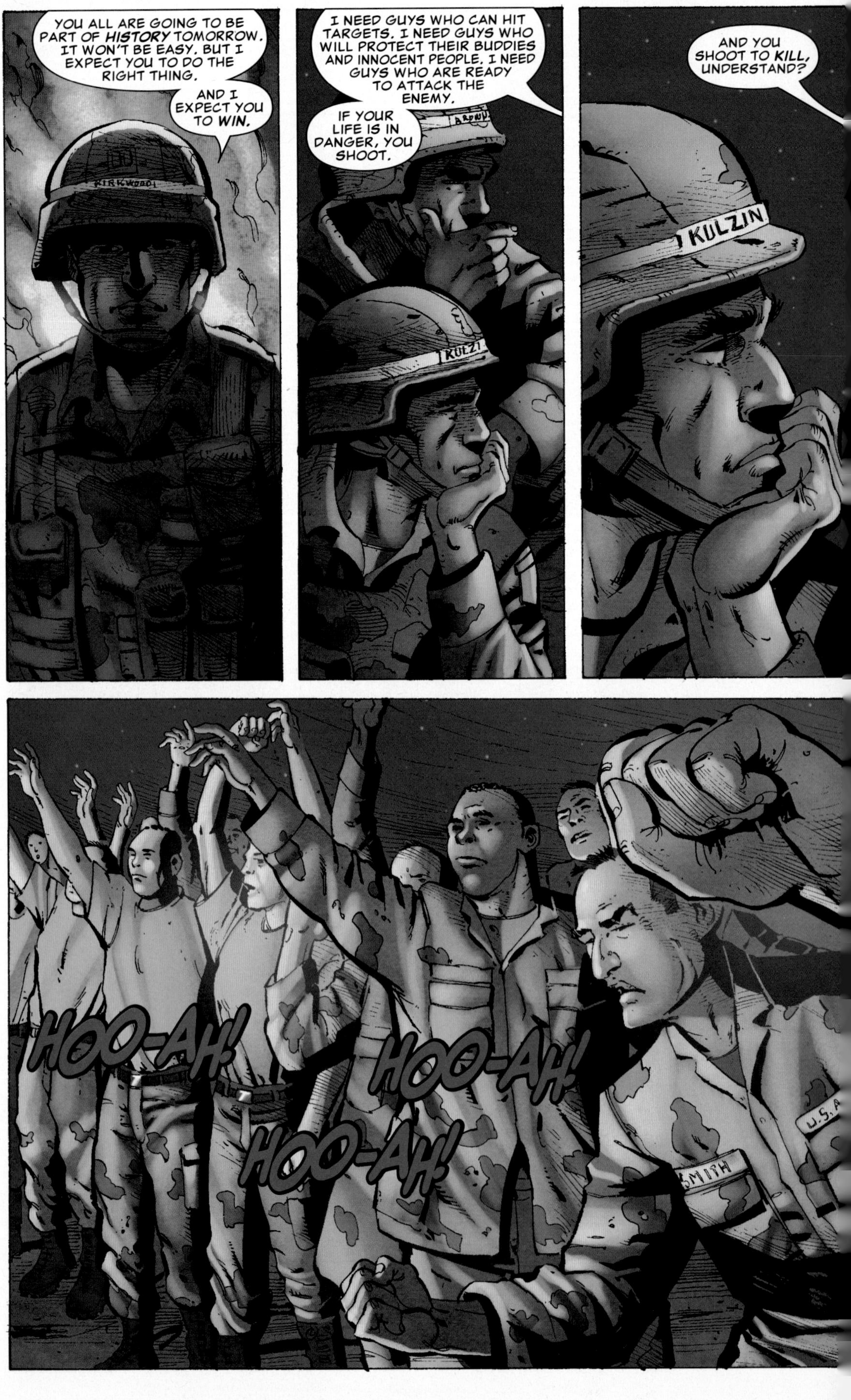
YOU ALL ARE GOING TO BE PART OF HISTORY TOMORROW. IT WON'T BE EASY. BUT I EXPECT YOU TO DO THE RIGHT THING.
AND I EXPECT YOU TO WIN.
I NEED GUYS WHO CAN HIT TARGETS. I NEED GUYS WHO WILL PROTECT THEIR BUDDIES AND INNOCENT PEOPLE. I NEED GUYS WHO ARE READY TO ATTACK THE ENEMY.
IF YOUR LIFE IS IN DANGER, YOU SHOOT.
AND YOU SHOOT TO KILL, UNDERSTAND?
KULZIN
HOO-AH!
HOO-AH!
HOO-AH!
SMITH

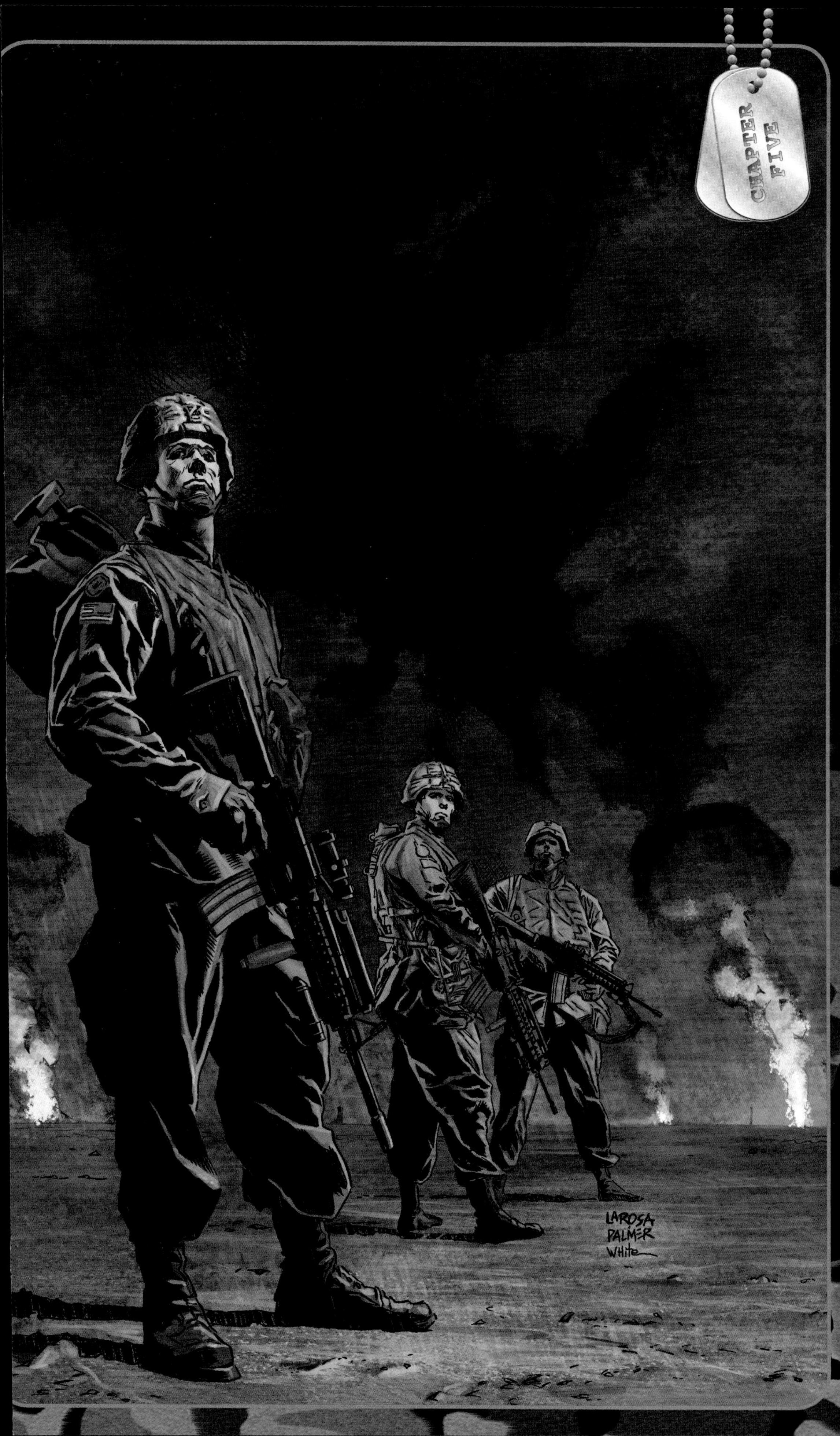
CHAPTER
FIVE
LAROSA
PALMER
White

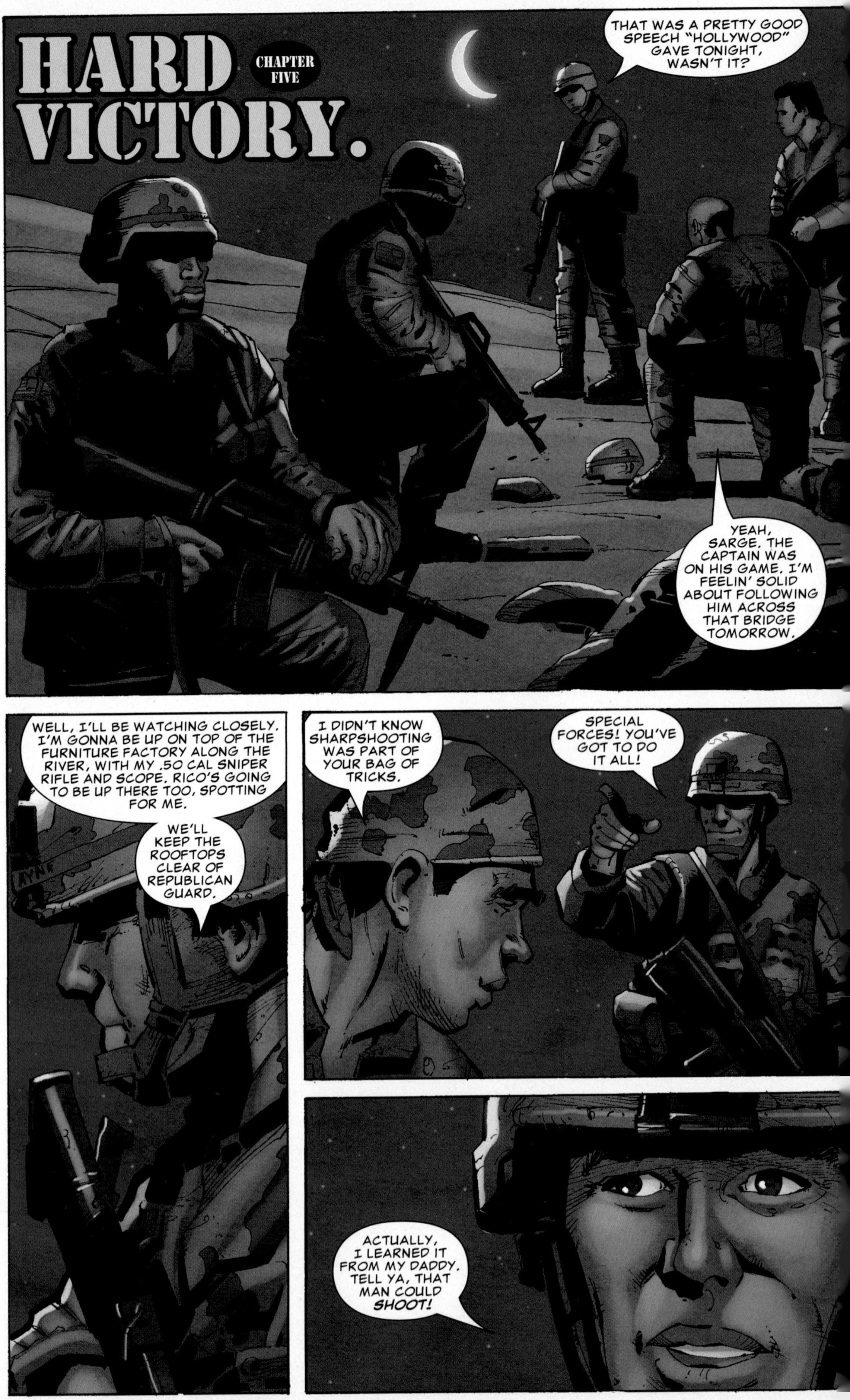
HARD VICTORY.
CHAPTER FIVE
THAT WAS A PRETTY GOOD SPEECH "HOLLYWOOD" GAVE TONIGHT, WASN'T IT?
YEAH, SARGE. THE CAPTAIN WAS ON HIS GAME. I'M FEELIN' SOLID ABOUT FOLLOWING HIM ACROSS THAT BRIDGE TOMORROW.
WELL, I'LL BE WATCHING CLOSELY. I'M GONNA BE UP ON TOP OF THE FURNITURE FACTORY ALONG THE RIVER, WITH MY .50 CAL SNIPER RIFLE AND SCOPE. RICO'S GOING TO BE UP THERE TOO, SPOTTING FOR ME.
WE'LL KEEP THE ROOFTOPS CLEAR OF REPUBLICAN GUARD.
I DIDN'T KNOW SHARPSHOOTING WAS PART OF YOUR BAG OF TRICKS.
SPECIAL FORCES! YOU'VE GOT TO DO IT ALL!
ACTUALLY, I LEARNED IT FROM MY DADDY. TELL YA, THAT MAN COULD SHOOT!

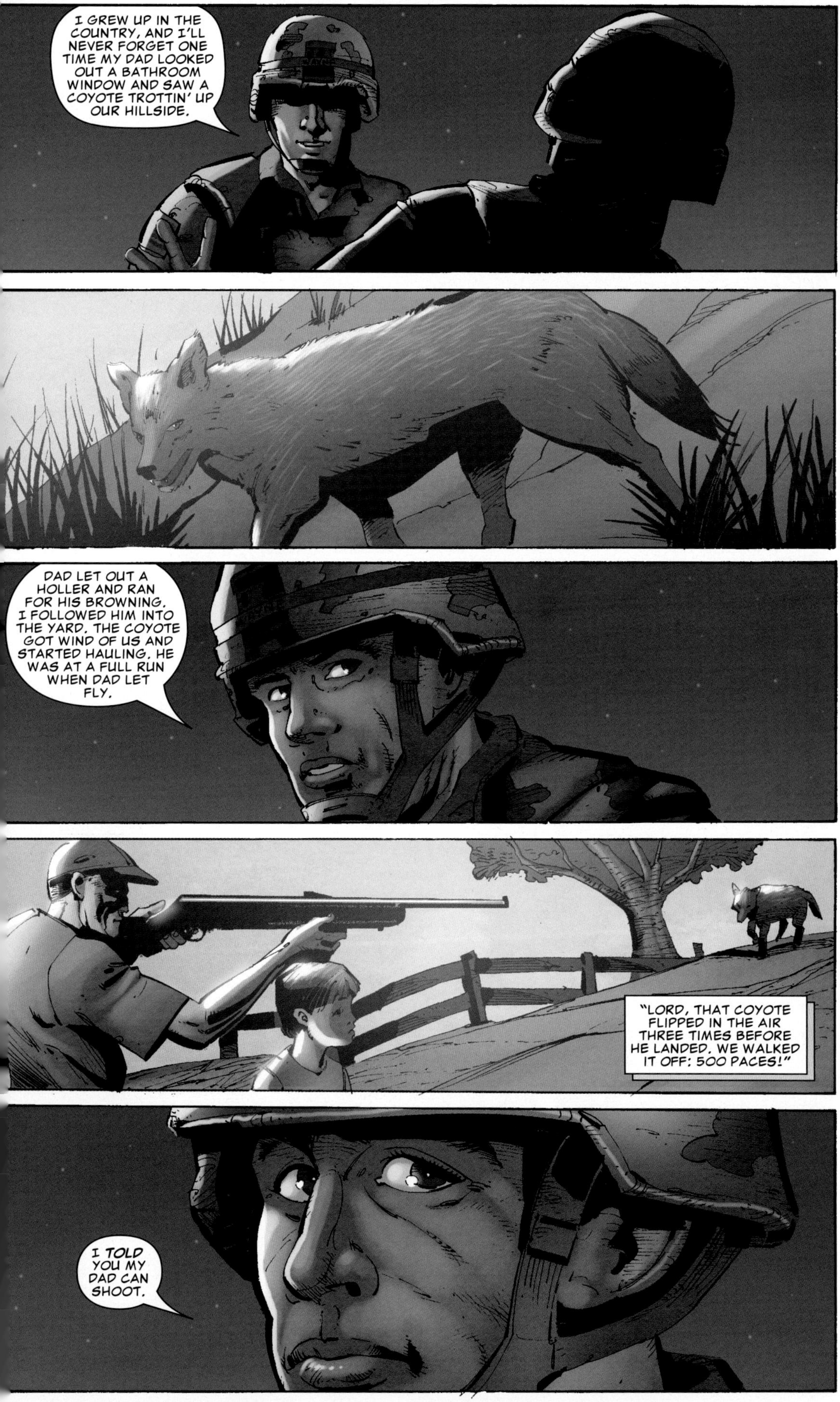
I GREW UP IN THE COUNTRY, AND I'LL NEVER FORGET ONE TIME MY DAD LOOKED OUT A BATHROOM WINDOW AND SAW A COYOTE TROTTIN' UP OUR HILLSIDE.
DAD LET OUT A HOLLER AND RAN FOR HIS BROWNING. I FOLLOWED HIM INTO THE YARD. THE COYOTE GOT WIND OF US AND STARTED HAULING. HE WAS AT A FULL RUN WHEN DAD LET FLY.
"LORD, THAT COYOTE FLIPPED IN THE AIR THREE TIMES BEFORE HE LANDED. WE WALKED IT OFF: 500 PACES!"
I *TOLD* YOU MY DAD CAN SHOOT.

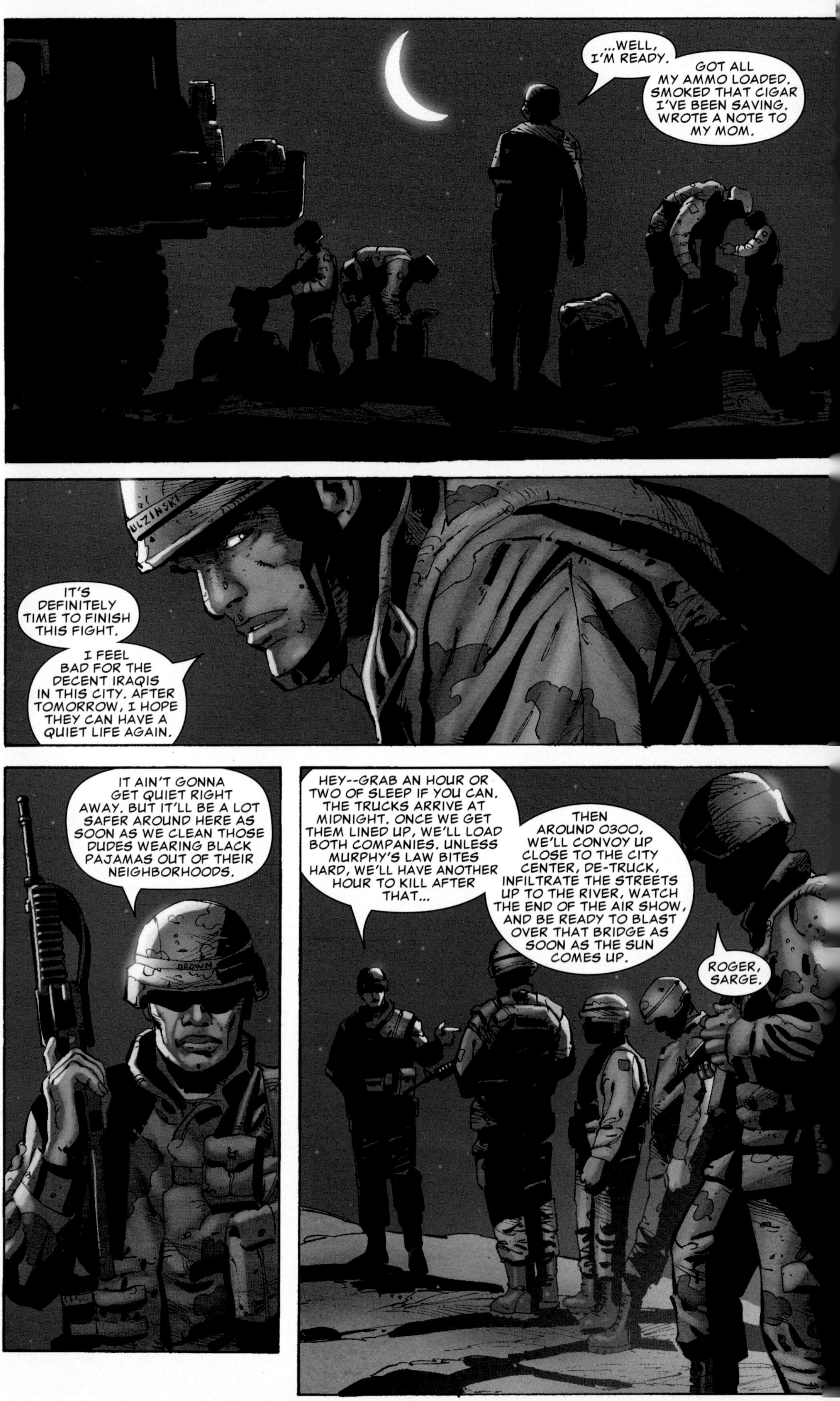

...WELL, I'M READY.
GOT ALL MY AMMO LOADED. SMOKED THAT CIGAR I'VE BEEN SAVING. WROTE A NOTE TO MY MOM.
IT'S DEFINITELY TIME TO FINISH THIS FIGHT.
I FEEL BAD FOR THE DECENT IRAQIS IN THIS CITY. AFTER TOMORROW, I HOPE THEY CAN HAVE A QUIET LIFE AGAIN.
IT AIN'T GONNA GET QUIET RIGHT AWAY. BUT IT'LL BE A LOT SAFER AROUND HERE AS SOON AS WE CLEAN THOSE DUDES WEARING BLACK PAJAMAS OUT OF THEIR NEIGHBORHOODS.
HEY--GRAB AN HOUR OR TWO OF SLEEP IF YOU CAN. THE TRUCKS ARRIVE AT MIDNIGHT. ONCE WE GET THEM LINED UP, WE'LL LOAD BOTH COMPANIES. UNLESS MURPHY'S LAW BITES HARD, WE'LL HAVE ANOTHER HOUR TO KILL AFTER THAT...
THEN AROUND 0300, WE'LL CONVOY UP CLOSE TO THE CITY CENTER, DE-TRUCK, INFILTRATE THE STREETS UP TO THE RIVER, WATCH THE END OF THE AIR SHOW, AND BE READY TO BLAST OVER THAT BRIDGE AS SOON AS THE SUN COMES UP.
ROGER, SARGE.

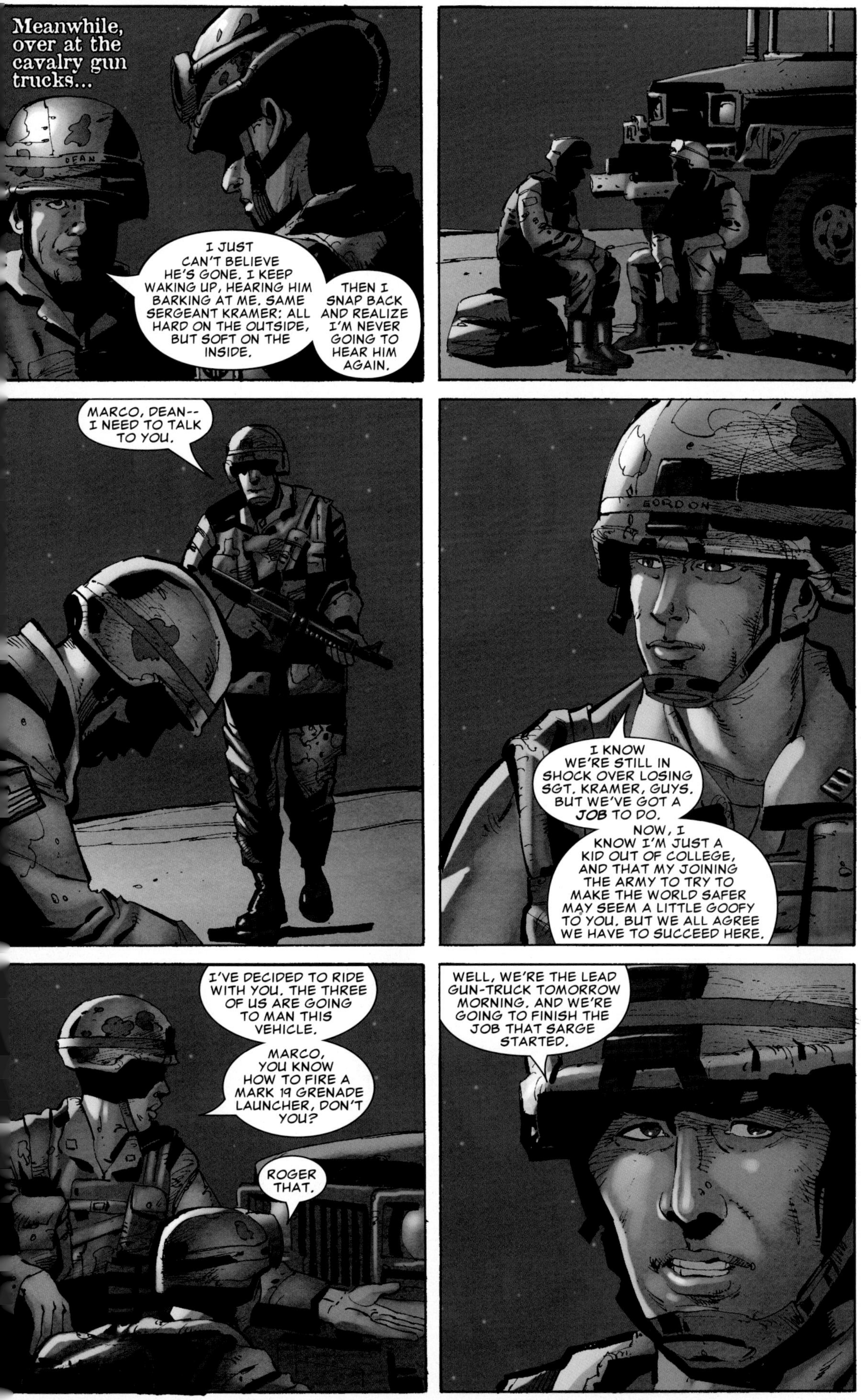
Meanwhile, over at the cavalry gun trucks...
I JUST CAN'T BELIEVE HE'S GONE. I KEEP WAKING UP, HEARING HIM BARKING AT ME. SAME SERGEANT KRAMER: ALL HARD ON THE OUTSIDE, BUT SOFT ON THE INSIDE.
THEN I SNAP BACK AND REALIZE I'M NEVER GOING TO HEAR HIM AGAIN.
MARCO, DEAN-- I NEED TO TALK TO YOU.
I KNOW WE'RE STILL IN SHOCK OVER LOSING SGT. KRAMER, GUYS. BUT WE'VE GOT A JOB TO DO.
NOW, I KNOW I'M JUST A KID OUT OF COLLEGE, AND THAT MY JOINING THE ARMY TO TRY TO MAKE THE WORLD SAFER MAY SEEM A LITTLE GOOFY TO YOU. BUT WE ALL AGREE WE HAVE TO SUCCEED HERE.
I'VE DECIDED TO RIDE WITH YOU. THE THREE OF US ARE GOING TO MAN THIS VEHICLE.
MARCO, YOU KNOW HOW TO FIRE A MARK 19 GRENADE LAUNCHER, DON'T YOU?
ROGER THAT.
WELL, WE'RE THE LEAD GUN-TRUCK TOMORROW MORNING. AND WE'RE GOING TO FINISH THE JOB THAT SARGE STARTED.

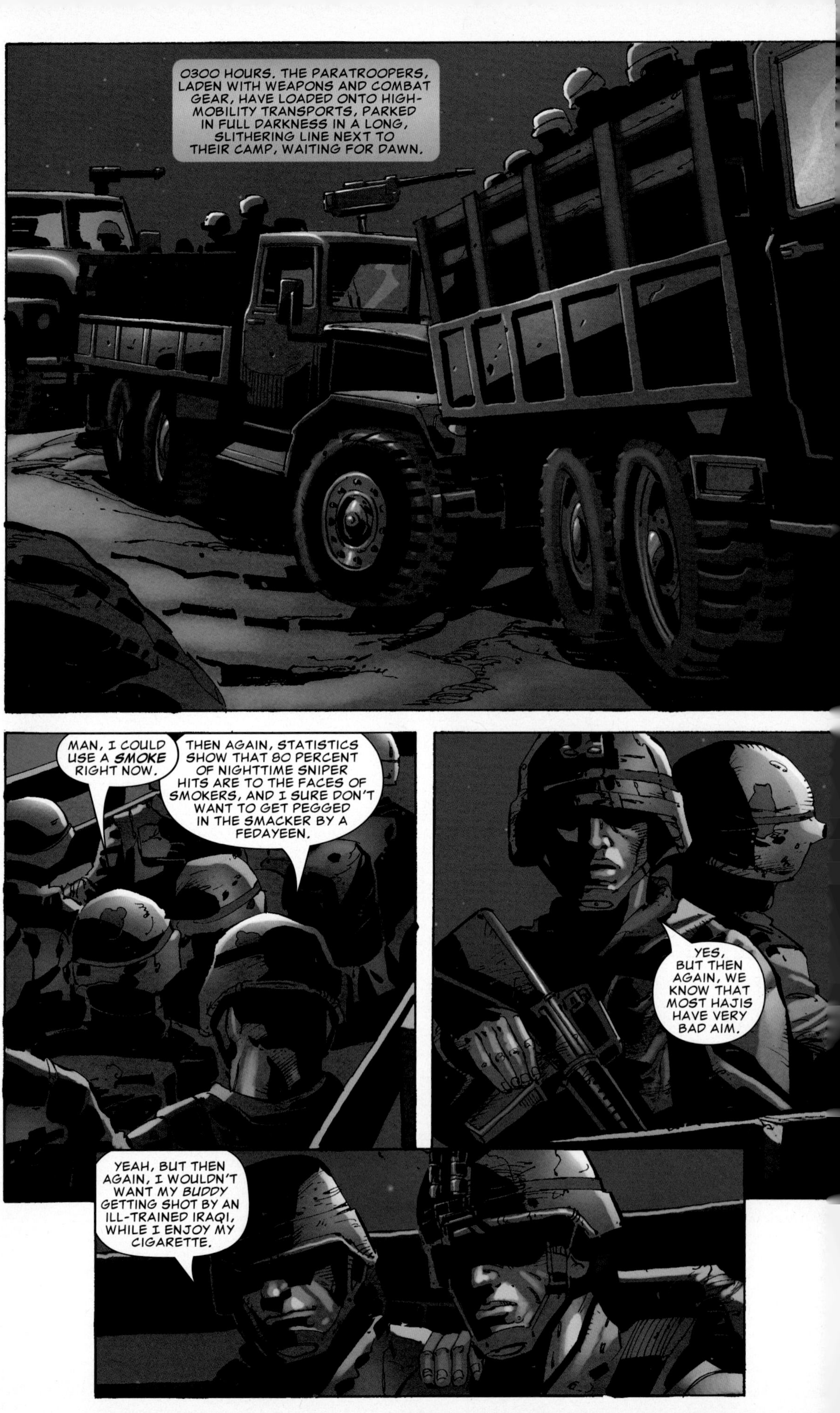
0300 HOURS. THE PARATROOPERS, LADEN WITH WEAPONS AND COMBAT GEAR, HAVE LOADED ONTO HIGH-MOBILITY TRANSPORTS, PARKED IN FULL DARKNESS IN A LONG, SLITHERING LINE NEXT TO THEIR CAMP, WAITING FOR DAWN.
MAN, I COULD USE A SMOKE RIGHT NOW.
THEN AGAIN, STATISTICS SHOW THAT 80 PERCENT OF NIGHTTIME SNIPER HITS ARE TO THE FACES OF SMOKERS, AND I SURE DON'T WANT TO GET PEGGED IN THE SMACKER BY A FEDAYEEN.
YES, BUT THEN AGAIN, WE KNOW THAT MOST HAJIS HAVE VERY BAD AIM.
YEAH, BUT THEN AGAIN, I WOULDN'T WANT MY BUDDY GETTING SHOT BY AN ILL-TRAINED IRAQI, WHILE I ENJOY MY CIGARETTE.

0330 HOURS. THE TRUCKS START UP. THE TROOPERS INSTANTLY FALL QUIET, AND FLIP DOWN THEIR NIGHT-VISION GOGGLES. A TOTALLY BLACKED-OUT CONVOY BEGINS ITS JOURNEY INTO THE CITY.

0400 HOURS. THE SOLDIERS POUR OUT OF THEIR VEHICLES AND DISTRIBUTE THEMSELVES IN A PRONE RIFLE POSITION ACROSS AN OPEN AREA NEXT TO INDUSTRIAL BUILDINGS. THE TAIL END OF THE AIR ASSAULT IS SOFTENING UP THE IRAQI GUN EMPLACEMENTS AROUND THE BRIDGE. F-15S FROM U.S. CARRIERS HUNDREDS OF MILES AWAY SCREAM AT THE TOP OF THE SKY. A COMPUTER-CONTROLLED HOWITZER THUNDERS FROM AN UNSEEN AC-130 CIRCLING OVERHEAD.

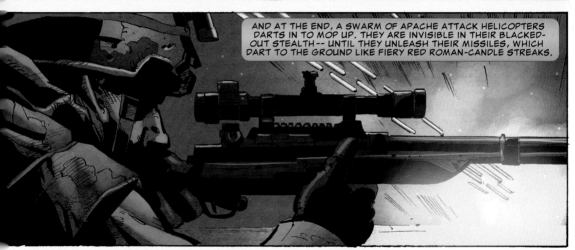

AND AT THE END, A SWARM OF APACHE ATTACK HELICOPTERS DARTS IN TO MOP UP. THEY ARE INVISIBLE IN THEIR BLACKED-OUT STEALTH -- UNTIL THEY UNLEASH THEIR MISSILES, WHICH DART TO THE GROUND LIKE FIERY RED ROMAN-CANDLE STREAKS.

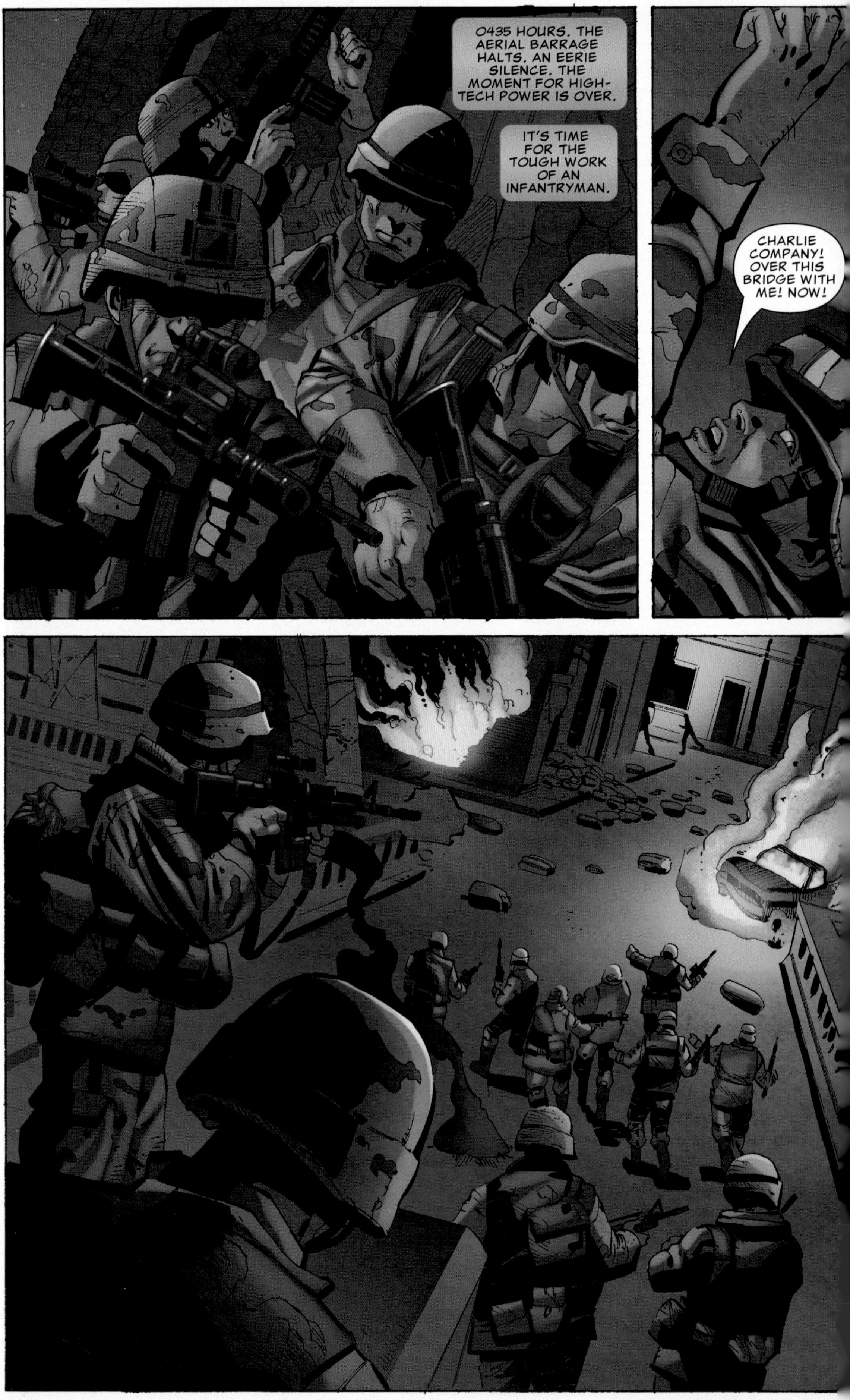
0435 HOURS. THE AERIAL BARRAGE HALTS. AN EERIE SILENCE. THE MOMENT FOR HIGH-TECH POWER IS OVER.
IT'S TIME FOR THE TOUGH WORK OF AN INFANTRYMAN.
CHARLIE COMPANY! OVER THIS BRIDGE WITH ME! NOW!

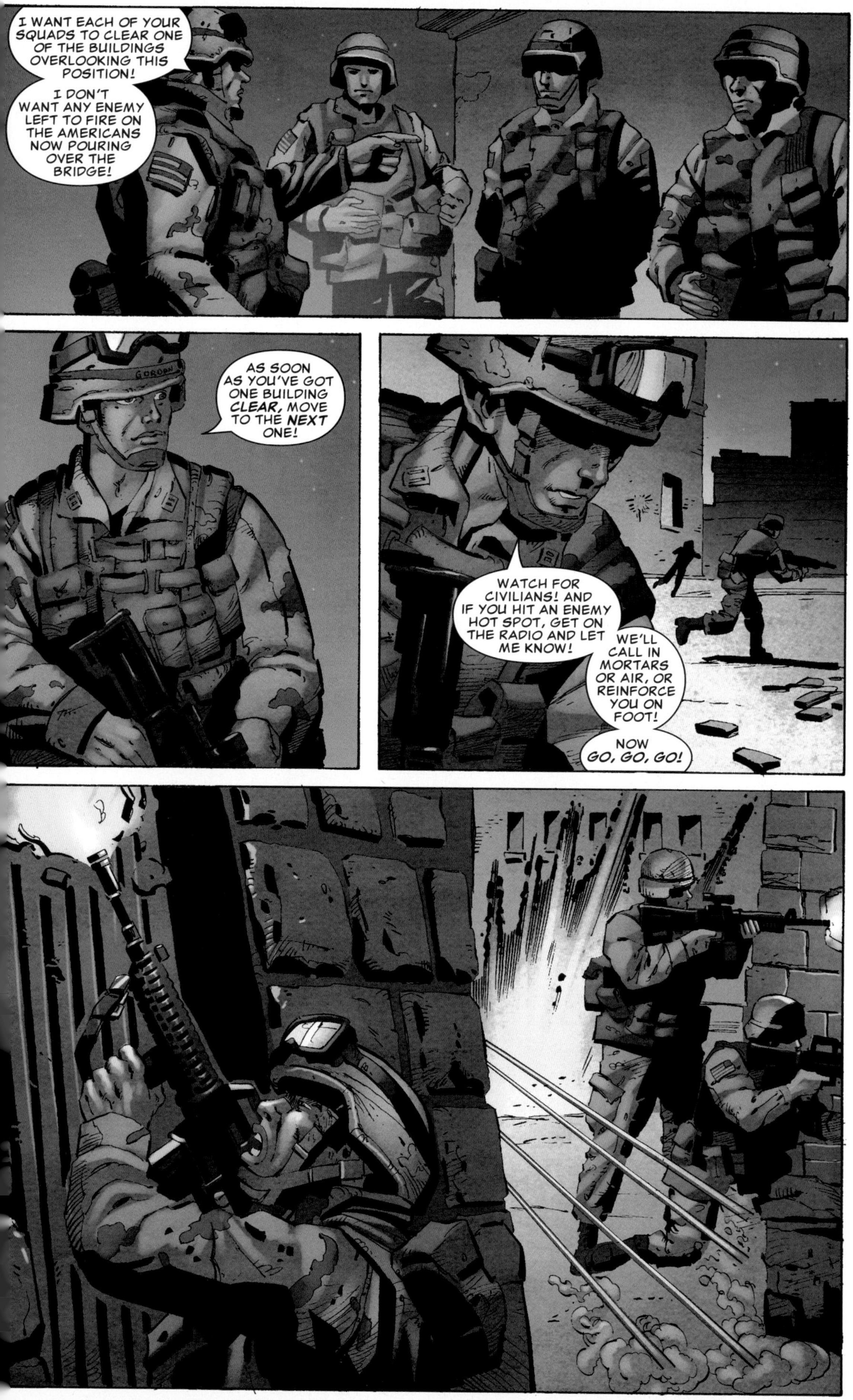

I WANT EACH OF YOUR SQUADS TO CLEAR ONE OF THE BUILDINGS OVERLOOKING THIS POSITION!
I DON'T WANT ANY ENEMY LEFT TO FIRE ON THE AMERICANS NOW POURING OVER THE BRIDGE!
GORDON
AS SOON AS YOU'VE GOT ONE BUILDING CLEAR, MOVE TO THE NEXT ONE!
WATCH FOR CIVILIANS! AND IF YOU HIT AN ENEMY HOT SPOT, GET ON THE RADIO AND LET ME KNOW!
WE'LL CALL IN MORTARS OR AIR, OR REINFORCE YOU ON FOOT!
NOW GO, GO, GO!

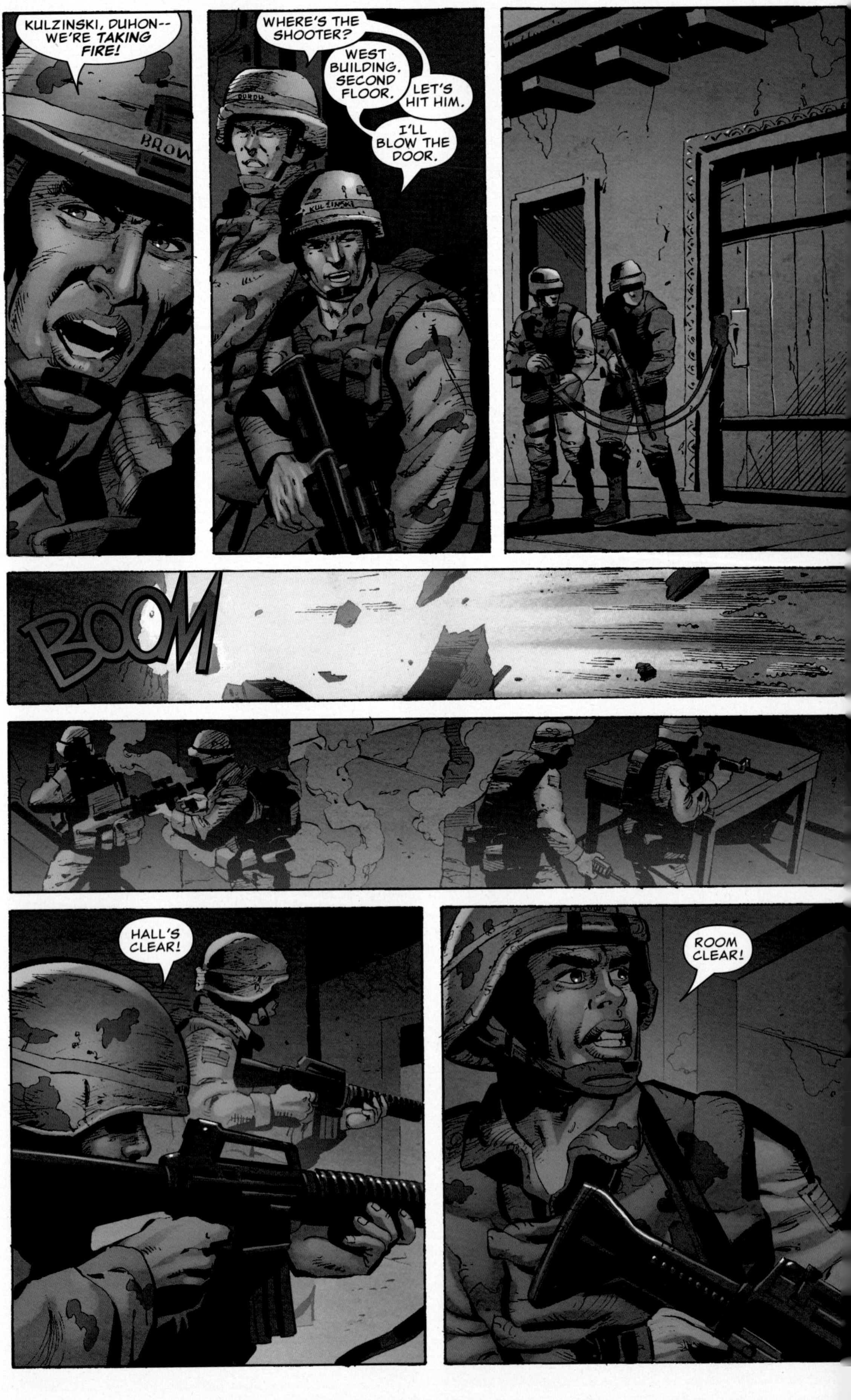
KULZINSKI, DUHON--
WE'RE TAKING FIRE!
WHERE'S THE SHOOTER?
WEST BUILDING. SECOND FLOOR.
LET'S HIT HIM.
I'LL BLOW THE DOOR.
BROW
DUHON
KULZINSKI
BOOM
HALL'S CLEAR!
ROOM CLEAR!

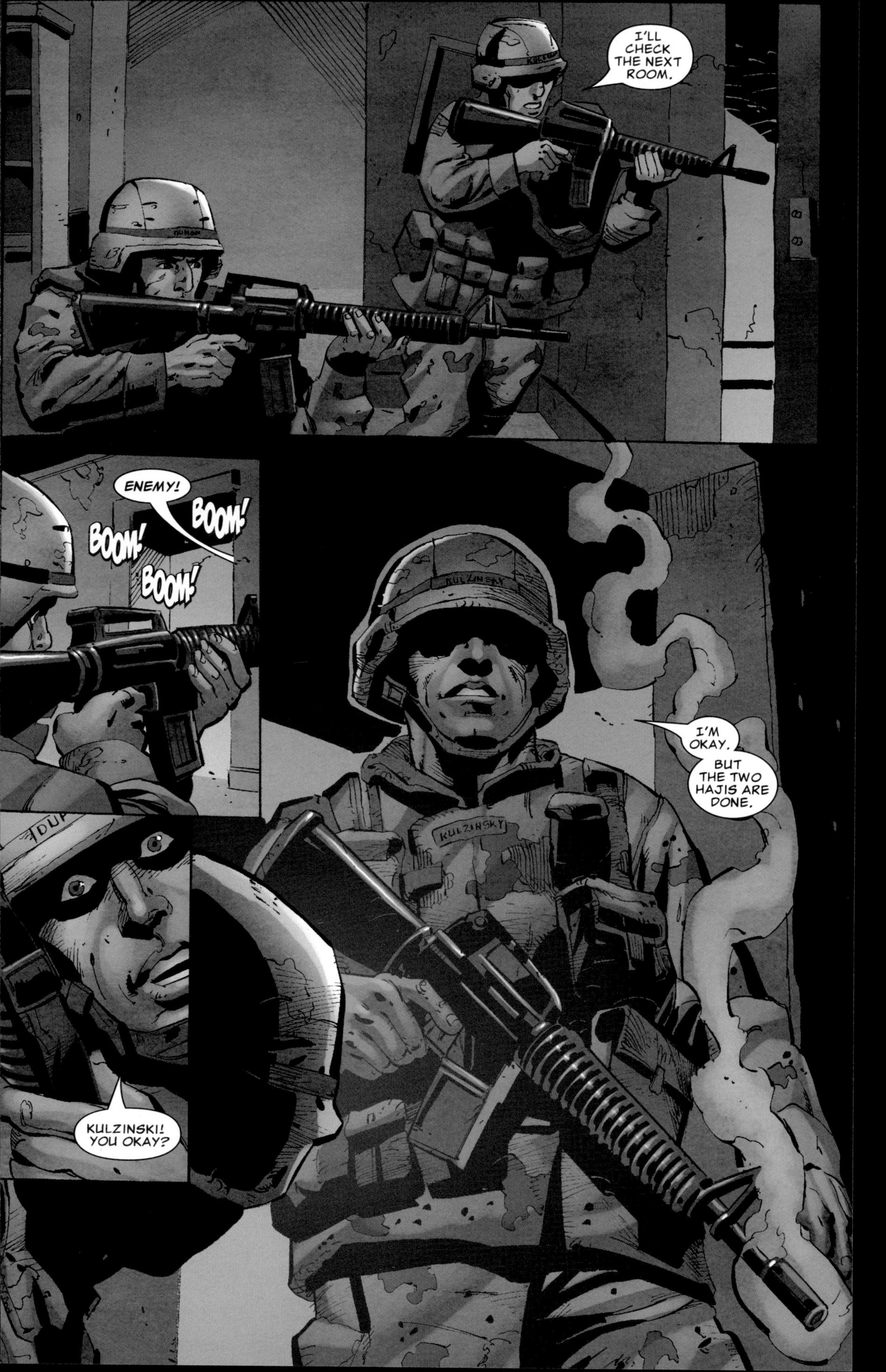
I'LL CHECK THE NEXT ROOM.
ENEMY!
BOOM!
BOOM!
BOOM!
I'M OKAY.
BUT THE TWO HAJIS ARE DONE.
KULZINSKI! YOU OKAY?

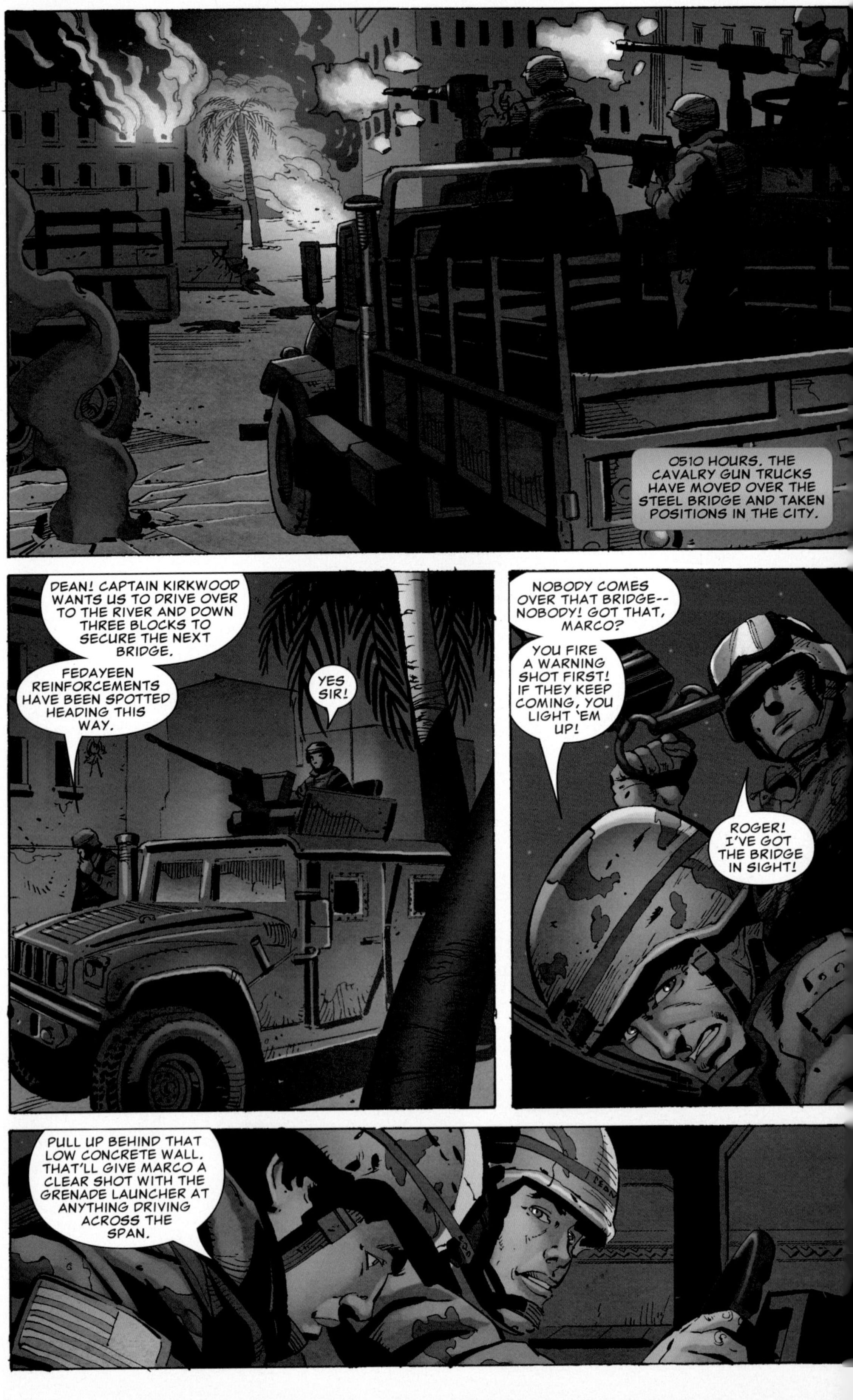
0510 HOURS. THE CAVALRY GUN TRUCKS HAVE MOVED OVER THE STEEL BRIDGE AND TAKEN POSITIONS IN THE CITY.
DEAN! CAPTAIN KIRKWOOD WANTS US TO DRIVE OVER TO THE RIVER AND DOWN THREE BLOCKS TO SECURE THE NEXT BRIDGE.
FEDAYEEN REINFORCEMENTS HAVE BEEN SPOTTED HEADING THIS WAY.
YES SIR!
NOBODY COMES OVER THAT BRIDGE-- NOBODY! GOT THAT, MARCO?
YOU FIRE A WARNING SHOT FIRST! IF THEY KEEP COMING, YOU LIGHT 'EM UP!
ROGER! I'VE GOT THE BRIDGE IN SIGHT!
PULL UP BEHIND THAT LOW CONCRETE WALL. THAT'LL GIVE MARCO A CLEAR SHOT WITH THE GRENADE LAUNCHER AT ANYTHING DRIVING ACROSS THE SPAN.

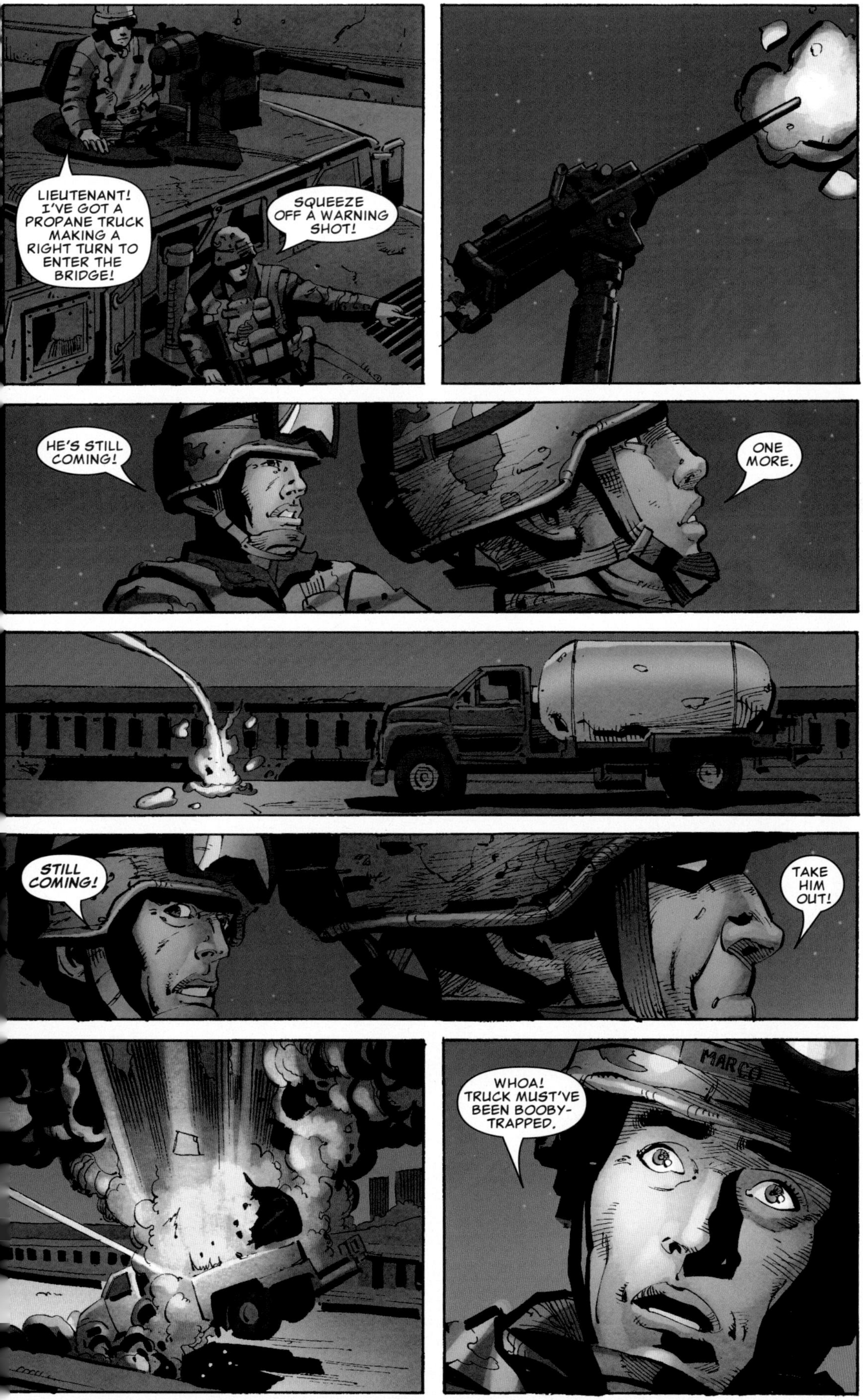

LIEUTENANT! I'VE GOT A PROPANE TRUCK MAKING A RIGHT TURN TO ENTER THE BRIDGE!
SQUEEZE OFF A WARNING SHOT!
HE'S STILL COMING!
ONE MORE.
STILL COMING!
TAKE HIM OUT!
MARCO
WHOA! TRUCK MUST'VE BEEN BOOBY-TRAPPED.

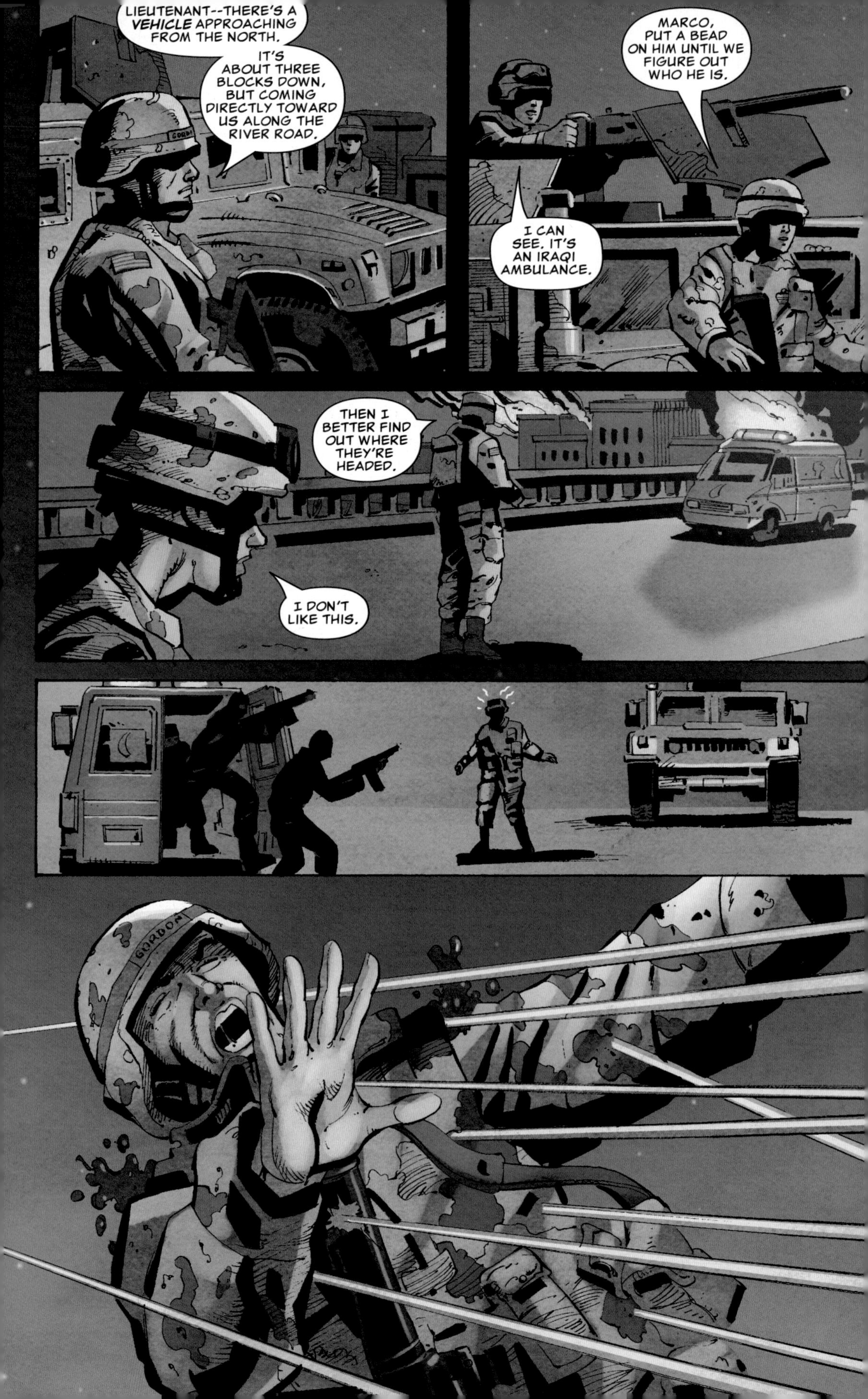
LIEUTENANT--THERE'S A VEHICLE APPROACHING FROM THE NORTH.
IT'S ABOUT THREE BLOCKS DOWN, BUT COMING DIRECTLY TOWARD US ALONG THE RIVER ROAD.
MARCO, PUT A BEAD ON HIM UNTIL WE FIGURE OUT WHO HE IS.
I CAN SEE. IT'S AN IRAQI AMBULANCE.
THEN I BETTER FIND OUT WHERE THEY'RE HEADED.
I DON'T LIKE THIS.
GORDON

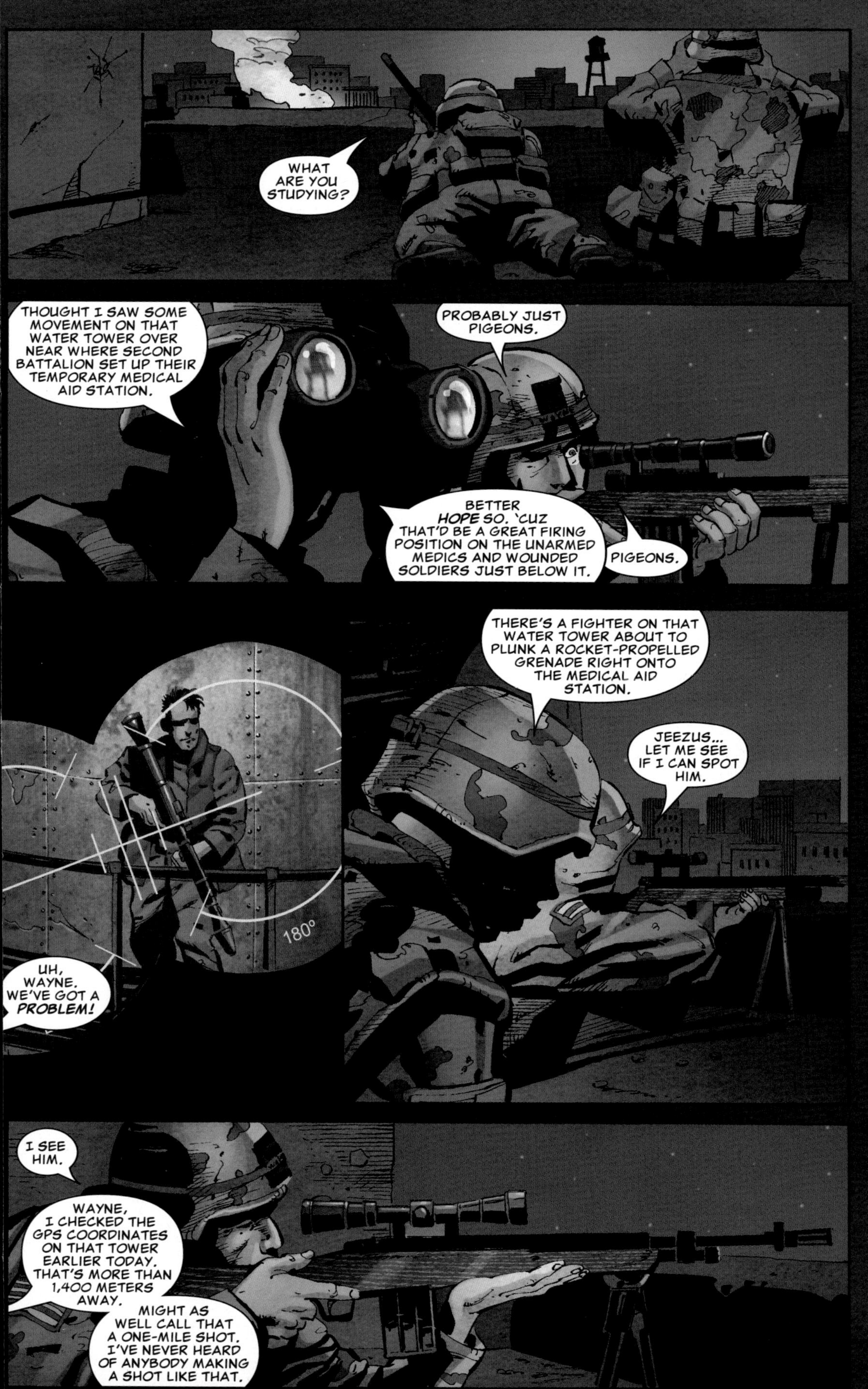
WHAT ARE YOU STUDYING?
THOUGHT I SAW SOME MOVEMENT ON THAT WATER TOWER OVER NEAR WHERE SECOND BATTALION SET UP THEIR TEMPORARY MEDICAL AID STATION.
PROBABLY JUST PIGEONS.
BETTER *HOPE* SO. 'CUZ THAT'D BE A GREAT FIRING POSITION ON THE UNARMED MEDICS AND WOUNDED SOLDIERS JUST BELOW IT.
PIGEONS.
180°
UH, WAYNE. WE'VE GOT A *PROBLEM!*
THERE'S A FIGHTER ON THAT WATER TOWER ABOUT TO PLUNK A ROCKET-PROPELLED GRENADE RIGHT ONTO THE MEDICAL AID STATION.
JEEZUS... LET ME SEE IF I CAN SPOT HIM.
I SEE HIM.
WAYNE, I CHECKED THE GPS COORDINATES ON THAT TOWER EARLIER TODAY. THAT'S MORE THAN 1,400 METERS AWAY.
MIGHT AS WELL CALL THAT A ONE-MILE SHOT. I'VE NEVER HEARD OF ANYBODY MAKING A SHOT LIKE THAT.

YOU GOT ANY BETTER IDEAS?

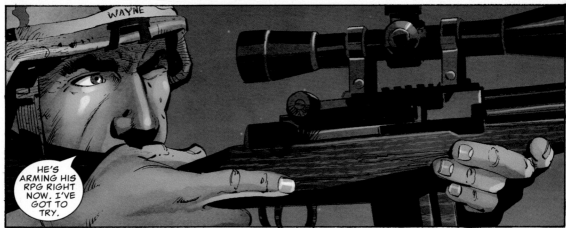

HE'S ARMING HIS RPG RIGHT NOW. I'VE GOT TO TRY.

CRACK!

GOOD LORD, WAYNE! YOU JUST DID YOUR COYOTE-HUNTIN' DADDY PROUD.

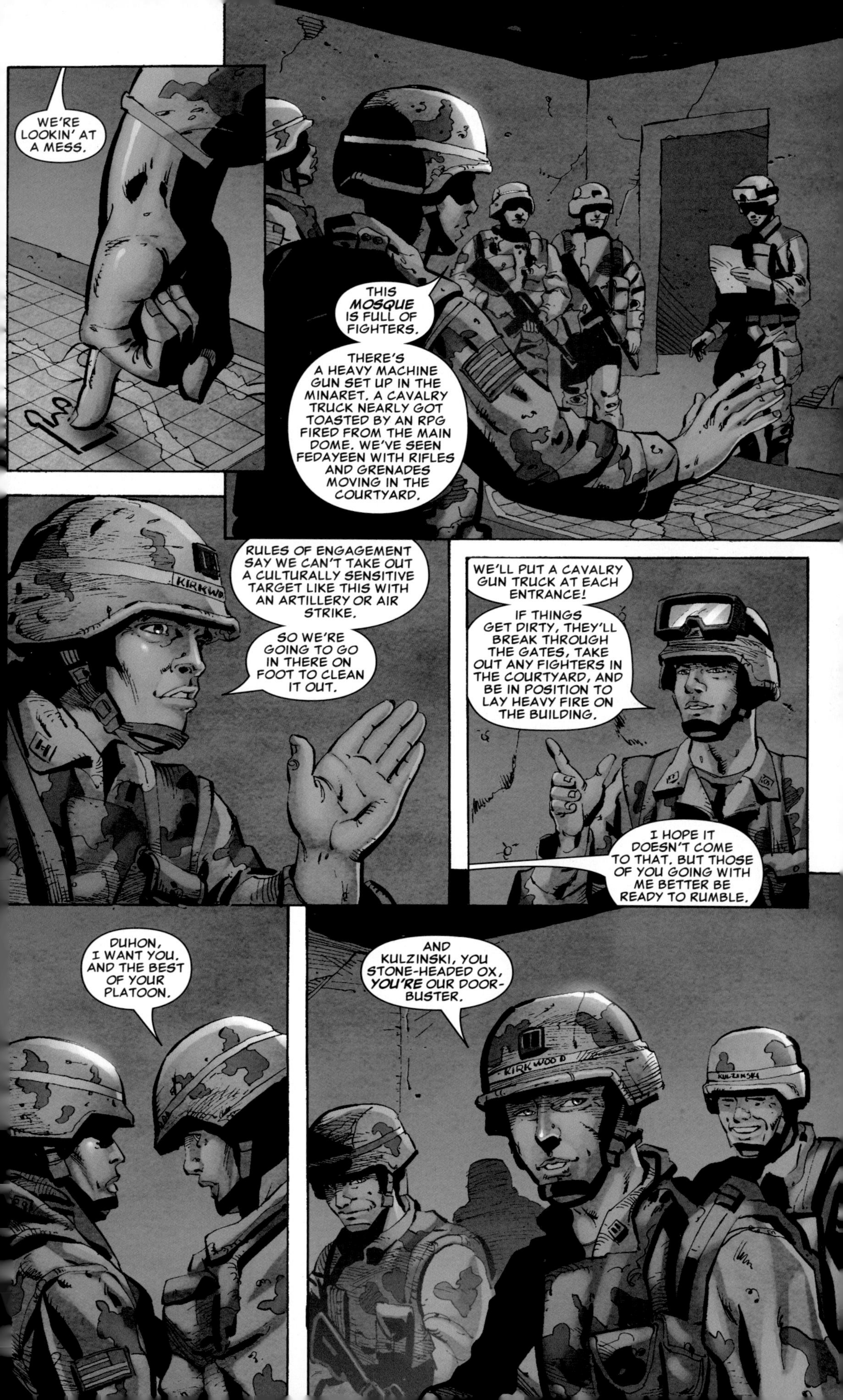
WE'RE LOOKIN' AT A MESS.
THIS *MOSQUE* IS FULL OF FIGHTERS.
THERE'S A HEAVY MACHINE GUN SET UP IN THE MINARET. A CAVALRY TRUCK NEARLY GOT TOASTED BY AN RPG FIRED FROM THE MAIN DOME. WE'VE SEEN FEDAYEEN WITH RIFLES AND GRENADES MOVING IN THE COURTYARD.
RULES OF ENGAGEMENT SAY WE CAN'T TAKE OUT A CULTURALLY SENSITIVE TARGET LIKE THIS WITH AN ARTILLERY OR AIR STRIKE.
SO WE'RE GOING TO GO IN THERE ON FOOT TO CLEAN IT OUT.
KIRKWOOD
WE'LL PUT A CAVALRY GUN TRUCK AT EACH ENTRANCE!
IF THINGS GET DIRTY, THEY'LL BREAK THROUGH THE GATES, TAKE OUT ANY FIGHTERS IN THE COURTYARD, AND BE IN POSITION TO LAY HEAVY FIRE ON THE BUILDING.
I HOPE IT DOESN'T COME TO THAT. BUT THOSE OF YOU GOING WITH ME BETTER BE READY TO RUMBLE.
DUHON, I WANT YOU. AND THE BEST OF YOUR PLATOON.
AND KULZINSKI, YOU STONE-HEADED OX, *YOU'RE* OUR DOOR-BUSTER.
KIRKWOOD
KULZINSKI

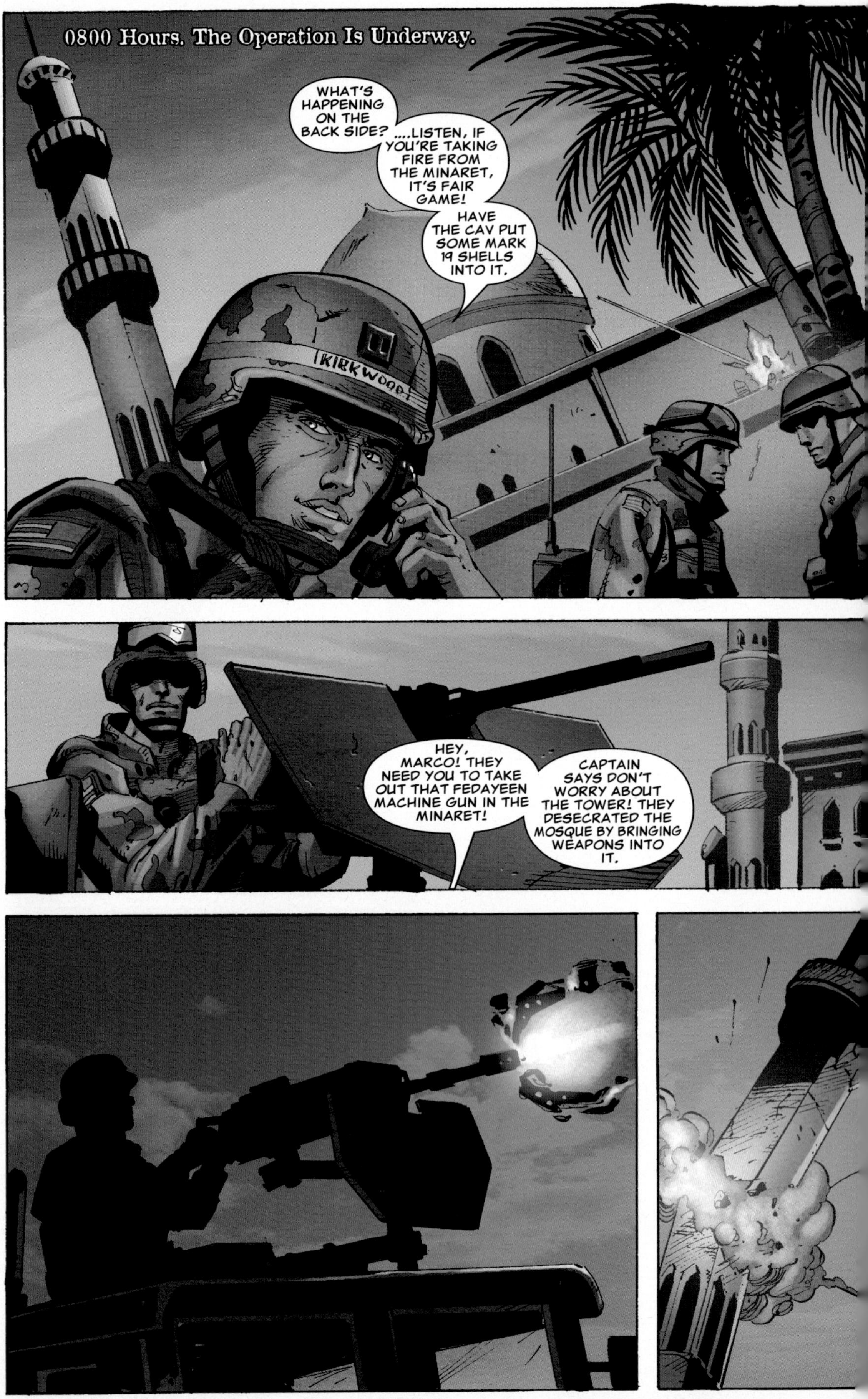
0800 Hours. The Operation Is Underway.
WHAT'S HAPPENING ON THE BACK SIDE?
....LISTEN, IF YOU'RE TAKING FIRE FROM THE MINARET, IT'S FAIR GAME!
HAVE THE CAV PUT SOME MARK 19 SHELLS INTO IT.
KIRKWOOD
HEY, MARCO! THEY NEED YOU TO TAKE OUT THAT FEDAYEEN MACHINE GUN IN THE MINARET!
CAPTAIN SAYS DON'T WORRY ABOUT THE TOWER! THEY DESECRATED THE MOSQUE BY BRINGING WEAPONS INTO IT.

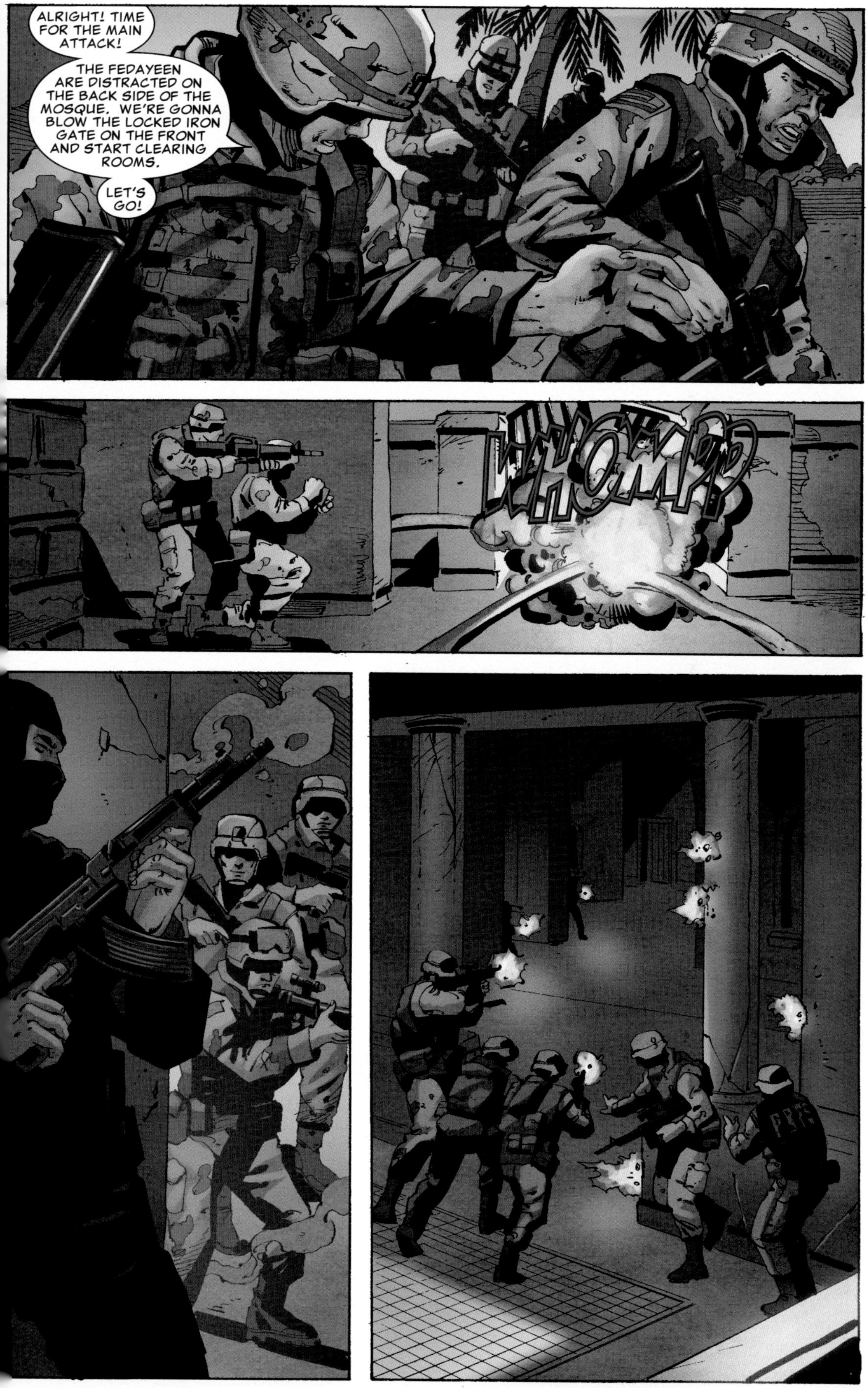
ALRIGHT! TIME FOR THE MAIN ATTACK!
THE FEDAYEEN ARE DISTRACTED ON THE BACK SIDE OF THE MOSQUE. WE'RE GONNA BLOW THE LOCKED IRON GATE ON THE FRONT AND START CLEARING ROOMS.
LET'S GO!
WHOMP!

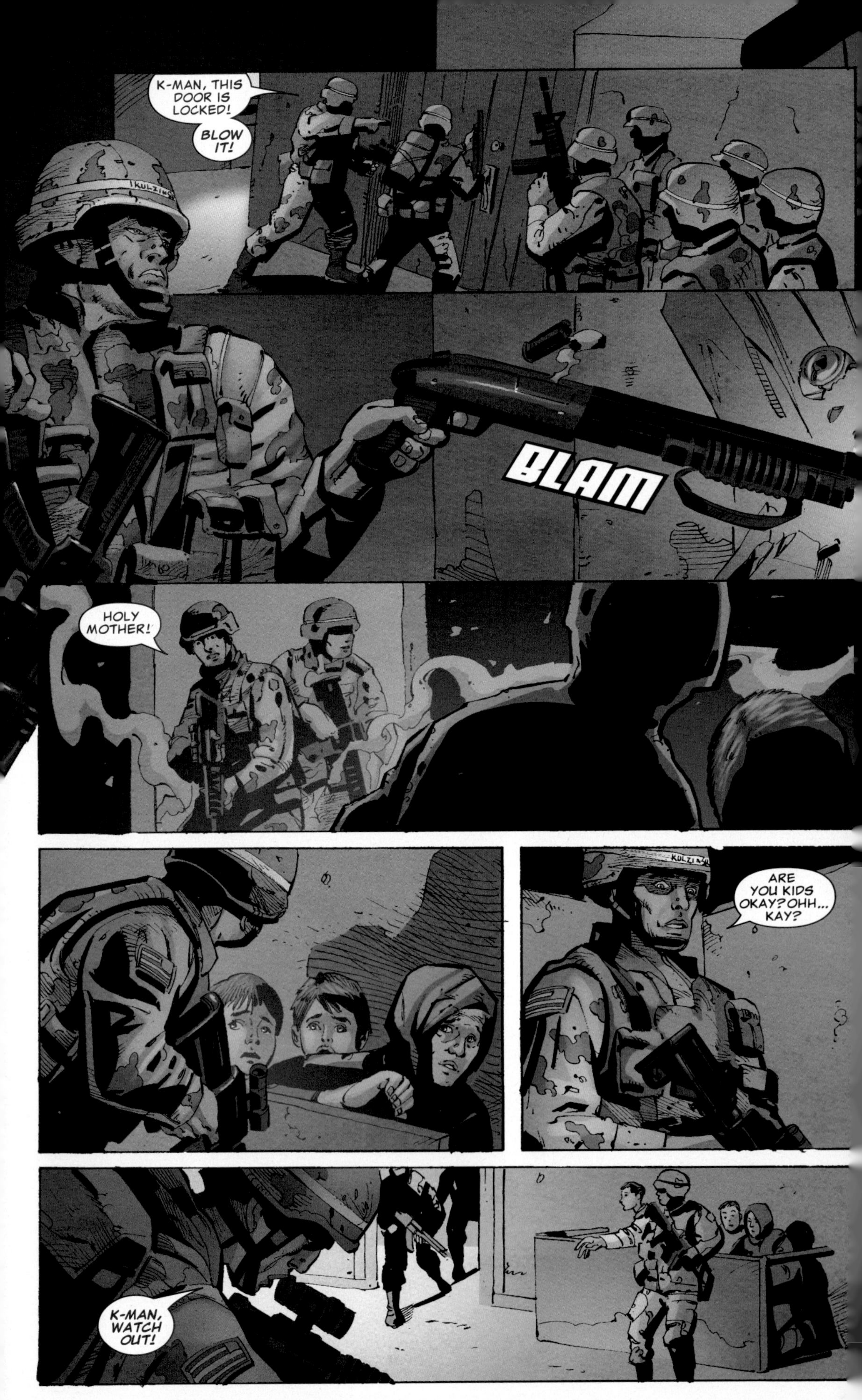
K-MAN, THIS DOOR IS LOCKED!
BLOW IT!
BLAM
HOLY MOTHER!
ARE YOU KIDS OKAY? OHH... KAY?
K-MAN, WATCH OUT!

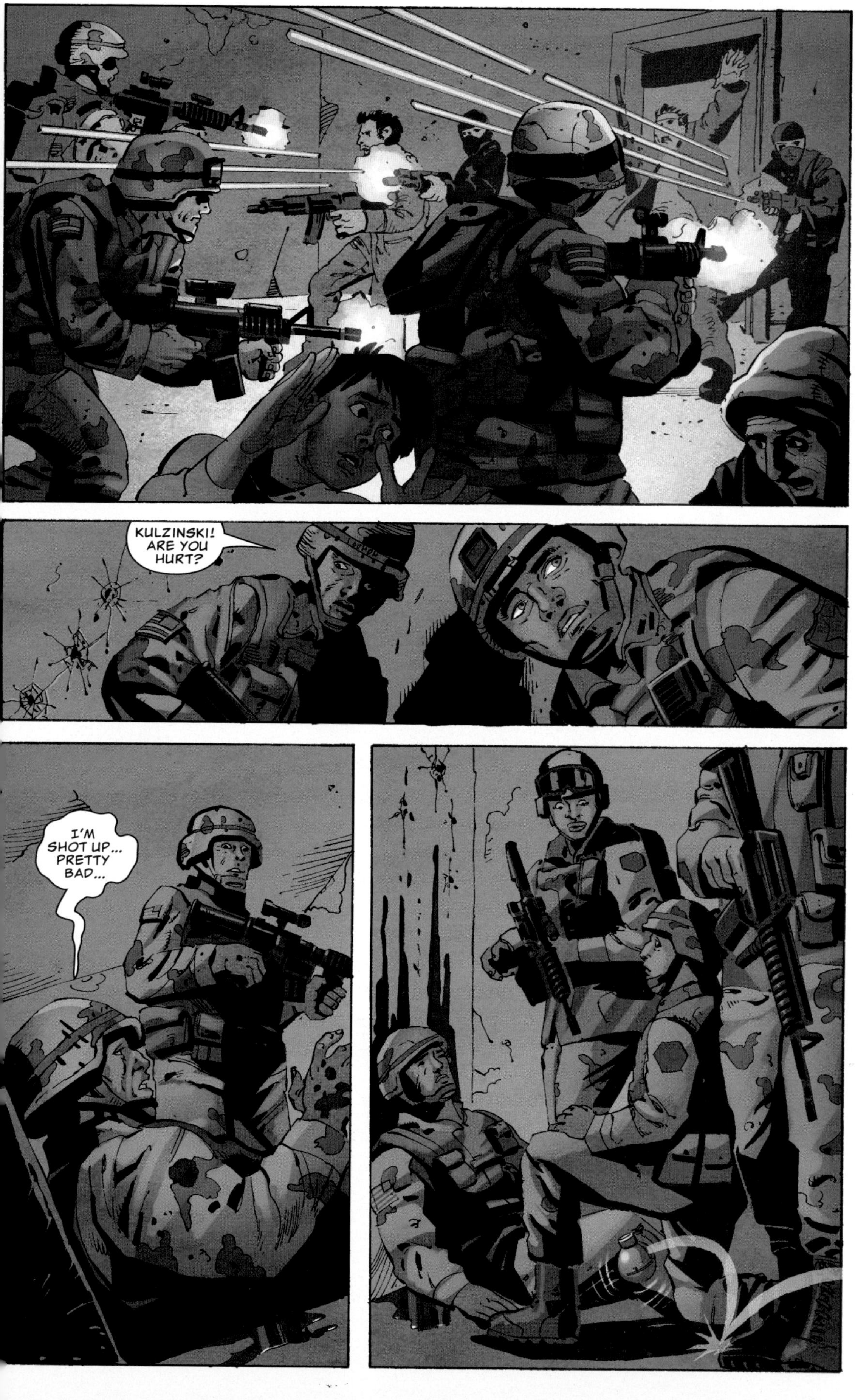
KULZINSKI! ARE YOU HURT?
I'M SHOT UP... PRETTY BAD...

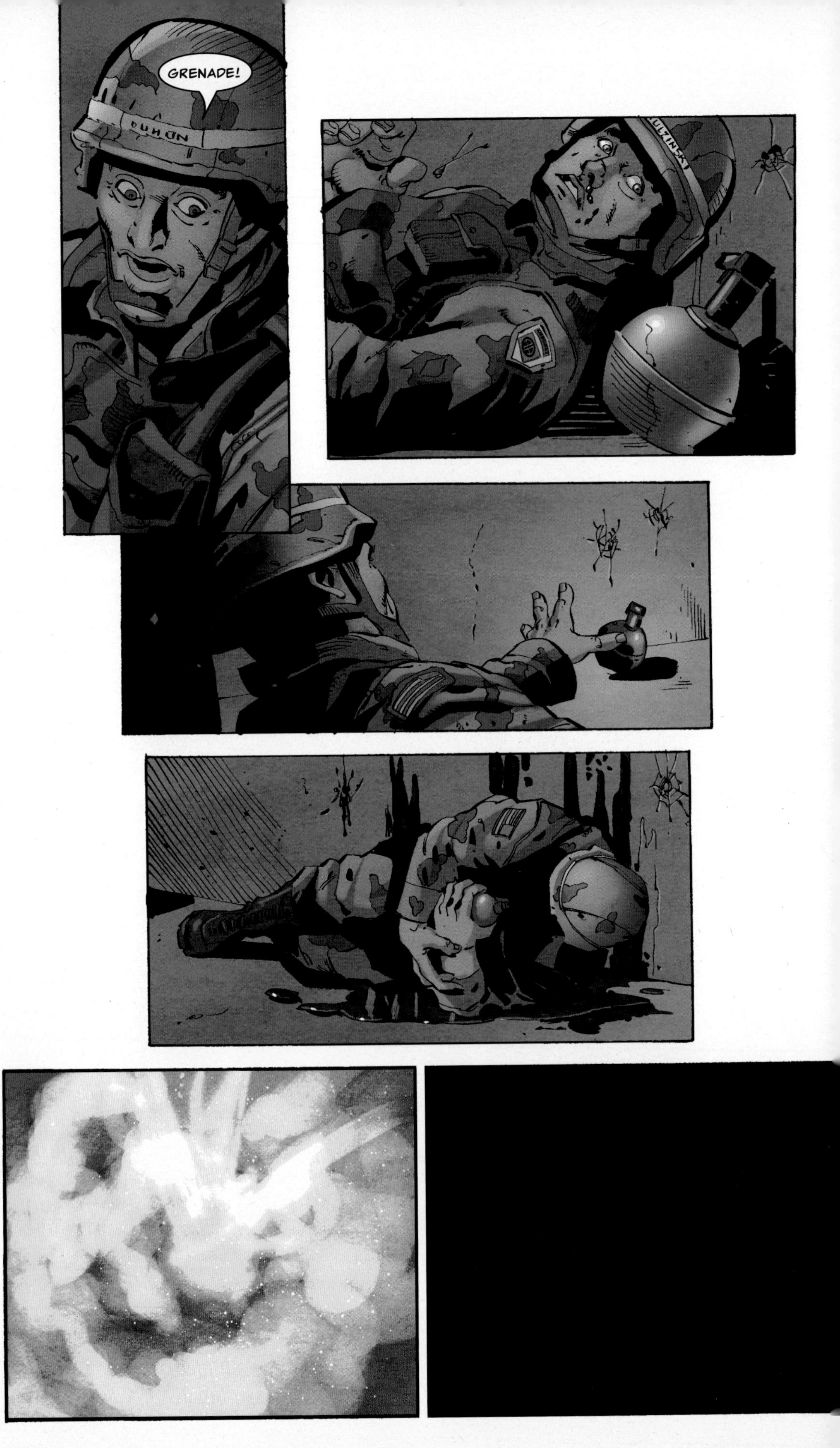
GRENADE!

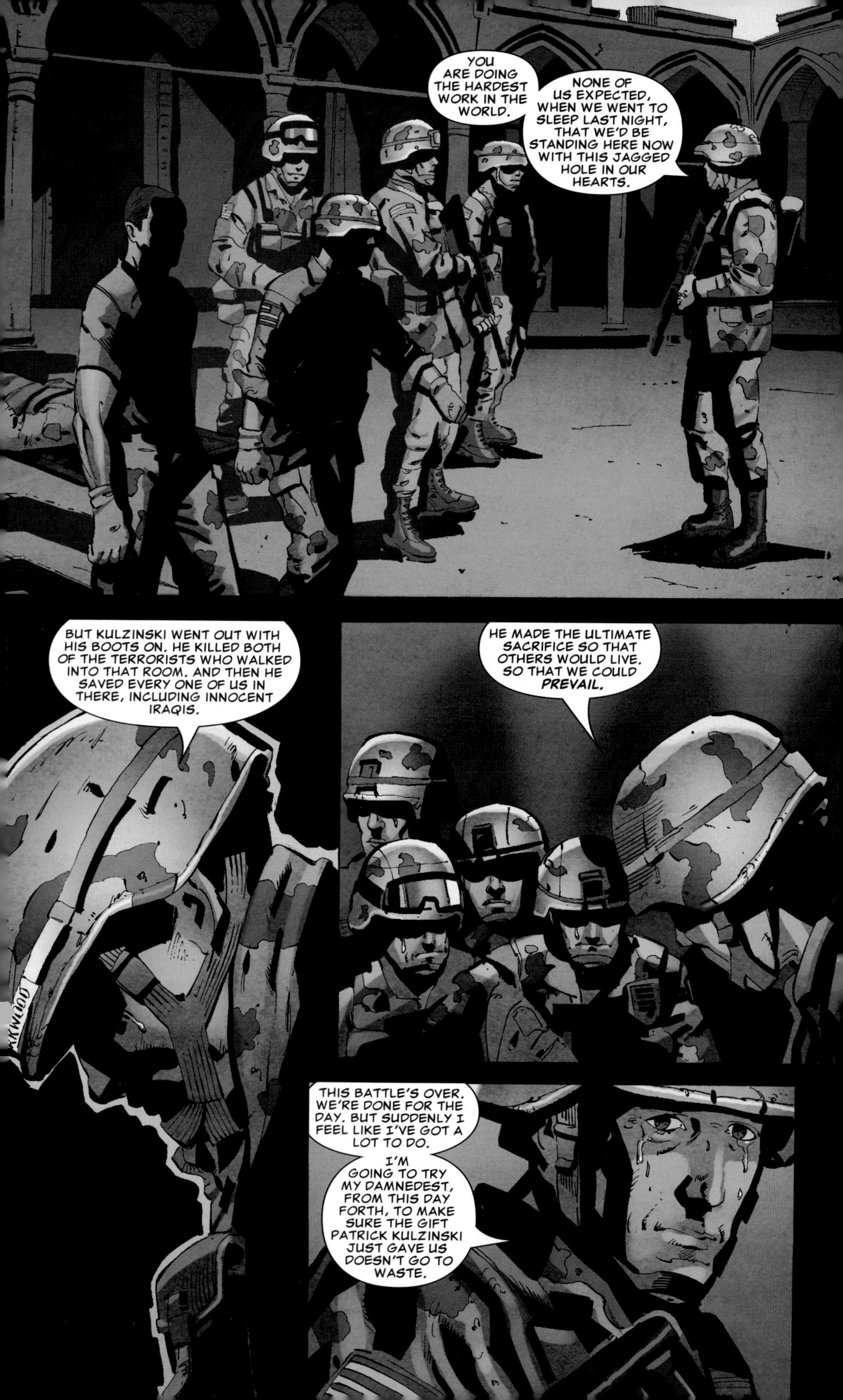
YOU ARE DOING THE HARDEST WORK IN THE WORLD.
NONE OF US EXPECTED, WHEN WE WENT TO SLEEP LAST NIGHT, THAT WE'D BE STANDING HERE NOW WITH THIS JAGGED HOLE IN OUR HEARTS.
BUT KULZINSKI WENT OUT WITH HIS BOOTS ON. HE KILLED BOTH OF THE TERRORISTS WHO WALKED INTO THAT ROOM. AND THEN HE SAVED EVERY ONE OF US IN THERE, INCLUDING INNOCENT IRAQIS.
HE MADE THE ULTIMATE SACRIFICE SO THAT OTHERS WOULD LIVE. SO THAT WE COULD PREVAIL.
THIS BATTLE'S OVER. WE'RE DONE FOR THE DAY. BUT SUDDENLY I FEEL LIKE I'VE GOT A LOT TO DO.
I'M GOING TO TRY MY DAMNEDEST, FROM THIS DAY FORTH, TO MAKE SURE THE GIFT PATRICK KULZINSKI JUST GAVE US DOESN'T GO TO WASTE.

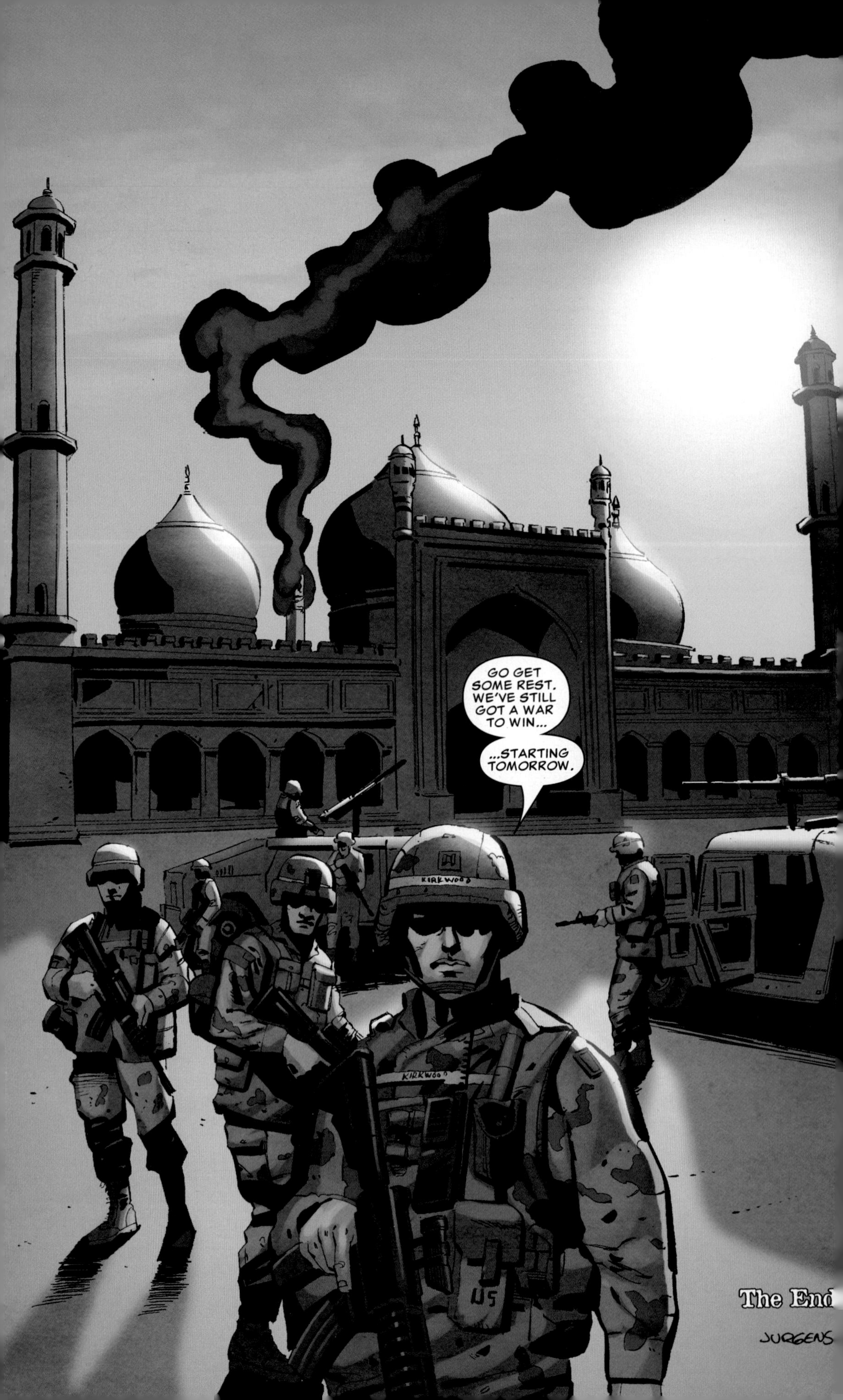
GO GET SOME REST. WE'VE STILL GOT A WAR TO WIN...
...STARTING TOMORROW.
KIRKWOOD
KIRKWOOD
US
The End
JURGENS